Happy Christmas
Love from Helen

FIRST FRIENDS

Paul and Bunty, John and Christine – and Carrington

RONALD BLYTHE

VIKING

VIKING

Published by the Penguin Group
Penguin Books Ltd, 27 Wrights Lane, London W8 5TZ, England
Penguin Putnam Inc., 375 Hudson Street, New York, New York 10014, USA
Penguin Books Australia Ltd, Ringwood, Victoria, Australia
Penguin Books Canada Ltd, 10 Alcorn Avenue, Toronto, Ontario, Canada M4V 3B2
Penguin Books (NZ) Ltd, Private Bag 102902, NSMC, Auckland, New Zealand

Penguin Books Ltd, Registered Offices: Harmondsworth, Middlesex, England

First published by Simon Lawrence at his Fleece Press, 1997
Published by Viking 1999
1 3 5 7 9 10 8 6 4 2

Set in 12.5 on 15.5pt Monotype Centaur
Typeset by Rowland Phototypesetting Ltd, Bury St Edmunds, Suffolk
Printed in Great Britain by Butler and Tanner Ltd, Frome and London

A CIP catalogue record for this book is available from the British Library

ISBN 0-670-88613-0

For Ursula Hamilton-Paterson

Contents

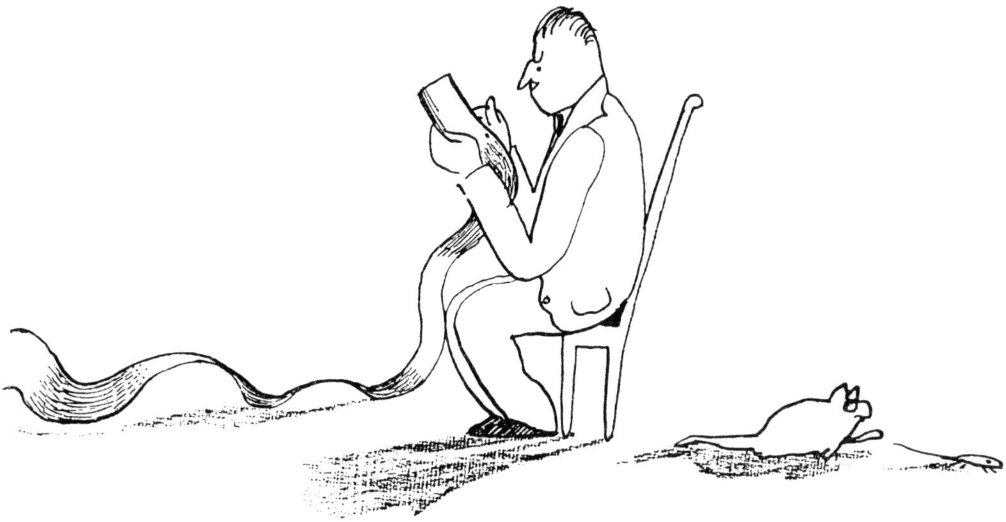

Above: John Nash to Carrington: 'A very good letter. Let us consider it.'

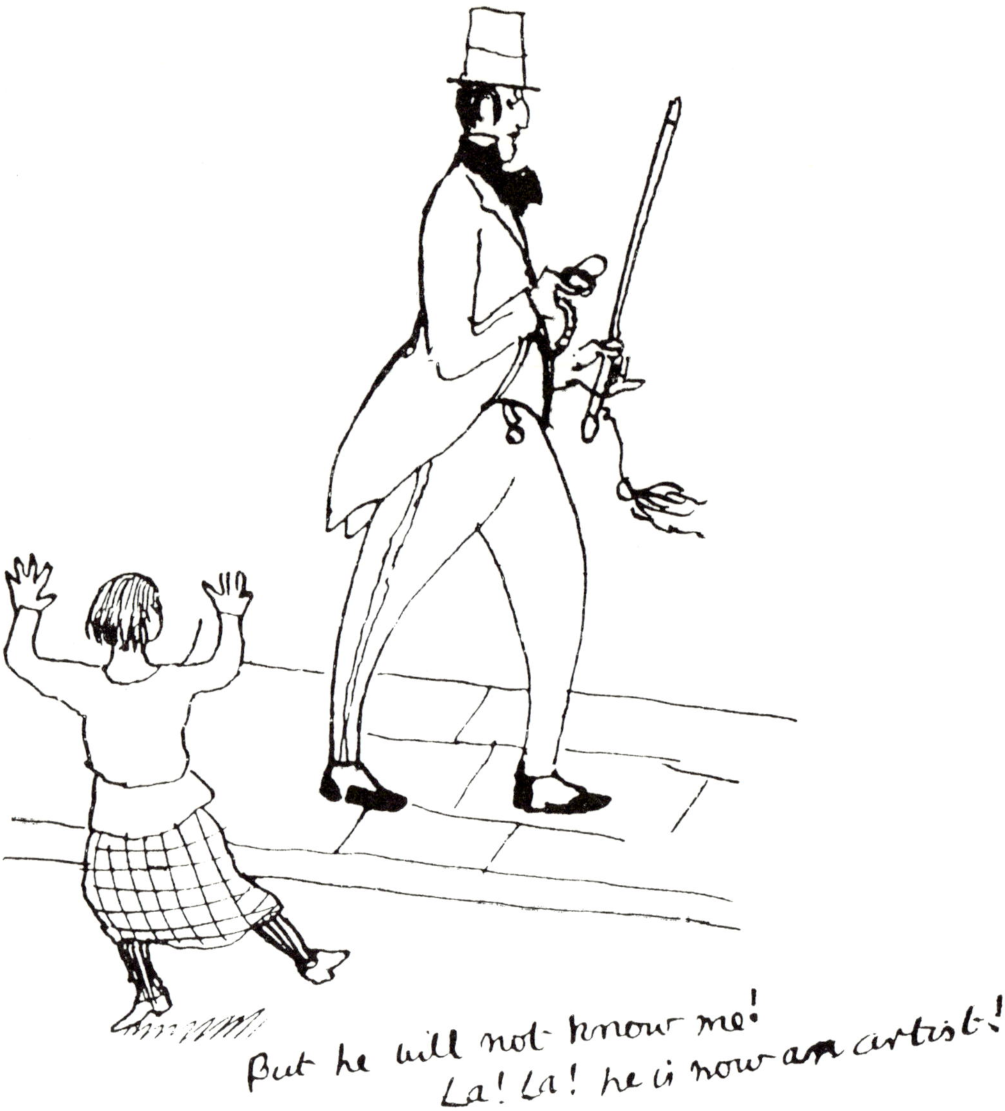

Carrington writes to tell John Nash that four of his pictures (*The Devil Watching his Theatre fill up*; *The Colonel's Wife Story*; *Well*; *Feeding the Chickens*) have sold at College Hall (1913):
'Already I see you bowing to me with much grandeur & dignity in the street, fingering a thick gold watch chain, with a tall, silk hat, grown stout with rich living & good wines!'

Introduction

I met John and Christine Nash soon after the war when they came to live in an old farmhouse at Wormingford in the Stour Valley. I was a youthful poet and short-story writer, and they were part of a large circle of artists who had been drifting towards the lovely countryside of the Suffolk–Essex borders since the Thirties, and which included Cedric Morris, Lett-Haines, Edward Bawden, Hugh Cronyn, John Aldridge, Joan Warburton, Roderick Barrett, Michael Ayrton, and many others. They were never a 'school' in the Newlyn sense but they all knew each other and created for me from my late teens onward a magic society.

It was Christine Nash who most encouraged me to write, who found a little house for me on the Suffolk coast and who – I suppose – inculcated in me her own somewhat severe work disciplines. She and John were my closest friends for over thirty years and it was inevitable that my writer's antenna should be especially alert when they talked about people they had known and things they had done before I was born. My first glimpse of Dora Carrington was in their photograph albums, a serious girl with heavy hair falling across her face, and often her feet bare in long grass. Her surname only was written in white ink under each Box Brownie snapshot.

After John's death in 1977 – Christine died ten months before – I discovered a tin trunk full of letters in the brick bread-oven at Bottengoms Farm. These were the letters which Paul, John, Christine and Carrington had written to each other since just before the First World War, and which continued, although less enthusiastically, throughout the 1920s. It was only after I had completed this book that Frances Partridge told me, 'It was in fact actually I who rescued Carrington's letters from a mouldering trunk after she had died and despatched them to their senders.' They are vigorous, funny, self-searching, tender letters which relate to what was really a growing-up, and the emergence of the Slade School and then war-divided friends, all of them much the same age, and each of them wonderfully gifted, and both troubled and released by the new freedoms of the period.

The 'image', as he called it, of Dora Carrington in Michael Holroyd's *Lytton Strachey* upset John Nash, and also decided her friend David Garnett to publish her letters and parts of her diary. When invited to include Carrington's letters to him, John told David Garnett that he had destroyed them. He had 'many warming memories of her so the destruction of her letters is more to be regretted'. However, his wife had about two dozen written between 1914 and 1918. 'These letters are in some trunk in a very cold place' – in other words the long-unheated bread-oven at Bottengoms Farm. When I asked Christine Nash why, in the light of all that she had told me about her friendship with Carrington, there was barely a mention of her in David's book, she said that she had sent him 'one or two letters but he had returned them'. What inference can be drawn from such reticence nearly forty years after Carrington's death is uncertain. What does emerge from this youthful correspondence is a vivid and sometimes painful account of artists finding their feet and then being caught up in the miseries of the First World War, and eventually finding very different paths.

In *First Friends* I have connected these youthful letters with the stories and memories told to me by John and Christine Nash during our own long friendship, and by Barbara Nash, John and Paul's sister. It is a book about student days, Western Front days and courtship days. The real passion which emerges is that for landscape.

R.B., Wormingford, November 1996

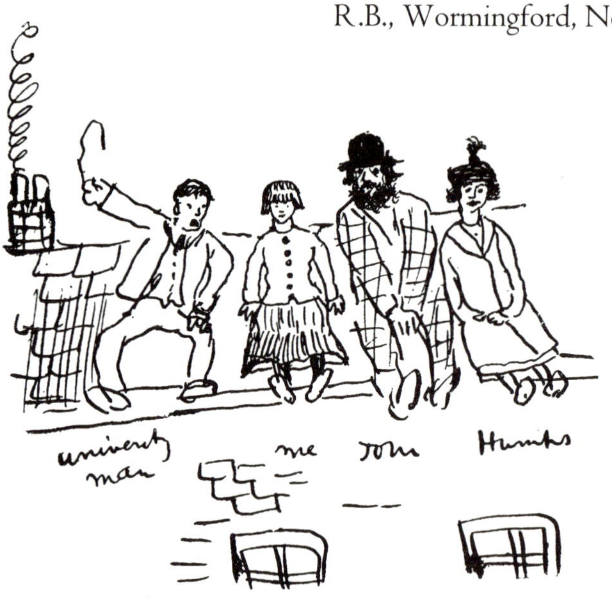

Carrington to John Nash: herself, Augustus John and Ruth Humphries on a roof at Hammersmith, watching the Boat Race.

Acknowledgements

There has been a great deal of assistance toward the making of this book, for which we are profoundly grateful. Many of the early pictures by the four young artists whose story this is, especially those pre-war pictures by John Nash, are now untraceable (and visually unrecorded), which is a pity. However, the letters, on which this story is based, are to be found at the Tate Gallery Archive, and we are indebted particularly for the kindly and enthusiastic help of the Archivist, Jennifer Booth, over several years. In the same spirit of generosity, Jennifer Wood at the Department of Art, the Imperial War Museum, has assisted with the Museum's material. To both Jennifers and both institutions we give our grateful thanks.

As Ronald Blythe mentions in the Introduction, it was Frances Partridge who returned the correspondence to the original owners after Carrington's death, which is indeed fortunate, and we thank her for her gracious permission to use material in which she holds copyright, through the good offices of her agents, Rogers, Coleridge and White (20 Powis Mews, London W11 1JN). Similarly, the permission of John Nash's literary executor, the late John Lewis, and his artistic executor, David Wolfers, together with that of the Paul Nash trustees (Clare Colvin, Dr Andrew Causey and Robin Langdon-Davies), has been freely granted. The help of all these has been most important.

Jane Hill assisted with information and advice about Carrington, particularly the location of pictures, and Jane Carrington and her mother gave permission to reproduce other Carrington material. Jeremy Greenwood started the whole thing off by a chance remark in Oxford about six years ago. Richard Garnett located a letter to his father from John Nash. Anne Tennent found a picture of Claughton Pellew. Brian Webb loaned a Paul Nash block for an early design of the binding paper, though in the end this was not used. The research by Alan Powers into the Ashridge House frescoes has been helpful. A good number of individuals gave permission to show pictures, and the help of Allen Freer; Anthony Spink of Spink-Leger Pictures; Edgar Astaire; Luke Gertler; Charles Newton and the Department of Prints and Drawings at the Victoria and Albert Museum; Melanie Gardner and David Clarke at Tullie House Museum, Carlisle; Richard Oram, Librarian at the Harry Ransom Humanities Research Center, Texas; Countess Camilla Chandon de Briailles, and lastly, Ashridge Management College is acknowledged with pleasure; the last two had pictures photographed professionally at their own expense. The owner of *Hill in Snow at Hurstbourne Tarrant* could not be traced, despite various efforts.

Some of the following acknowledgements refer specifically to the Fleece Press edition. David Edwards, at Leach and Company in Brighouse took especial pains to ensure that photographic work was of the highest order, as did Douglas Atfield when photographing *The Picnic*; Bristol and West Graphics made the line-blocks for the drawings. Peter J. Sanderson expertly set the type at Whittington. The printing of the plates has been done with care by J. W. Northend of Sheffield, whose Managing Director Keith Stubley has taken an especial interest in this project even though the day before I took him the transparencies, his company had taken on forty-six new orders for work; Ian Wright went the extra mile in preparation of the images for printing. Ken Smith and Brian Settle have made their customary effort to ensure an excellent binding. To everyone who has helped, we give our hearty thanks.

Ronald Blythe and Simon Lawrence, September 1997

Bibliography

Bluecoat Gallery, Liverpool, *An Honest Patron: A Tribute to Sir Edward Marsh*, 1976.
Blythe, Ronald, *A Painter in the Country*, BBC2, 1968. Directed by John Read.
Blythe, Ronald, *John Nash at Wormingford*, Aldgate Press, 1992.
Colvin, Clare, *John Nash Book Designs*, Minories, Colchester, 1986.
Eates, Margot, *Paul Nash: Paintings, Drawings and Illustrations*, Lund Humphries, 1948.
Garnett, David (ed.), *Carrington: Letters and Extracts from her Diaries*, Jonathan Cape, 1970.
Hill, Jane, *The Art of Dora Carrington*, Herbert Press, 1994.
Holroyd, Michael, *Lytton Strachey: A Critical Biography*, Heinemann, 1967–68.
King, James, *Interior Landscapes: A Life of Paul Nash*, Weidenfeld and Nicolson, 1987.
Lewis, John, *John Nash: The Painter as Illustrator*, Pendomer Press, 1978.
Nash, John, *The Artist Plantsman*, Anthony d'Offay, 1976.
Nash, Paul, *Outline*, Faber and Faber, 1949.
Proust, Marcel, *Time Regained*, translated by Stephen Hudson, Chatto and Windus, 1931.
Sieveking, Lance, *The Eye of the Beholder*, Hulton Press, 1957.
Stevens, Anne, *Claughton Pellew*, Ashmolean Museum, 1990.

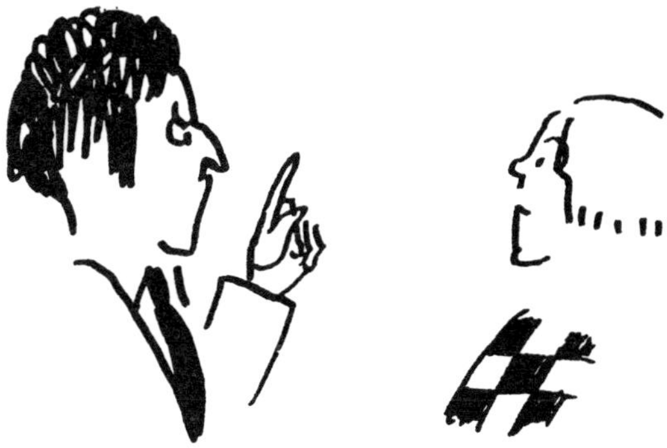

FIRST FRIENDS

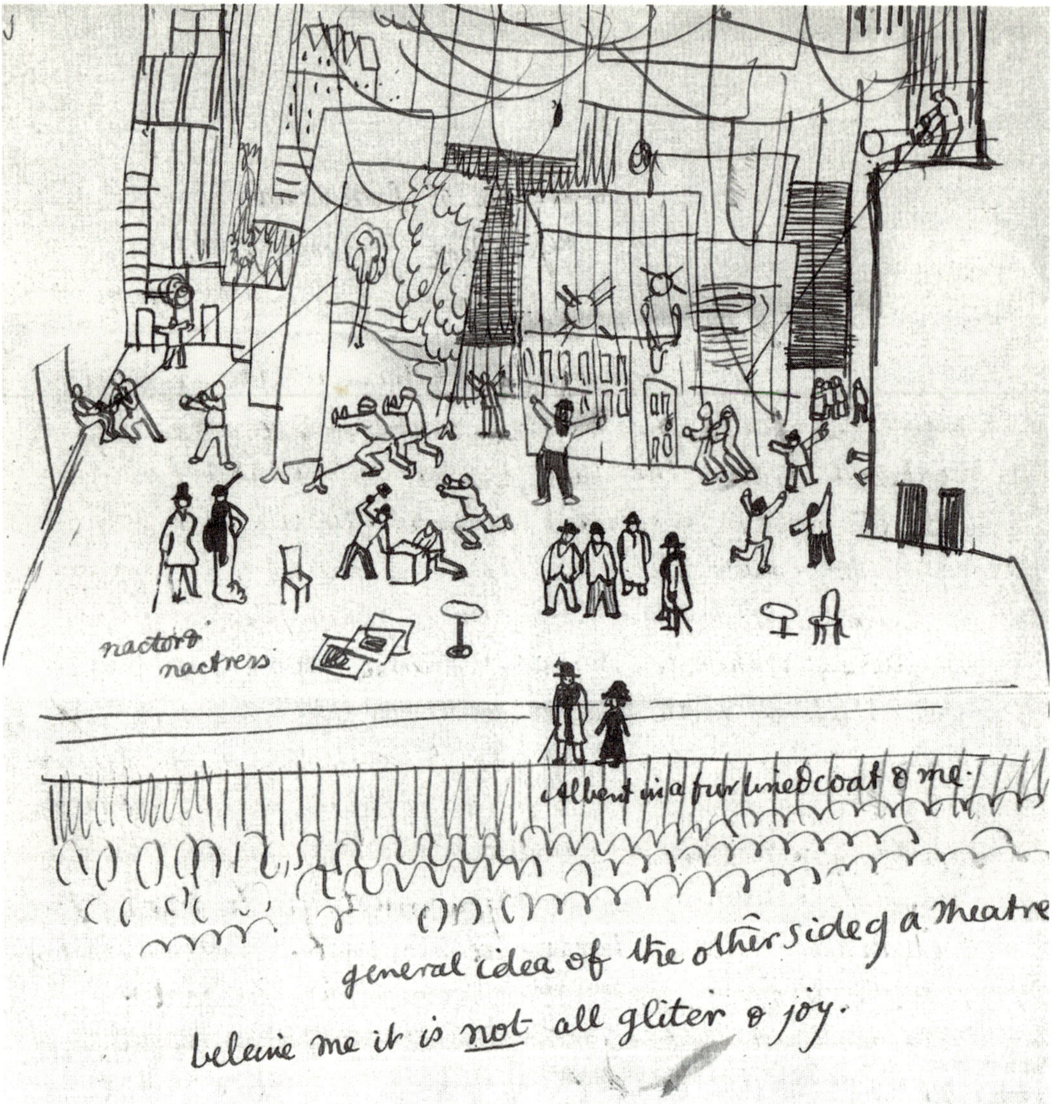

Dora Carrington to John Nash; a view of a theatre set with herself and Albert Rutherston. 'You must go to "The Doctor's Dilemma". It is Shaw at his best, most excellent conversation, and my scene isn't so bad. Of course Albert really does it all, & occasionally lets me have a word here & there. It is great fun running about between rehearsals, & seeing the great G. B. Shaw rehearsing them, and watching the switch light man. The scene shifters are wags – & good swearers.' Tate Gallery Archive.

In the Beginning

This is essentially a student story, a tale of first friendships and their consequences. The four students, Dora Carrington, Paul Nash and his brother John, and Christine Kühlenthal, came together at the Slade School of Painting, Drawing and Sculpture in the years just before the First World War. John Nash was not registered on the Slade's books but as did other teenagers hung around the School unofficially. Its ethos was that of the classic European painter's workroom in which pupils sat at the feet of the master, learning their trade and exercising self-discipline. It was now just over thirty years old and at a peak of excellence and excitement which would not again be reached. It had been named after Sir Felix Slade, who had died in 1868 leaving £35,000 to endow professorships of art at Oxford, Cambridge and London Universities. Its pre-1914 fame owed everything to the triumvirate of Wilson Steer, Frederick Brown and especially Henry Tonks. Paul Nash registered at the Slade in October 1910, having been told that Paris was not 'the least use', Dora Carrington the same year and Christine Kühlenthal in 1912. Paul was twenty and the girls both seventeen. John Nash had been advised by his brother to avoid formal art-school training because it would destroy the fresh 'innocent' vision and line which were to remain the hallmark of his work. He and Dora Carrington were born in the spring of 1893; he was just a month her junior. Paul was born in 1889 and Christine in 1895. In old age John would boast to his friend Cedric Morris, 'We are Victorians, old boy!' and would receive a grim look. But the Empire certainly stamped all their childhoods, with the Nashes living at Ghuznee Lodge, Kensington, Christine at Krishna Villa, Harrow, and Dora amid the oriental bric-à-brac brought home to Bedford by her elderly father who had been building Indian railways as long ago as the Mutiny in 1857.

All four young people would have emotional difficulties with their backgrounds. Dora Carrington's were no secret. She openly despised her mother, who in crude Victorian terms had been an old maid governess who had caught a well-off old bachelor in need of settling down in the shires after long years abroad. Whilst Mrs Carrington could be oppressively conventional, always keen on doing the right thing, it has to be said that she brought up five attractive and intelligent children and that her now famous heavy hand where her daughter was concerned was no more than might be expected of a woman of her time with an unchaperoned daughter in London. Dora has left a scathing portrait of Charlotte Carrington, with her churchgoing, tastelessness and 'what will people think' obsessions. She puts her mother firmly in the 'Balkan' ('trouble' – 'Trouble in the Balkans' was a headline in the newspapers) camp and gives her no credit for putting nothing in her way when she wanted to leave Bedford High School for Girls to be a Slade student. And this when both her parents were ill, her father partly paralysed by a stroke and her mother rheumatic and lame.

Paul and John Nash's difficulties with their mother would never reach letters or diaries. They were too terrible for that. Caroline Nash died in a mental asylum on St Valentine's Day, 1910, only a few months before Paul registered at the Slade. Her many years of suffering, and the expense of a series of retreats and nursing-homes, had crippled her family in all sorts of ways. John never spoke or wrote of her, more out of love and pity for her than from 'shame'. Insanity in the family was among the unspeakable illnesses then. Only a few years before his own death Paul summoned up his courage to write, '... our dark Beautiful but delicate mother who used to be so quick and gay ... my dearest memories of her are fraught with a sense of disquiet. I see her great agate eyes change and become overwhelmed with misery and anxious distress at the reminder of something dreaded. Perhaps already the horrid disease was at work preparing the cruel doom which was to overshadow all.'

Not only were John and Paul, and their sister Barbara, harrowed by their mother's sickness, but the boys had added to it the ritual suffering of their Edwardian schooling, Paul's at a sadistic naval crammer's, John's at Wellington College, then a dreadful place from which he more than once ran away. 'You wouldn't mention art there unless you wanted your head knocked off!'

Opposite, top left: *W. H. Nash* (1848–1929), Rupert Lee, June 1913. Pencil, 254 × 207 mm. Ronald Blythe. Top right: Caroline Nash, (died 1910). Ronald Blythe. Below left: Claughton Pellew, *c.*1915. Anne Tennent. Below right: Portrait of *Wilhelm Kühlenthal*, Christine's father; Rupert Lee, *c.*1918. Pen and ink and wash, 443 × 250 mm. Ronald Blythe.

Over, left: Slade students in fancy dress on a London taxi, *c.*1910. Tate Gallery Archive. Carrington is wearing a headband and short-sleeved flapper dress, standing on the taxi roof. Right: Dora Carrington, *c.*1910, before she became a 'crophead'. Tate Gallery Archive.

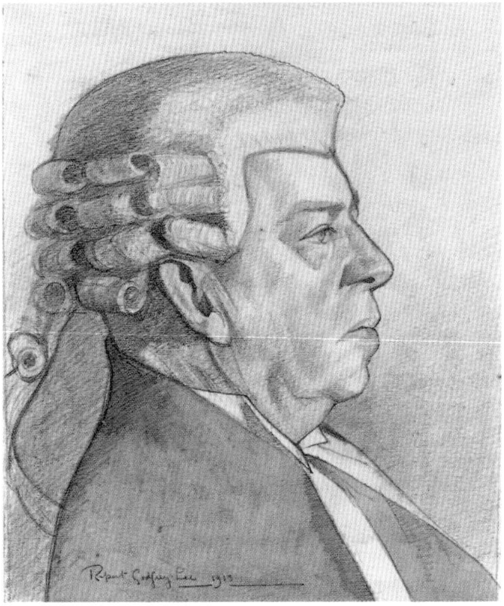

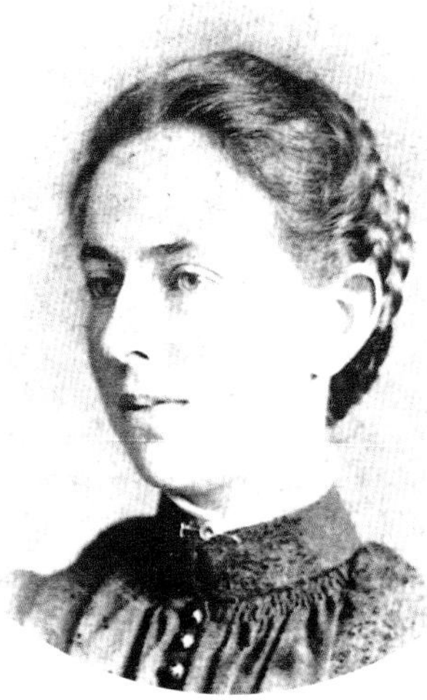

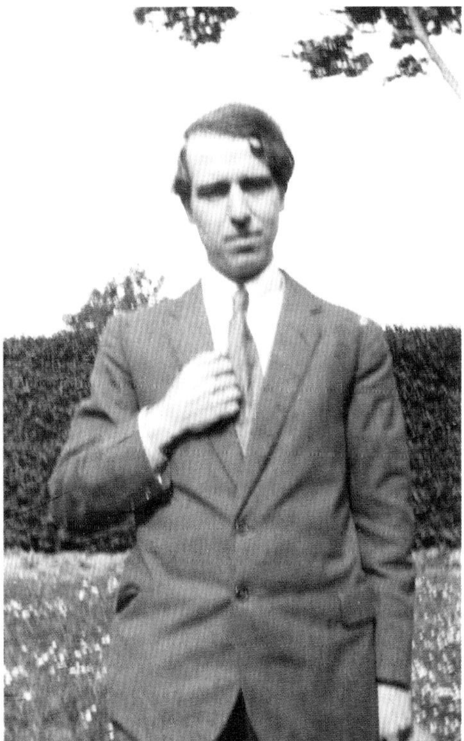

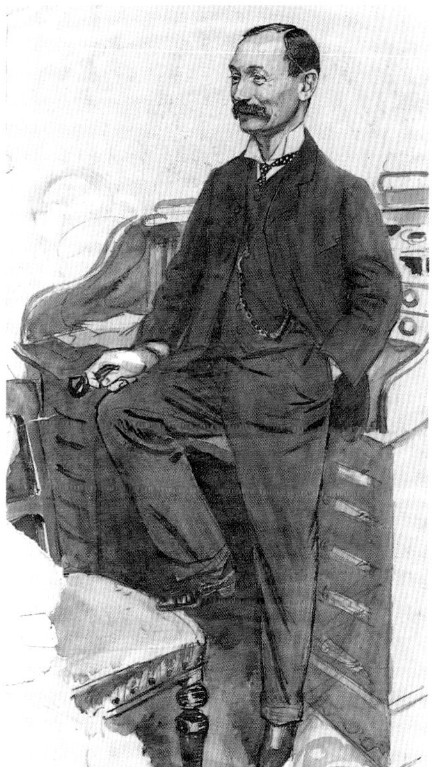

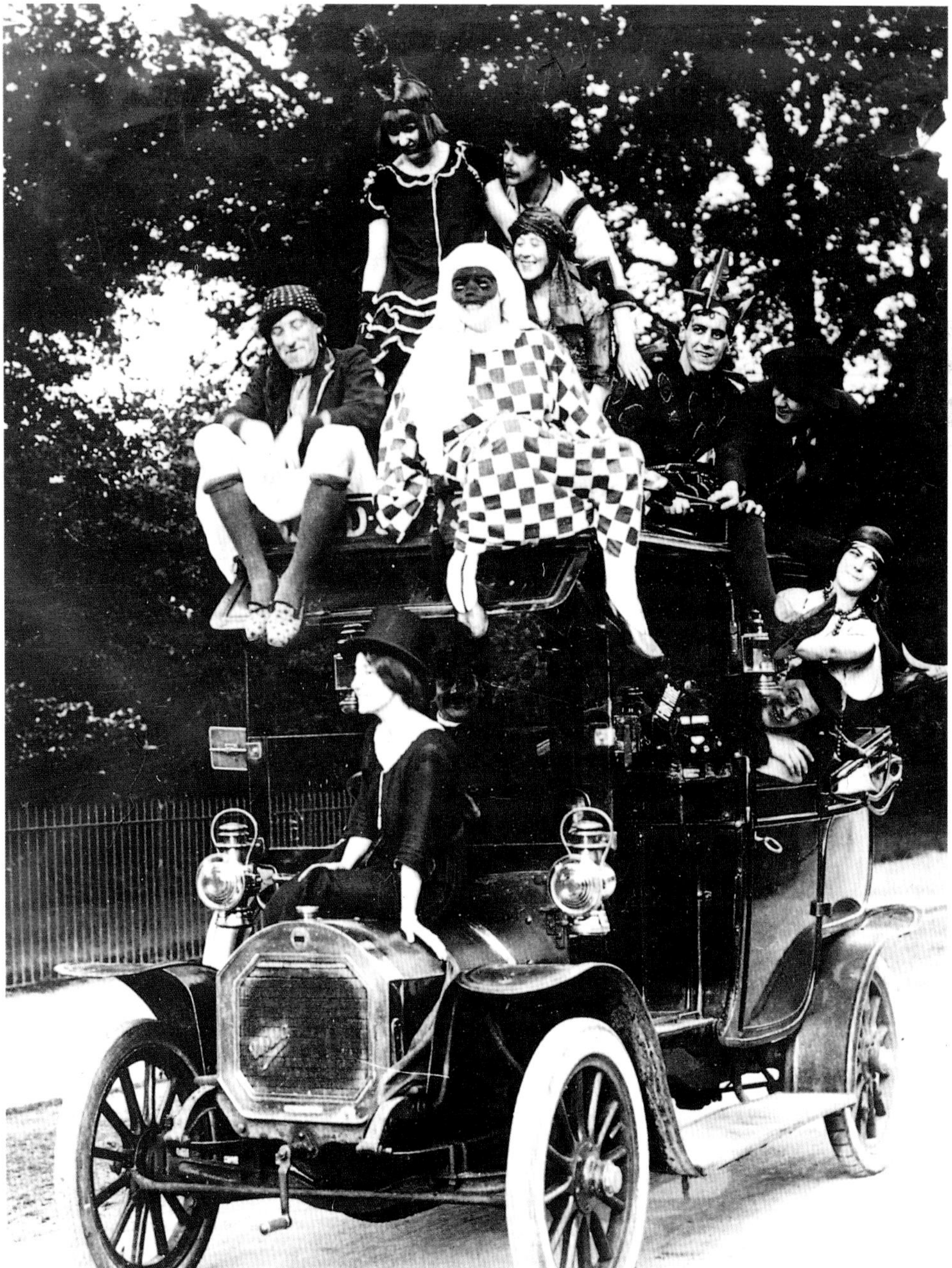

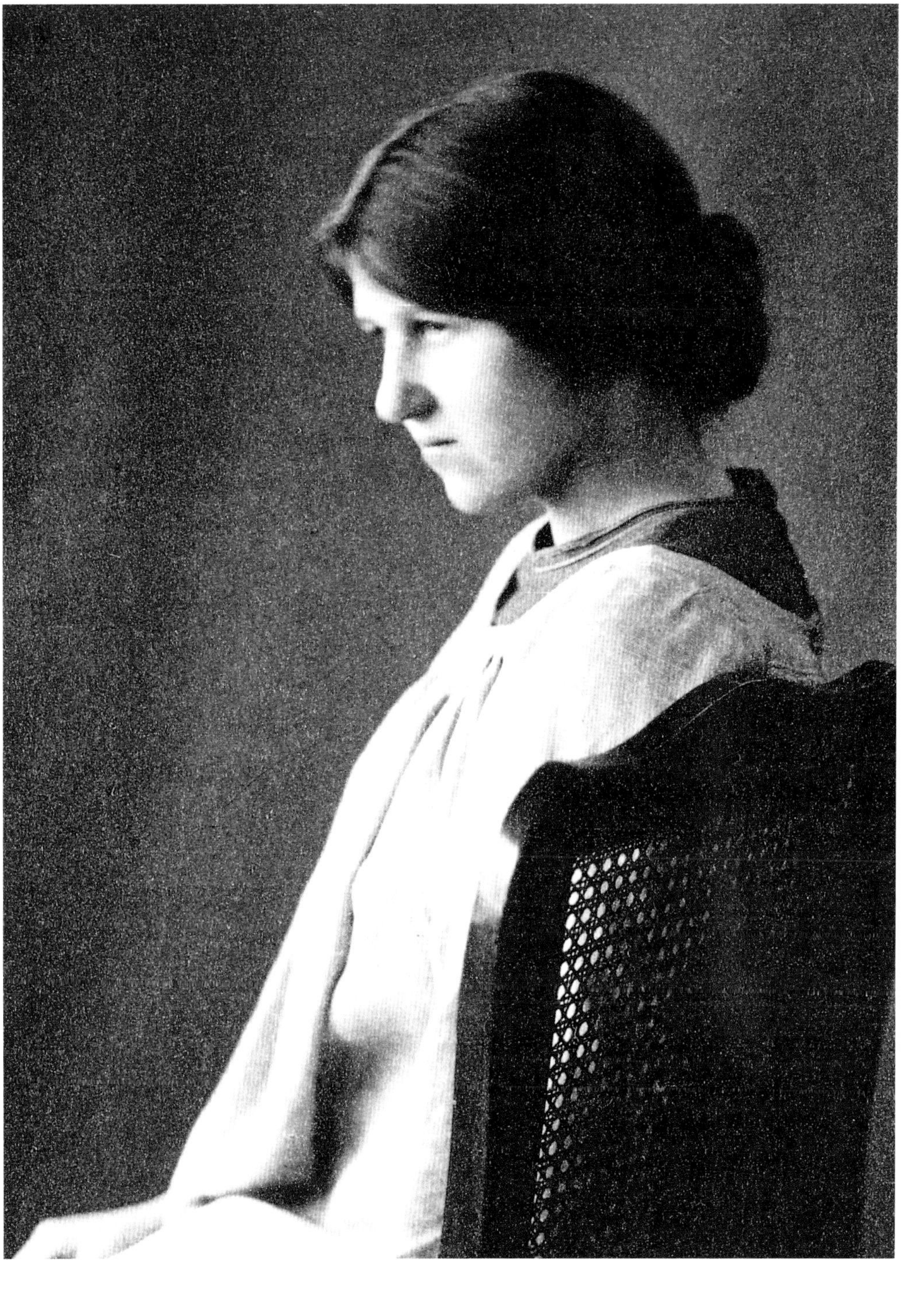

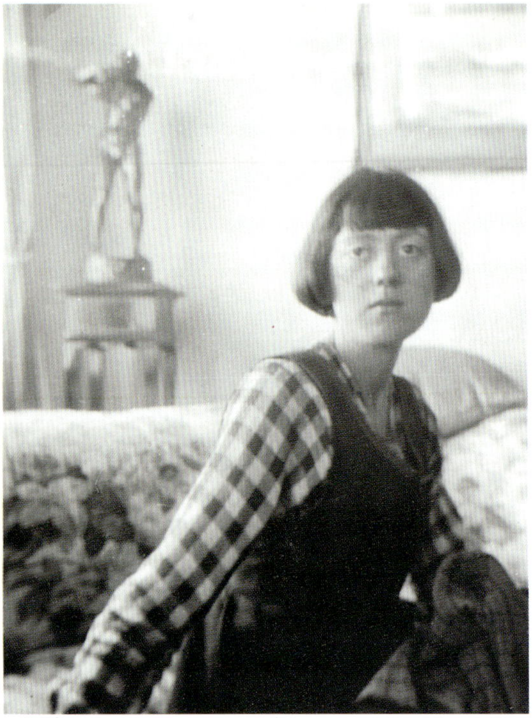

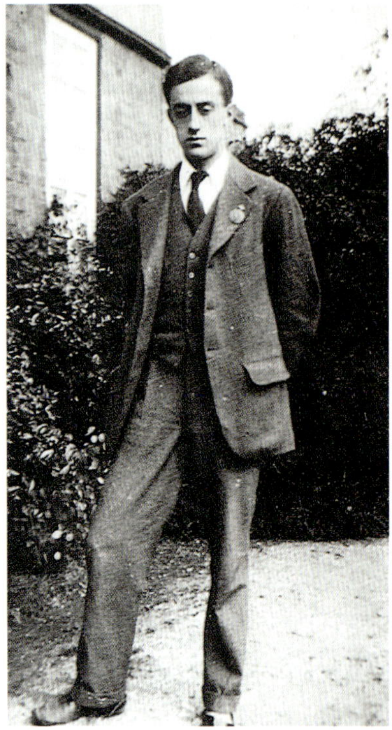

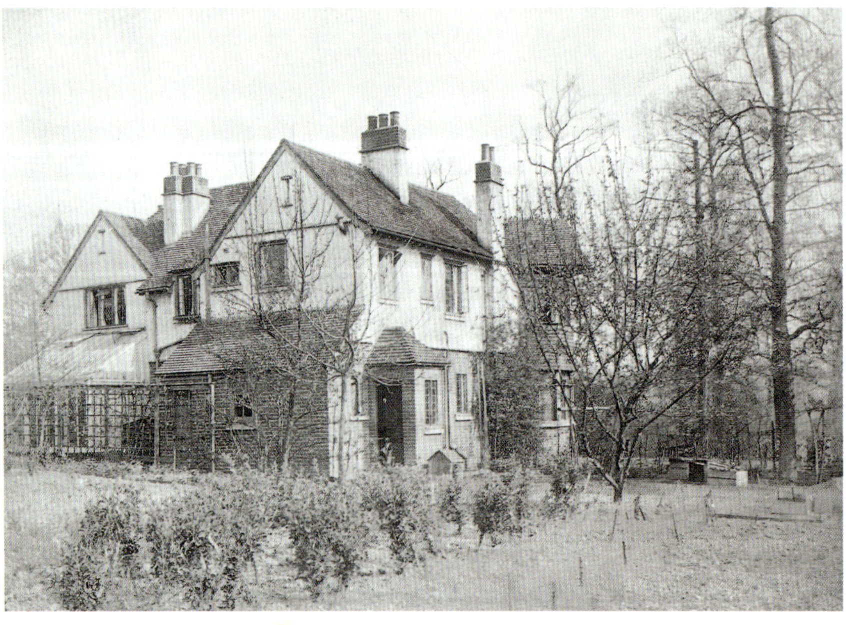

Christine's background contained a time-bomb. Her father was an unnaturalised German merchant chemist married to a Scottish wife. If Carrington's mother was 'Balkan', Christine's father was one of E. M. Forster's Schlegels, as indeed was Christine herself. But this would not save them from persecution after August 4th, 1914. King George would change his German name to Windsor; the Kühlenthals kept theirs and were condemned to the full stench of *Daily Mail* and *John Bull* generated Hun-hatred, and were only saved from this, and from more official harassment towards the end of the war, by the Nash brothers persuading their friend Eddie Marsh to use his influence on behalf of the guiltless family. Right up to the war, to be a German living in England was to be part of an intellectual élite, but after August 1914 it was to be a criminal. Much has been made of Carrington's insistence on her surname but all the Slade women similarly addressed each other – Brett, Humphries, Lloyd. But never 'Kühlenthal' for the simple reason that nobody could get their tongue round it. John gave up when he first had to mention her in a letter to Carrington – 'Miss K' followed by a snaky tailing off. Carrington herself, Christine's close friend, wrote 'Küthenthel' always. In 1916 after her brother Teddy had been killed on the Somme there was no way of taking 'Miss Küthenthel' to meet her parents at Hurstbourne Tarrant, so would Christine mind being introduced as Miss Penn or Penzance 'or any extravagance you choose?' Christine bore the embarrassment of her name stoically throughout these ghastly days. She had long rid herself of her first name, Dorothy. As for the Nash boys, Paul became even more magnificently Paul, John was Jack or Jacko, and Carrington during the war toyed with the notion of turning the loathed Dora into 'Doron'. John wrote it in Greek for her, ΔΩΡΟΝ.

However, the names which threatened the Slade in 1910 were those of Manet and the French Impressionists whose paintings Roger Fry had brought to the New Grafton Galleries. It was England's first sight of them. 'Keep away!' Henry Tonks warned his students. Paul was immune. That year he had discovered his curious mentor, the north country poet Gordon Bottomley, who was many years his senior and still a Pre-Raphaelite. At this moment John was still very much Jacko the little brother, having in the financial straits following their mother's death to get himself some kind of job. Christine was still at school in Gerrards Cross and better known as

Opposite, top left: Christine Nash, 1919. Top, right: John Nash, *c.*1918. Below: Forestholme, Gerrards Cross, Buckinghamshire, 1907. The Kühlenthals' house. All Ronald Blythe.

a dancer than as a prospective artist. Although it is true at the beginning when John decided to paint that Paul advised against the attendance at an art school, the state of affairs at their home Wood Lane House was such as to make John himself recognise that there was little money to fund him at the Slade or anywhere else. In old age their sister Barbara still grumbled about Paul's 'extravagance' and all the worry it caused at home – 'But never Jacko, he took nothing.'

Three months after leaving the Slade, on 26th March 1912, Paul wrote to 'Miss Carrington' reminding her that they had been properly introduced so that 'if this letter seems impertinent forgive me. I am carried out of myself. Happening to come here [the Slade] this evening I found [Claude] Miller about the pack up your two drawings . . . thus I saw your drawing of a girl sitting on a bed. I think it is one of the most beautiful things I remember to have seen, but it is beautiful *now* and *final* and no line or touch can improve it. It *must* spoil it. That is why I write, because I feel terrified you are about to carry it further. . . . Please be content to pause and see what you have done, if you do not already realise it. Oh I am sure you have created a marvellous thing, tremendously alive and strong, simple and full of great feeling, and beside all this as fine a piece of decoration as can be desired by any eyes. You'll think I exaggerate but this is about half what I am feeling.' Soon afterwards came invitations to Wood Lane House, Iver, now no longer the confused vacuum left behind by poor Caroline Nash but in the process of being translated into two kinds of imagery by her sons, Paul's symbolic and poetic, John's botanically and agriculturally informed. Moreover, although their father never pretended to know the first thing about art and remained domestically conventional and sedate, Carrington was to discover a far more acceptable atmosphere at Iver than she did at Hurstbourne Tarrant or Bedford. Mark Gertler's response to it reveals its unoppressive nature, and its being a place where an artist could work. He wrote to Carrington:

> I enjoyed my visit to the Nashes very much indeed. What a splendid way to live. What beautiful surroundings. How beautiful the country is. It will be my ultimate aim to live in the country. We went for a walk and got caught in the rain, but it was very splendid all the same. [Paul] took me to see the lake. Before I went Jack gave me some flowers to take away and said perhaps my mother would like them.
>
> After tea the sister played the piano and then a wonderful rainbow appeared in the sky. . . . In the garden there was a little tree full of brilliant white blossoms

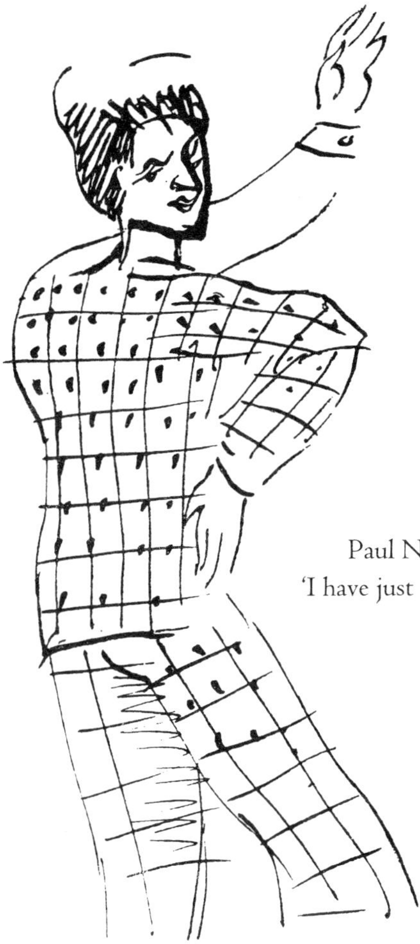

Paul Nash to Carrington, on his love of fine clothes:
'I have just got a brown check suit that will stagger humanity.
My word it is a check suit.'

which stood out strong and light against the sky .... [In the wood] one trunk looked like a bundle of many-coloured snakes.

Having got out of London, Paul himself was in a dream of elms, of slender girls in the cage of his 'bird garden' and of magical prehistoric mounds. At the Slade he had deliberately cut a dandiacal figure with his thick black hair and dressy suits, a figure and face which were somehow arranged to be seen in profile, if possible. Having already studied at two previous art schools, and having unknown to them passed through some of the worst adult experiences, he was seen by Carrington as a little awesome. He made her feel awkward and gauche yet by so sincerely praising her work he also made her feel remarkable. She found him disturbing and he knew it. He frequently needed to put her at ease. He was not, unlike his brother, in pursuit. 'My dear golden Carrington – what a good letter to me – it has greatly delighted me – I have no time this moment to answer you as I would, but Jack and I are to be in Town tomorrow and I will call at the Slade and see if you'll have us to tea that afternoon. All I will say here is – never fear to be "friendly" with me – I am an extraordinary harmless affectionate animal – probably of the anteater tribe – and as for being offended by your naive conclusion upon my appearance – pouff, Carrington, what nonsense.'

None of this was exactly true, of course. Further letters might address her as Carrington Regina but they also suggested that, although he was happily married to Bunty, Carrington qualified as one of his 'wives'. Neither of the Nash brothers knew the meaning of sexual faithfulness nor ever attempted to. Paul first saw Carrington across the Antique Room where students of both sexes came together to draw from plaster casts of classical sculpture: 'One of the Slade girls who was both clever and good-looking to an unusual degree [attracted me] ... and when she cut her thick gold hair into a heavy golden bell, this, her fine blue eyes, her stutter, her turned-in toes and other quaint ... attributes combined to make her a conspicuous and popular figure.' This memorable initial glimpse of Carrington occurred in the months following Paul's etherial love affair with a girl named Sybil Fountain and preceding his enthralment with Margaret Odeh, the girl he would marry. His friendship with Sybil was a shy, elusive business, a boy's romantic pursuit of someone he was still not mature enough to deal with. She was like the women in the 'bird garden' cage, remote from men. He had actually met her on his home ground, so to speak, when she was visiting Buckinghamshire and, longing to see her again, he followed her back to London, finding the street but not the complete address. 'I did not know the number of the house, I felt only a strange certainty that we should meet. As I came into the street the sunshine was still warm on the pavements. When I entered the third square I saw her walking towards me. We met with the most obvious pleasurable surprise on her part; but I looked in vain for the slightest hint of any deeper emotion.' There was a reversal of such seeking during the early months of Paul's and Carrington's friendship but Carrington was not to find what she was half-hoping for, something closer, something greater than which was in any event her first important relationship with a man. He was playful and mocking and profoundly admiring all at the same time. He teased her and complimented her both at once. In time – a short time – she appeared to be thankful that things had not taken the course she had briefly hoped they would.

John Nash's pursuit was a very different story. He and Carrington had met when Paul brought her to Iver and he was almost immediately plunged into a desire so painful that he could think of little else. He had neither his brother's good looks nor his panache but he did have wit, and something near to genius where a feeling for the English countryside was concerned. Both endeared him to Carrington. Landscape would be their true love affair. Not that John wanted such a sublimation. What he wanted was her body – her to be his. They were both nineteen and he was tormented and overwhelmed by her. His first letter to her was decorous. He had to come nearer but without scaring her off:

Dear Carrington,

I am sending you these wallflowers. I thought they might be rather pleasant in London. I grow them in a little plantation just as a coffee planter grows his coffee trees though my plantation is more interesting and sweet-smelling. I hope your little band [of Slade girls] are all well. If you should want some more flowers I should like to send them, I have such a lot.... John N. Nash.

She replied so openly and delightfully, and at such length, as to encourage him into believing that she had seen something in him which she liked, something more than 'Paul's brother'.

Dock House, Beaulieu, Brockenhurst.

Dear Jack,

Thank you very much for your two letters and the flowers. They were very beautiful and I loved getting them, especially the wallflowers.... Hurray! I am glad you sold at Leeds and the London Group. I am very happy here, and miserable at having to leave tomorrow to return to that town of ill fame – London.

We spend most of the day sailing and picking primroses, in wonderful woods. Yesterday I drew a head all day. Heads are difficult to draw. Mrs Stuart Wortley [the sitter] is very interesting. She was a great friend of Whistler, Gilbert and Sullivan, Ellen Terry, Oscar Wilde and all the persons of wit and beauty belonging to that wonderful epoch. So the company and the food are both good here, whilst outside the country surpasses all belief.

Thank Paul for his wonderful letter. I felt, do not tell him, bad pangs of jealousy, that Bunty [Margaret Odeh, his new girlfriend] must have stacks of such letters whilst I have but few!...

The woods are very wonderful to draw, and a river which is blue, flows by the

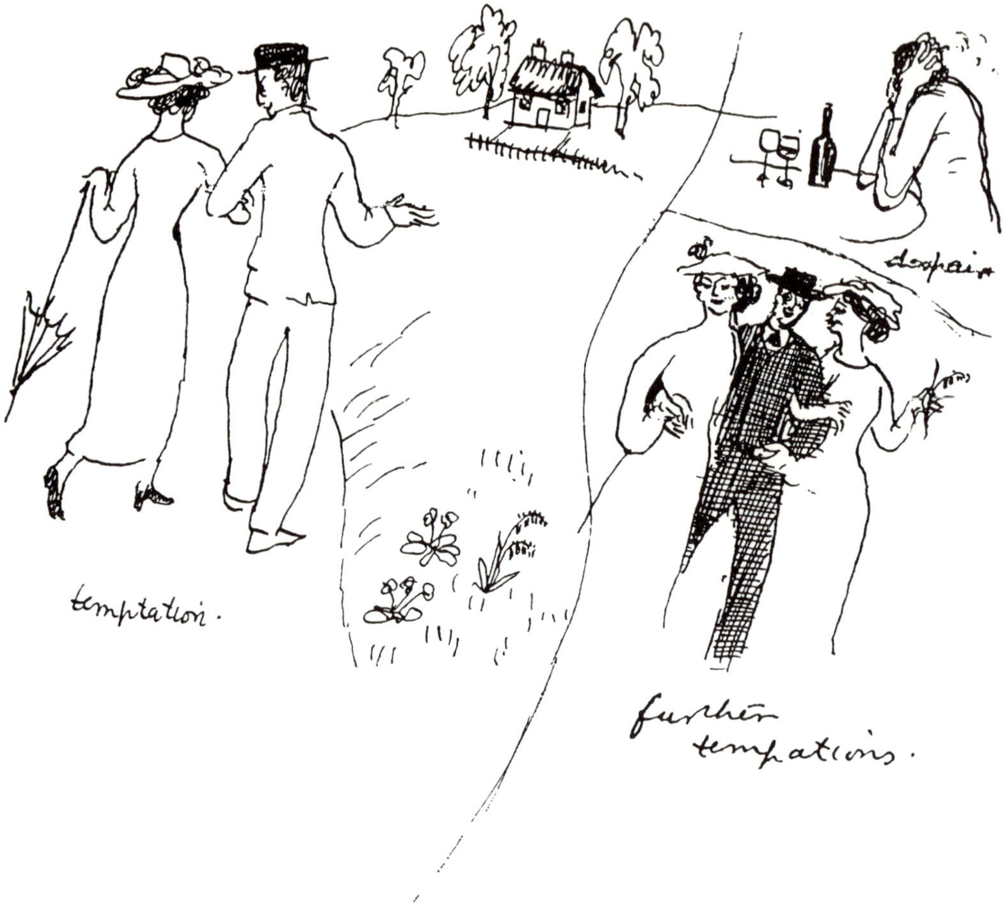

Carrington depicts John Nash's supposed vices:
'*Quotation from the letter of John Nash Esq* "I daresay you will hear *all kinds* of rumours about me from the Slade" – to put it mildly.'

trees, and stiff marsh marigolds and primroses grow erect on its banks. I can now sail a boat with no little skill, a thing which gives me much pleasure to think of. I am just going out to draw the mill and this afternoon I shall draw the men making bricks in the brick kiln by the river. They are all made by hand, in silence, just like the Israelites made bricks. Three men, working quite silently, in an old shed, grey the clay they use, and dimly lighted through the chinks in the walls, and by the side of the river and primrose woods.
This is no letter . . . Carrington.

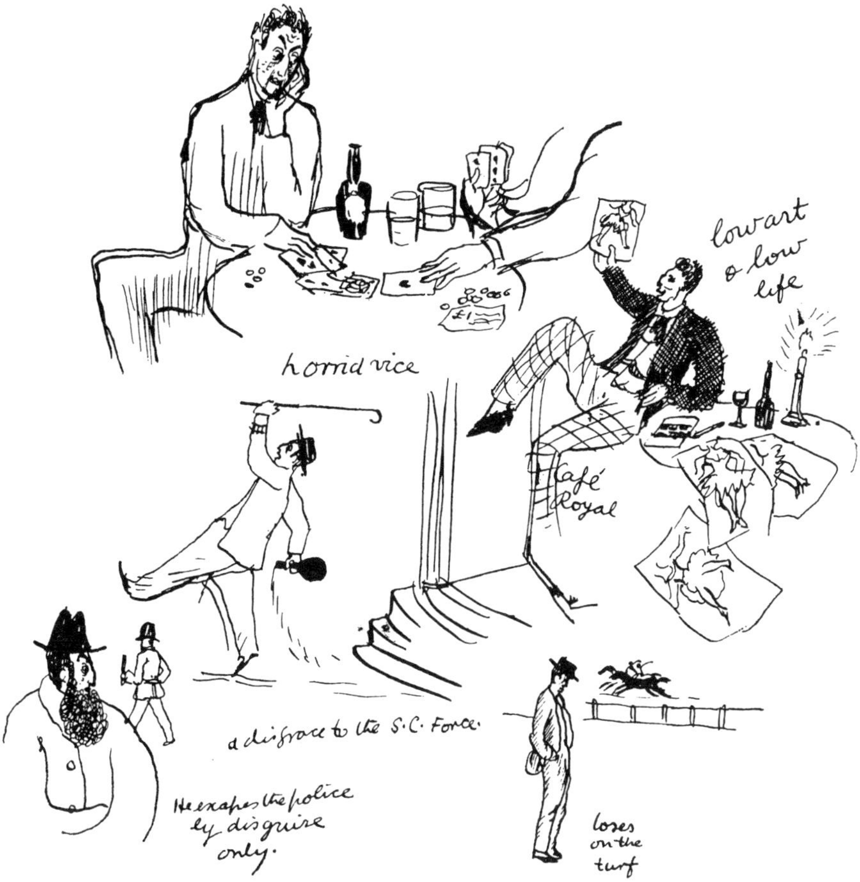

1913 was for John the year of frustrated wooing and bewilderment, and for Carrington her first year of battling to retain her independence as a free person and a dedicated artist. Her myriad ways of putting him off baffled and enraged John, who simply needed a lover. Their for-and-against arguments on this subject were obfuscated by their having no proper (improper) sexual language in which it could be discussed. So that John could only confess to being 'passionate' and Carrington could only take shelter in flight and neglect. As they were equally driven by a determination to be artists (although John's drive was still in hiding due to the financial situation at Wood Lane House), they recognised that they had much in common. Although less charismatic than his brother, John knew his own worth. He was slight, witty, well-read, with a strangely measured way of talking. Carrington could also have noticed with alarm a certain dependency upon others in his nature, a demand rather than a hope that he should be cared for. Unlike her, he and Paul were not torn between the conventions of their home and the exhilarating unconventionality of the world opening before them as artists in London. On the contrary, they used Wood Lane House as first base, as it were, to where they intended to go, and whilst being reticent about their mother's tragedy, they never got themselves into Carrington's kind of muddles when she made her 'home or away' engagements. Her brother Noel wrote of her devising 'a makeshift system of alibis, based on painting commissions or visits to approved friends' and how 'all this led to a complicated calendar of deceptions which became a second habit even when no longer necessary'.

She and John were together at Iver and other country houses. They walked and bicycled, and exchanged pictures, went to the music hall and to the theatre, also to concerts and lectures. But there were times when she didn't arrive or, if she did, hurried on with one of her marvellous smiles. Once, taken to task, she burst out in a letter, 'Don't ever ask me to make any arrangement or appointment as it is a mental impossibility for me to fix anything.... It's a silly idea, arrangements and fixtures – and I have so much to draw, hens, appletrees and people. And yet again more people.' What she rarely neglected to do was to answer a letter, so that when she did John knew that he really was in her bad books. It was fearful – 'I wait in vain for a letter. I will keep my promise of patience to you. I was glad to see you t'other day for even that short moment in which you found time to administer a rebuke no doubt deserved.... When will you write? I feel inexpressibly dull.... Oh, postman, postman, is there a letter from Carrington with you?'

As the Slade years passed she became somewhat notorious for her evasions, but when one considers her shifts from address to address – and her compulsion to make any room she inhabited beautiful, thus endless toil painting and decorating – her having to feed herself and to travel miles by foot, train and bicycle, to cope with all the student activities at the Slade and, most of all, to fight hard to find time for her own work, her fibs and excuses become less reprehensible. John was hurt by them because he so much wanted to be in love with her. He believed that she need only respond in the normal female way for them both to be happy, since they had so much in common. But the months of 1913 passed and she never did. When he was old and was asked directly whether they ever did sleep together, he confessed, wryly, that the closest he had got to her was when their knees joggled together under the rain-apron of a London bus. A chilly grin.

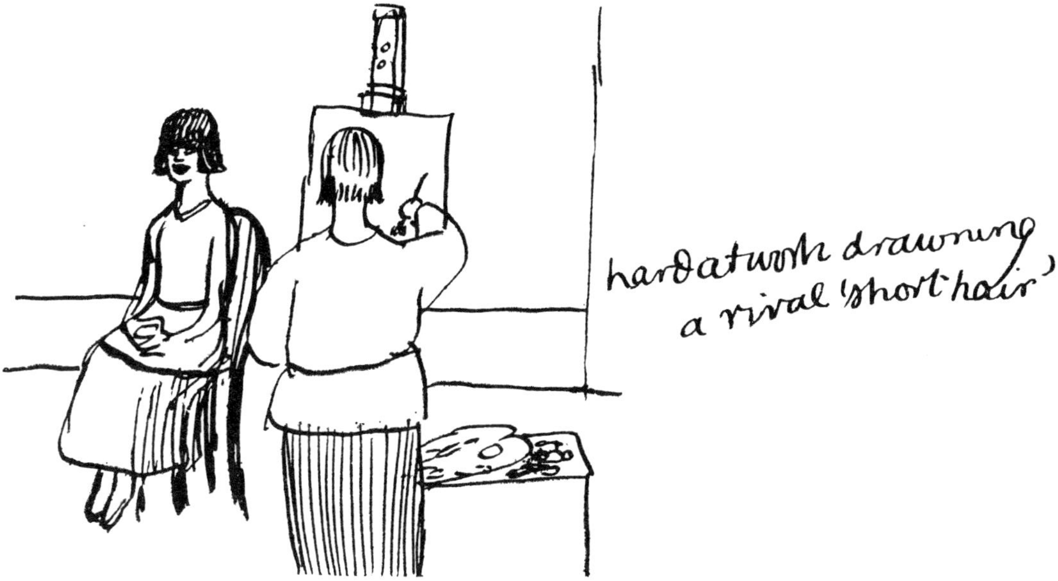

Carrington to John Nash: portrait of herself at work.

From woundings to some kind of immunity to her prevarications: 'I write this in indelible pencil. You notice therefore let some parts which I will underline be engraved on your mind. Your soliloquy on the frailty of mankind received and filed. ... *Now* re *Landscape* [Carrington's gift of one of hers to John] I am overjoyed to hear that it is finished and I beg you will let me have it as soon as possible as I am shortly taking my rooms.... Please do send it to me and don't keep it back because I have disappointed you, for after all, sakes alive and "marry-come-up", I know how to take care of myself, don't I? And as I have told you before, I know all women are *Artfull* and a man who has that one and only fact as a firm basis of his opinions towards 'em can't be led into much trouble, can he?... If you do think of marrying I should not marry a sergeant [her joke] or any form of soldier-piece. But I know better than to be tricked by your chance witty remarks, young woman. I daresay you have, or will hear, all kind of rumours about me from people at the Slade. All such like should be taken *cum grana salis* (Cerebos is the best).' Carrington's reply accepted the challenge to depict John's 'vices'.

Stifling desire so that it should not become an unwanted attention is about the worst thing a twenty-year-old can be asked to do. And never a thank-you either. John was upset.

Enter Claughton

Paul knew that he too was an artist after watching a boy at his school 'who lived not as other men lived but like a bird, rather, on a perch, knocking off likenesses of the plaster casts and whistling tunelessly the while'. The boy's name was Eric Kennington. John needed to be told and convinced that he was one. His saviour was one of Paul's fellow students at the Slade, Claughton Pellew. Paul was indebted to Claughton for befriending him on his arrival and taking him back to his comfortable home in Blackheath. 'Among the few people at the Slade who seemed in the least interested in what I was doing was a slight dark man with a strange voice. It was rather high-pitched and curiously uneven in tone, yet in its uneven, slightly sing-song progression oddly attractive. He had profound magnetic eyes ... and hair that was dark and thick above a high bony forehead.' Paul thought he had a look of George Borrow, his hero.

Until Claughton persuaded him otherwise, John appeared resigned to an office of sorts. Something having been said about journalism, he purchased Pitman's shorthand and practised it on the fly-leaves of novels, then apprenticed himself unpaid to the local paper. Or maybe he should be a chartered accountant, he told Carrington. 'It will mean giving up your yellow collar and wearing a bowler,' she replied, 'have you thought of this?' He had, but resignedly. 'Lucky' Paul! But soon John was quoting Cicero to her, '*Amicus cercus in ne incerta*' [*sic*] – 'A true friend appears in need of our uncertain business.' Claughton, of course. His father was not unlike Carrington's father, an Empire engineer. Claughton had spent his early childhood riding the Canadian Pacific Railway but was at this moment turning himself into a Franciscan. He was a man of certainties and tremendous courage. They sent him to Dartmoor in 1917 for refusing to fight – his conscientious objection to being called up had been refused by the tribunal – and the physical abuse he received in prison affected his health for the rest of his life.

Paul and Claughton were to have a walking holiday in Norfolk during the summer of 1912 but Paul was unable to go at the last minute, so John went instead. It was his salvation.

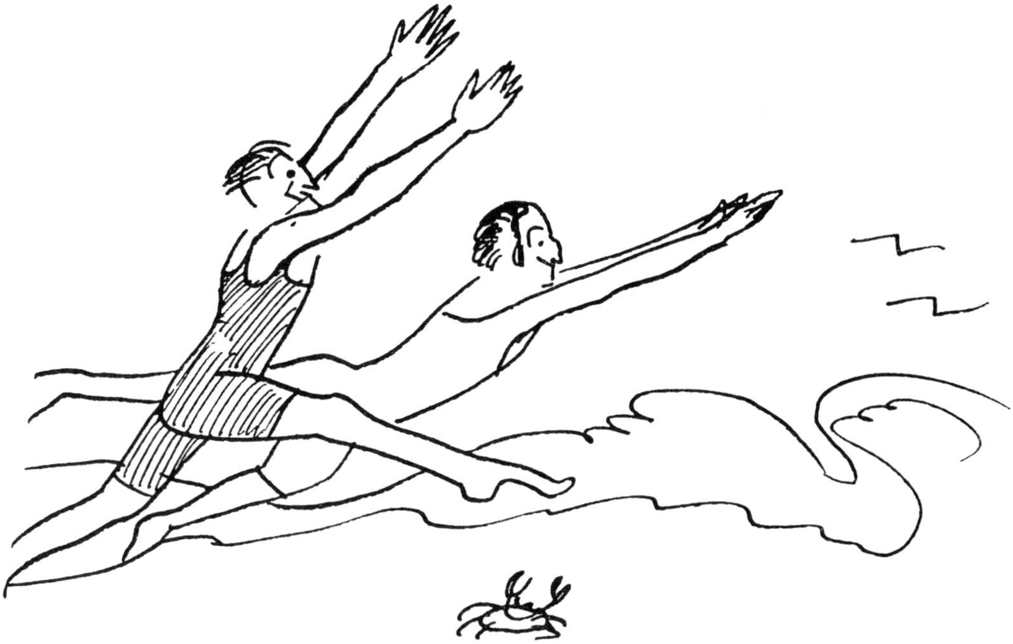

John Nash to Carrington: 'I bathed with Pellew in Norfolk rushing into the sea with leaps & bounds.'

'You *are* an artist, Jack,' Claughton told him. Not 'You could be an artist.' John returned somewhat apprehensively to Wood Lane House, dreading what his father would say to this startling commitment. Mr Nash listened, thought for a bit, then swept a space clear on the dining-room table and said, 'So you want to paint too. Well, you had better do it here.' Just before setting out on this momentous holiday John and Carrington had patched up a small misunderstanding. 'It seems to me that if you can forgive me that one insinuation which you have proved to me to be false we might remain good friends, better in fact than before, since we must necessarily know each other's temperaments better. It is unnecessary for *me* to say that I like you very much, for that you should know. Of your work, as you also know, I can say very little. What then can possibly stand between our being friends? I *will* be friends with you. [Much crossing out.] Please excuse this. It is difficult to write a good letter. Imagine it as hedges or distant woods instead of crossed-out words. I am going away on Wed. with Pellew. My address after then will be c/o Mrs Harrison, Overstrand, Norfolk. *I* wanted to go to Berkshire, he to Norfolk; *we* can't go without each other.

I was overruled but not before I had put up a gallant verbal fight in Eustace Miles' restaurant. ... I have been so serious-minded of late that I have done no drawings in my letters. Perhaps they will return though. JN.'

Carrington's response to John's decision to be an artist was as matter of fact as his father's. She had never regarded him as anything else. Nor did she question him about where he would train. Paul had written her an arch letter on the eve of his brother's setting out on this wild adventure, signing it 'Paul and John Nash'. 'It is late tonight. Bunty has fallen asleep in a chair near-by and Jack is packing a bag for his journey to the Norfolk Broads with Pellew. They go tomorrow. My wit has waned with the evening; all dinner we have been in a high state of hilarity listening to Paul's recital of his past love affairs, but now the laughter has died away and Coma, semi coma and now High Coma are set in. So to bed.... To you and Brett and Meyer we send our unanimous obedience and respect tinged with affection.' It pleased Paul at this time to take a detached look at himself and to be ironically judgmental. Also in his letters to Carrington to bring his brother forward a little. She in turn mocked the Nash family for being tribal.

By far the most influential part of the family where the artist brothers were concerned resided at Sinodun House, Wallingford. Aunt Gussie had been engaged to Edward Lear, and Paul and John had been brought up on the comic wonders which hung on its walls. The latter showed John the absurdity of life, and how he could deal with it. His letters to Carrington became under-written, as it were, with Lear–Nash drawings which reduced their tensions to laughter. She too would add an exquisite drawing to her execrable spelling and enchanting style.

If Overstrand and Claughton marked John's commitment to painting, Wittenham Clumps would be the place where Paul found what he had always been looking for, the timelessness and mystery which dwelt in landscape – those elements which continued to motivate a scene beyond or within 'nature'. He wrote of the enormity of the Clumps and how 'they eclipsed the impression of all the early landscapes I knew.... They were the pyramids of my small world.'

John stayed on at Sinodun House after his brother and sister had gone home and, as so often happened with him when left alone, the day darkened. He wrote to Carrington, 'There is an organ on the staircase which the gardener's boy blows for me besides many fine landscapes and very good Wallingford ale, to speak of baser material. The organ is difficult. I wonder if I shall ever be able to play well on it.... Yes,

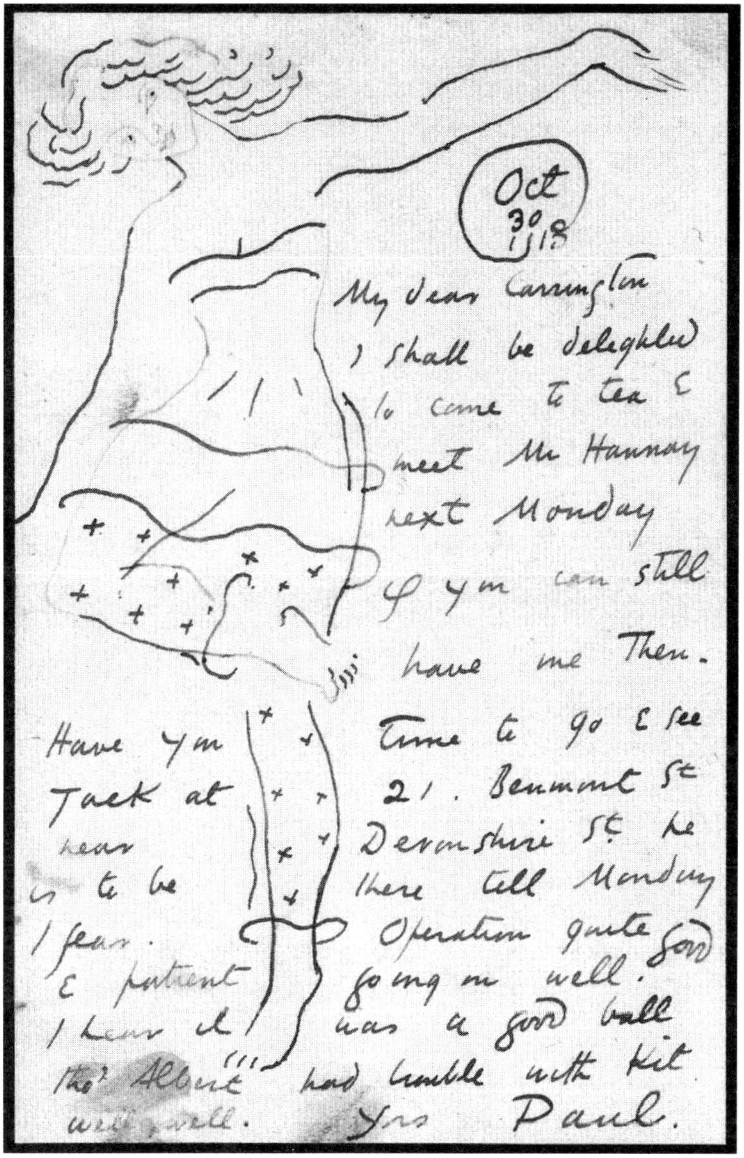

Oct 30 1918

My dear Carrington
I shall be delighted to come to tea & meet Mr Hannay next Monday if you can still have me then.
Have you time to go & see Jack at 21. Beaumont St Devonshire St. he is to be there till Monday I fear. Operation quite good & patient going on well. I hear it was a good ball tho' Albert had trouble with Kit well, well. Yrs Paul.

Paul Nash accepts an invitation to visit Carrington.

this is the very uncle who at an advanced age pursued my aunt with matrimonial intentions. We have family prayers morning and night and all that sort of thing. It is almost too windy to draw and cold but I hope to do some sketches.... I could not stay here for long, obliging and kind as the uncle is. It is so lonely and I don't like the people here very much, or perhaps they don't like me. I went to the top of Wittenham Clumps this morning: it was very windy but fine. Do not fear for my painting. I promise you I will not become a purple-green young man. Yes, I do miss you. It is more lonely now Paul is gone.... And now goodbye Carrington. I am going to practise a little fugue on the piano, my organ blower having gone out.... I write this in the absence of the uncle who might wonder why I wrote outside the family. How varied is human nature to be sure. Yours ever, Jack.'

In November this year, 1912, Paul had his first one-man show of twenty-one landscape drawings at the Carfax Gallery, arriving for the private view in full morning-dress, top-hat, malacca cane and all. On the walls Wittenham Clumps had become a swelling sea threatening the pyramids of Egypt. A few weeks later, in February 1913 at his friend Rupert Lee's flat, he met Margaret Odeh, who had spent her childhood in Cairo and who was part-Arab. They became engaged in April. He wrote to Carrington:

> I have fallen somewhat precipitably in love – no, that sounds too violent and blind, and mine is sure and fast and happy, and I am what the vulgar call engaged.... I can say no more. I do not propose to rapturise or to tell you that I am dizzily happy. I will reveal myself when I see you. You will give me the pleasure of introducing 'Bunty' to you. Yes? If you would like to know her real name it is Margaret Theodosia O'deh – when may I come and stand blushing before you? Do write a little letter – and forgive me. [He had broken an engagement of another kind.]
>
> The coming of you and yours to the house in Bird Garden must be a little postponed I'm afraid, but the weather will suit it better in three weeks.

Bunty Odeh was exotic, learned and formidable. She had been born in Jerusalem and was the daughter of the Reverend Naser Odeh, a part-Arab clergyman who was then chaplain to the bishop. After Cheltenham Ladies' College and St Hilda's, Oxford, where she took a degree in modern history, she had become a suffragist and was when Paul met her the organising secretary to the Committee on Social Investigation and Reform, with a particular dedication to the rescue of 'fallen women', i.e. the many thousands of London prostitutes. She was vivid, theatrical, full of tantrums, a person who lied with ease when it suited her not to tell the truth and altogether desirable. The night he met her at Rupert Lee's flat Paul noticed her tiny gloved hand 'running down the bannister rail like a little black mouse', and was caught. Their marriage was a turbulence with spaced-out calms. He called her 'Mouse', Paul's friend Rupert called her 'a charming little humbug'. Christine used to say, 'Oh, Bunty . . . '.

Paul described her: 'She was small and extremely slender with small feet and hands, but the remarkable feature of her appearance was the head which seemed large in proportion to her slight body. This impression was partly due to a cumulus of dark hair, grape-black in colour, which mounted round her brow. The whole structure of the head was vigorous, from the capable forehead to the firm chin. The eyes were large and wide-spaced and the mouth rather full.' Carrington was rather un-nerved by her, John stirred by such a clearly 'passionate' relationship.

Whether Paul ever tried his youthful hand at match-making between his brother and Carrington is debatable, but he did in his courteous, mannered way seem now and then to speak up for him: 'It now begins to seem long ago since I sat upon a check cushion in your brilliant circle – There's a line in the Blessed Damozel which, misquoted, suits your charming company rather well "Circle wise sit they, with shorn locks and foreheads garlanded . . . ". What I set out to say was – may Jack and I come to tea on Thursday somewhat. . . . May we come? You must say at once if my visits are becoming too sudden or too often but this time it is in my brother's behalf.'

When John began to understand the nature of the only friendship which Carrington would allow, he wrote to her as follows:

Dear Carrington,

> I find it terribly difficult to explain to you. I must own I am sceptical about platonic friendships unless each person is as it were sexless but I am not so and my nature is not adapted for it to my mind. I look forward not unnaturally to at last meeting someone who would be a friend and more to me. I am always, perhaps foolishly, building castles in the air. I cannot but admire the sureness with which you express yourself for I feel you 'know yourself' so well. You are eminently sensible and I will try to be so too now that I know your views, but I beg we may be friends, not acquaintances in future; for now that I have lost a vague possibility, if there ever was one, of your being more than a friend, surely I must

> not lose your friendship altogether. You are really stronger than me, less effeminate in mind, and more independent by virtue of your nature. I feel that independence in one's work and life is one of the greatest things. And now I can say no more because it is too hard to think of much. I am afraid I have expressed myself very badly. I must also again ask your pardon for disturbing your peace of mind in any way . . . Jack.

Two years later Carrington would write to the beautiful and in love Mark Gertler, 'Yes I know that your real love is "beautiful and not low". Do not think I ever doubted that. Only I *cannot* love you as you want me to. You must know one could not do what you ask, sexual intercourse, unless one does love a man's body. I have never felt any desire for that in my life: I wrote only four months ago and told you all this, you said you never wanted me to take any notice of you when you wrote again; if it was not that you just asked me to speak frankly and plainly I should not be writing. I do love you, but not in the way you want. Once, you made love to me in your studio, you remember, many years ago now. One thing I can never forget, it made me inside feel ashamed, unclean. Can I help it? I wish to God I could. Do not think I rejoice in being sexless. . . . It gives me pain also.'

Throughout 1913 Paul regarded John and Carrington's relationship rather hopefully. Writing to her about William Blake and George Borrow, he ends his letter, 'Best love from me and Bunty and Father and Barbara. Jack sends you enough on his own I daresay, *mine* has to come in company.'

After Carrington's refusal to see their friendship as an affair and John's bleak self-analysis there was an effort on both their parts to discover safe ground, as it were. Hers was easy to find, it was reading, drawing, the countryside, an entire universe of thrilling prospects and engagements. Be an artist! she was telling him. Who could possibly want to be more or other than this? But her mixture of bullying and

---

Opposite: *The Wittenham Clumps*, Paul Nash, 1913. Ink, pencil, chalk and watercolour, 308 × 397 mm. Carlisle Museum and Art Gallery. Over, left: *Picking Vegetables*, fresco panel by Dora Carrington at Ashridge House, Berkhamsted, 1912. 1.83 × 1.52 m. Ashridge Management College. Right, top: *Bedford Market*, Dora Carrington, *c*.1911. Pencil, ink and watercolour, 43 × 67 mm. Photograph courtesy of Tate Gallery Archive. One of Carrington's earliest surviving pictures. Right, below: Dora Carrington, *c*.1920. Hulton Getty.

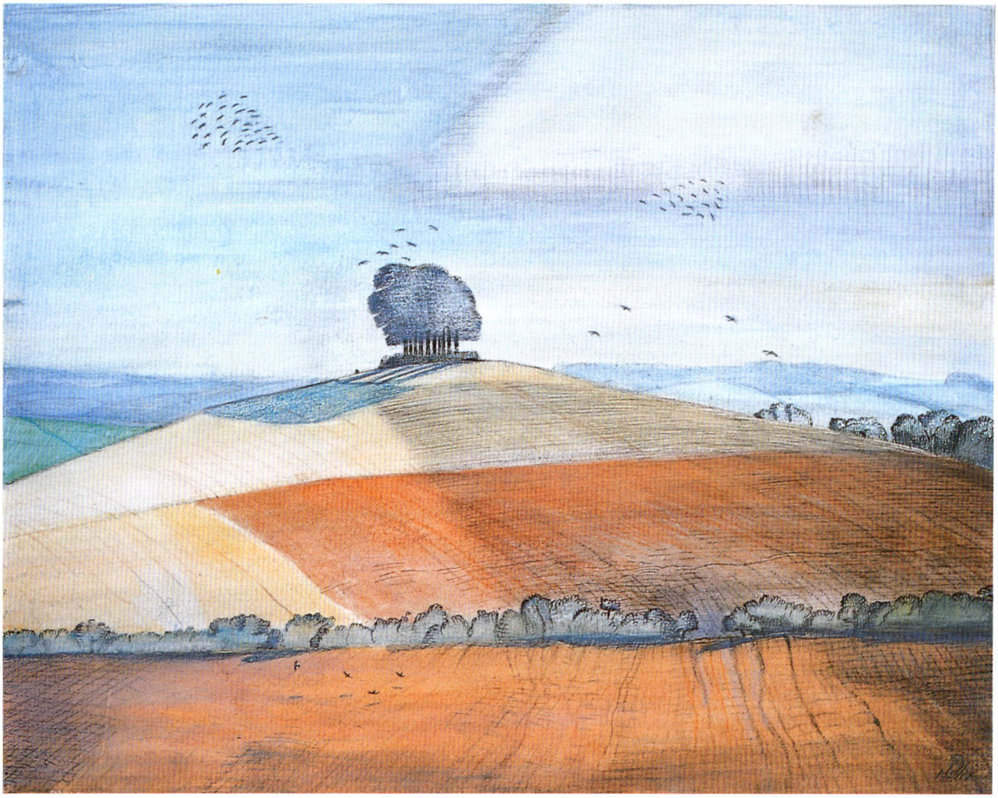

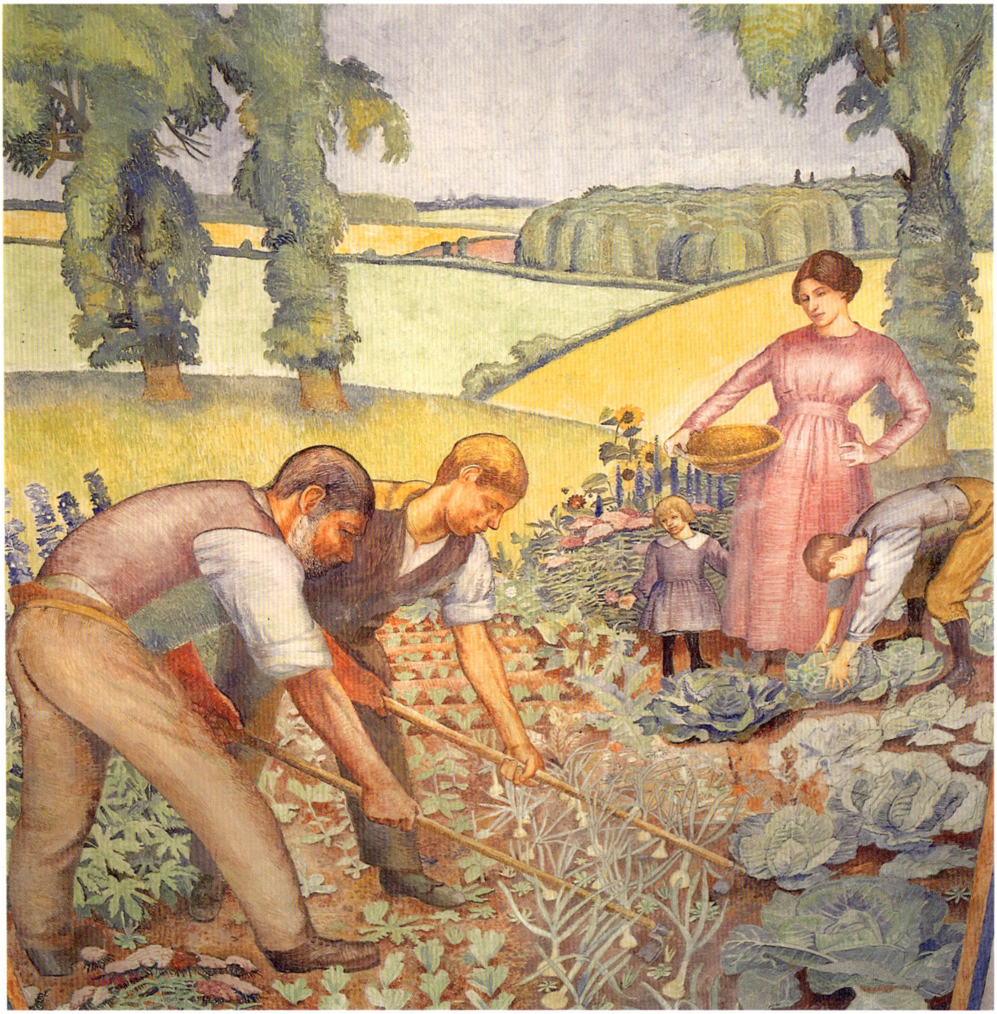

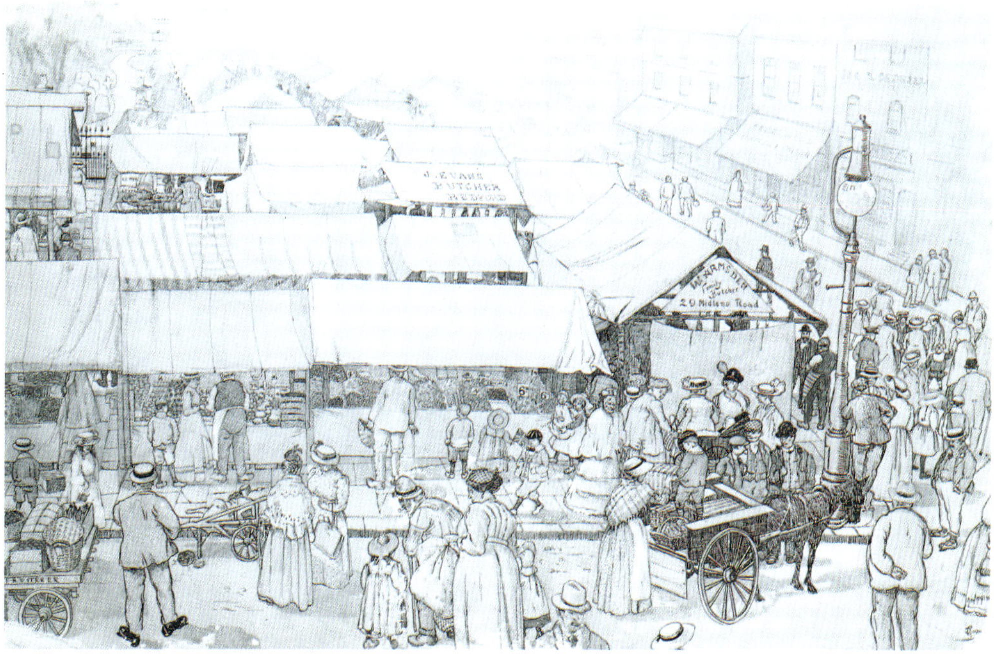
J. EVANS
BUTCHER
Family Butcher
29 Midland Road

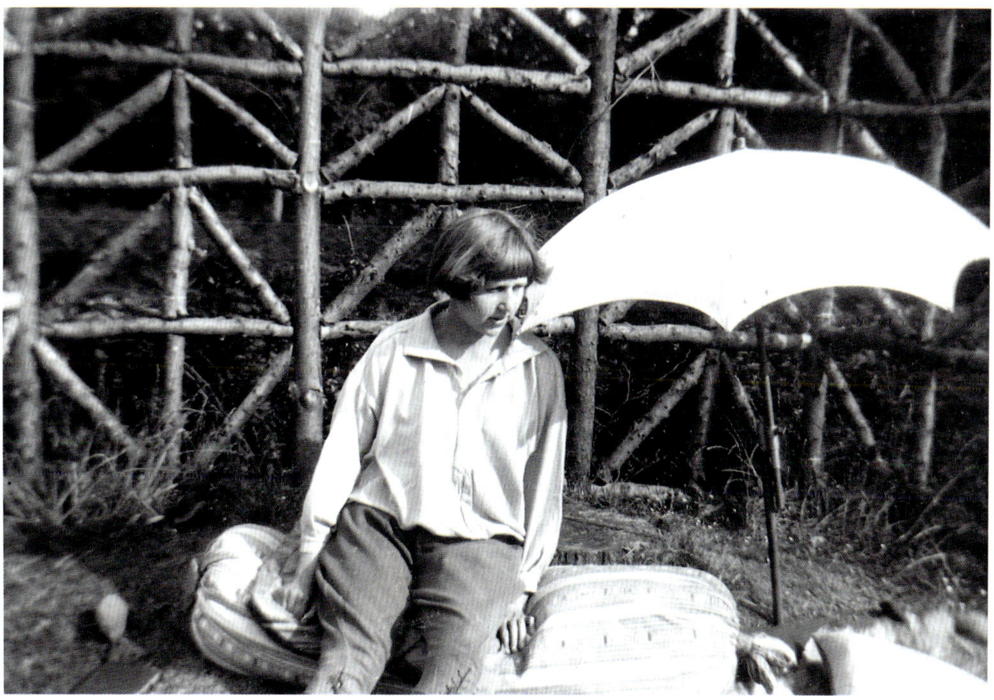

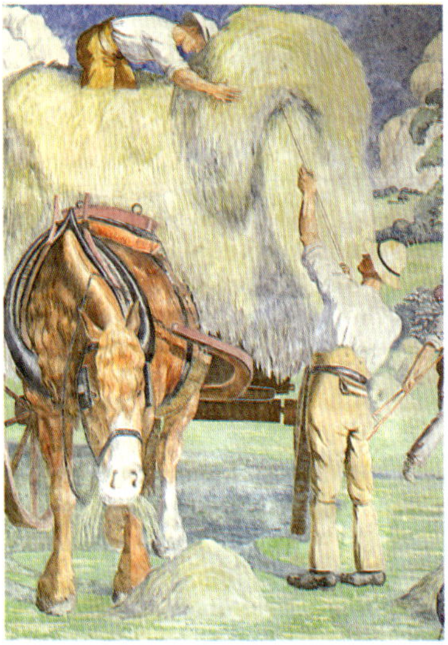

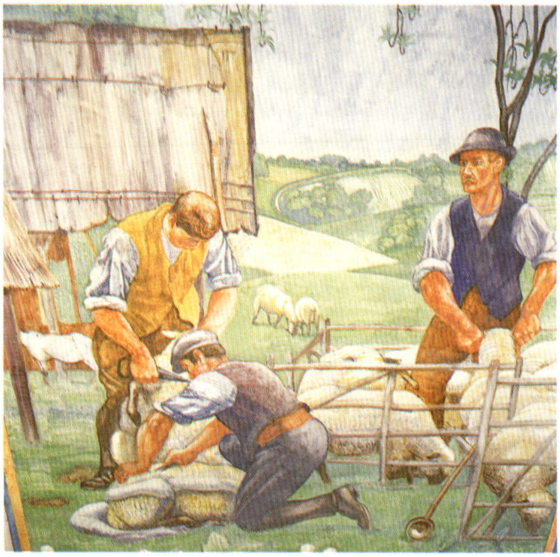

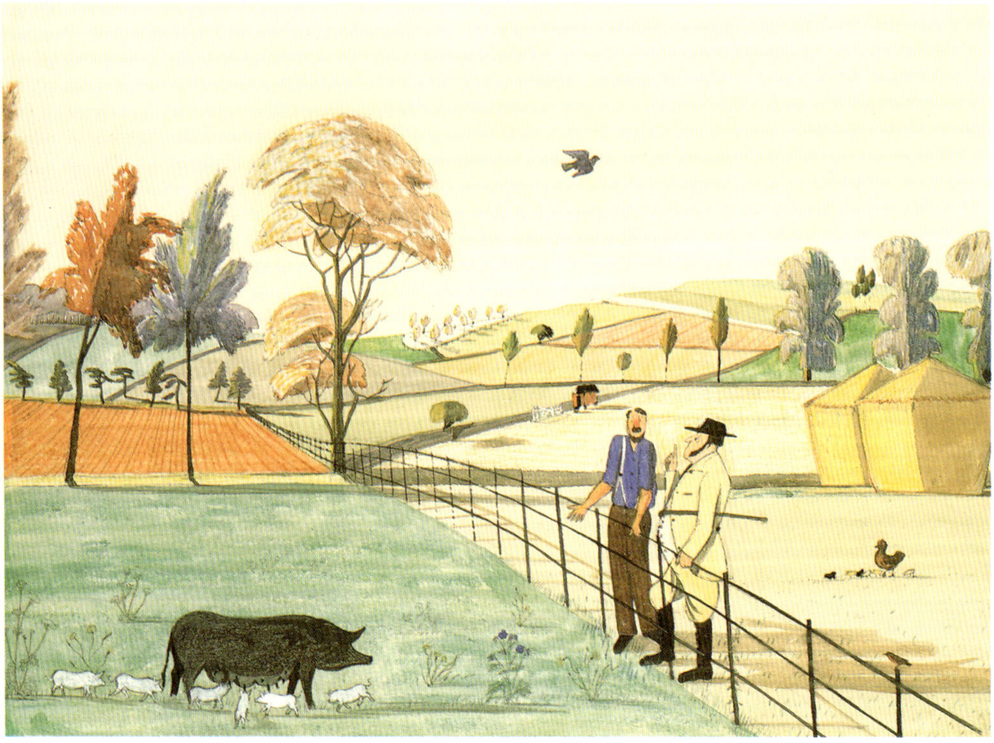

charming him into 'work' alone increased her fascination. They walked, bicycled, were weekend guests together and all the time he was finding her closeness what he most longed for, yet unbearable.

The situation began to improve when Carrington encouraged John's teaching impulse – she liked being told things. Taking the role of dunderhead, she found a way of letting him come near to her via lessons on this or that. When he wasn't plunged into 'Nashish' gloom he was a funny young man with a sharp wit, and she enjoyed this. Banter kept things in check as the letters between them grew more frequent and consequential. Her difficulty was that she thought she had made her position plain to him, although she never had, never could, not with John or with any man who desired her.

The Home Counties countryside proved to be the best of all safe ground. Still virtually carless and with its flora still intact, it caused them to compete with each other in their descriptions of it as well as their sense of freedom in it. Iver Heath was only fifteen miles from London but it was still far from suburbanised. John wrote that it was 'a large untidy village in the Colne Valley without much interest, except in a small corner where a bridge crossed the Colne under a very happy arrangement of trees'. These Buckinghamshire trees, the elms of Aylesbury Plain and the Chilterns beeches, had somehow held onto the country's ancient remoteness. The chalk too offered a pure contrast with London's filth from a million coal fires. A few stations down the line and one was well out of it.

Poets like W. H. Davies (*Autobiography of a Super-Tramp*, 1908) and artists such as Augustus John tempted students to become travellers. The Nashes' friend Rupert Lee sang the Open Road. Paul illustrated Borrow, and Carrington told John 'how we went with [Augustus] John and saw the gypsies. What a day! What a night! We sang lustily, a little flat, songs of Romany with them. They are a good race of people.' And John was to continue loving George Borrow so much that he took him to the

---

Opposite, top left: *Haymaking*, fresco panel probably by Dora Carrington and Constance Lane, 1912 or later. Top, right: *Sheep Shearing*, fresco by Constance Lane, 1912. Ashridge House, Berkhamsted. Ashridge Management College.

Below: *About a Pig*, John Nash, 1913. Pencil and watercolour heightened with bodycolour, 280 x 384 mm. Courtesy of Spink-Leger Pictures. A fine early example of John Nash's love of comic subjects, set in a landscape influenced by his visits to Norfolk. Writing from Callander in mid 1913, Carrington asks 'How did the drawing of the sow and family come off?'

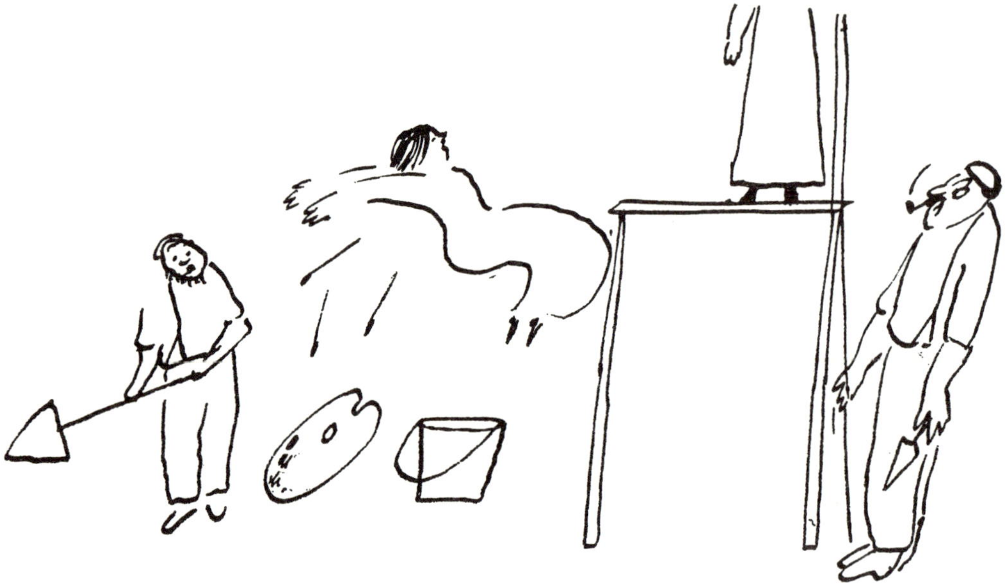

John Nash enquires after Carrington: 'I am pining for a letter from you; have you fallen from a scaffolding during fresco painting.'

trenches. Writing to Carrington from France in 1916 – 'My dear Duckie' – he tells her, 'I am reading *Lavengro* again, what a book! *The Bible in Spain* was the only book I could bring out on me with full pack, water-bottle, haversack outbulging, extra food-bag, additional haversack full of tins of corned beef, rifle, tin hat, water-proof sheet and 120 rounds of ammunition – there remains very little room for libraries.... A kind man however who had more room upon him stowed it [*Lavengro*] away and brought it safe with him here. Blessings on him. What a book again!'

Carrington would discover one of the peak landscape joys in the Chilterns, although not with John. It would be one of those moments in her life when she came as close as she could to what she needed for her happiness before, as so often happened, it vanished like a will-o'-the-wisp. During the warm summer of 1913 she was invited by her friend Constance – 'Cooee' – Lane to collaborate with her in painting some frescoes on the library wall of Lord Brownlow's romantic mansion at Ashridge. They were to live at Mrs Lane's house in Nettleden – just outside Hemel Hempstead – and bicycle each day to Ashridge. Her cup overflows.

Since Monday I have been here, oh, but it is a most wonderful country! You and Paul should just see the trees, and green fields like lettuces, you could almost eat them they are so luscious. And black sheep making patterns on the green fields, and amazing little deer which leap together on the hill like in a Psalm. It is altogether a very happy place. We go up each day to Ashridge (an ancestral seat with a most amazing early Italian garden, and trees) to do our fresco. I am drawing the big cartoon hard, 6 ft. by 5 ft. It *is* a job. But so exciting. I spend the mornings in fields drawing big heavy elms for it, and small village boys come and pose in the garden in the evening. Today the mason gave me a lesson in plastering. It is good to do. Mixing maltha and sand, then slapping it on the wall with 'floats' and making it as smooth as marble. About six workmen are running about erecting scaffolding and carrying buckets. Lane and I feel like great masters controlling this band of men and having the big wall to cover

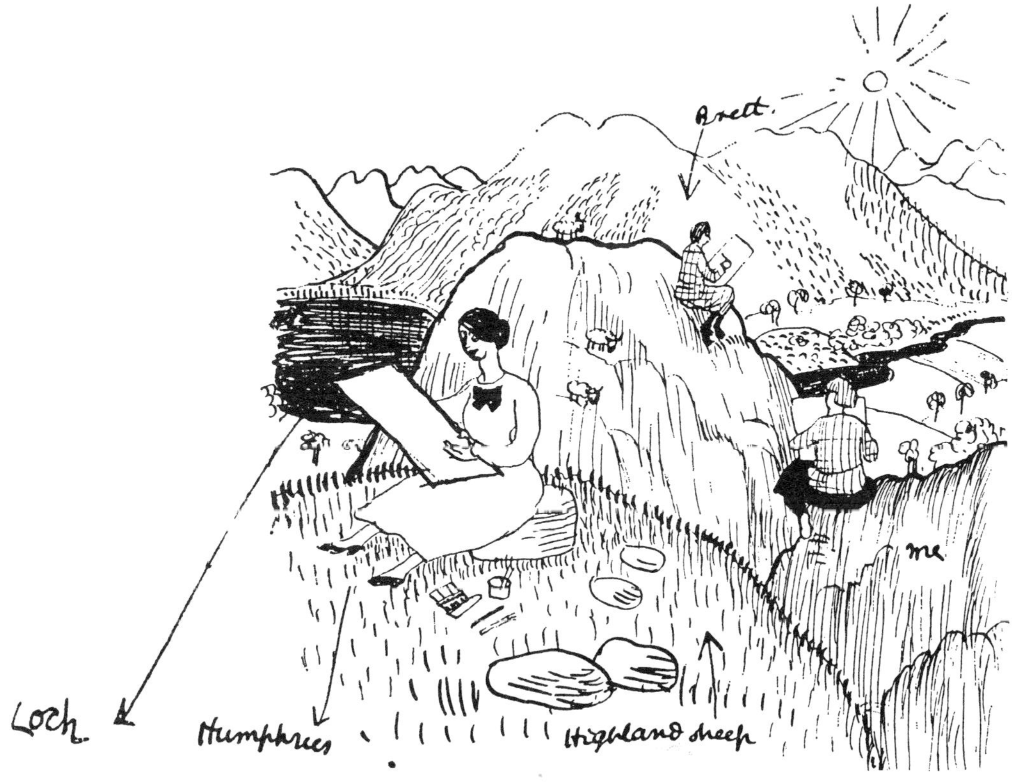

Carrington to John Nash while on holiday at Callander.

with our works of art. Fresco painting is awfully hard. All this afternoon I have been struggling to learn. But the best time is after it is all over at seven o'clock in the evening, when I can trudge home wearily across the fields, with the black sheep and the woods on the slope, and the little deer and big deer hopping and running.

Lane and her mother have gone away and left me all alone here. I am happy. They have gone to London till Saturday. It is fun now, as I can do exactly what I like and not be tidy and have clean hands. But I have to work at fresco every day to become proficient. What work are you doing now, and Paul? Are you going away this summer? Yesterday we found a Giotto nativity shed. It is wonderful. I want to do a nativity picture. The sheep and the oxen were there too. ... I am sorry to have written so much but I am very excited with the country....

This isn't really a p.s. only a continuation, only I had to tell you. It has been a wonderful evening. I went out at a quarter to nine by myself and saw some amazing landscapes. Each four ways there was a good one. The best was a long-shaped upright panel with a moon on a sky glazed with many colours, first green, then blue-pink over that, and then a dull mauve with a few little clouds round the moon.... What good shapes the trees make in this light. The other [landscape] was a long one. A road and grass either side and a railing, and dark masses of trees against a pale yellow sky, orangey at the bottom, and dark, dead grey clouds going clump, clump across the sky, and like little puffs of smoke at the top. Oh, but you should have seen it!

The grass was too wet to sit on but I managed to get two drawings, only it was very dusk to see the paper. I am terrifically excited about it all ... I love being alone here. I wish Lane and her mother weren't coming back tomorrow evening ... I think I must get Lane to ask you here one day. You would like her, for she is most charming in her thoughts and very beautiful to look at ... Carrington.

On 22nd July 1913 the frescoing was interrupted by a Scottish holiday with Brett at Lord Esher's house at Callander 'N.B.' – North Britain. Since Carrington's blissful outpouring of her contentment at Nettleden to John there had been an unintentional silence. He was worried. 'I am pining for a letter from you; have you fallen from a scaffolding.... Are you still at Hemel Hempstead? I have thoughts of riding over and surprising you in your raptures ...'. He tempts her with the pleasures of Wood Lane

House, croquet, larkspurs, fishing, a sow with her litter. The panache of her reply – from Scotland! – could not have comforted him. He had been ill with minor surgery on his famous nose. There also seemed to be pressures on him to find an occupation as well as that of artist. At any rate it would have been a help to find a friend in a similarly struggling boat, instead of which the sheer energy and enterprise of Carrington's splendid Scottish epistle must have left him feeling at a disadvantage. They were both twenty but she was 'away', and in spite of all her mother's efforts to hold her in check.

Dear Jack,

I am sorry to have been so long answering your letters. But it was such a whacking long one last time that I thought a little rest would be pleasant to you. I will now answer them. I am grieved to hear about your nasal appendage. . . .

Our elms at Nettleden show their ankles and are of all elms the best, the like of which are not to be found in any kingdom . . . [John, Paul and Bunty had been to Epping Forest where there were 'elms better than ours because they show their ankles so' – a drawing].

How exciting the pre-Raphaelites being back again. . . . Oh isn't *The Hireling Shepherd* amazing! I really think they got there. Wouldn't you like to do a real picture like that? [John had told her, 'I saw the loan exhibition of Pre-Raphaelite paintings at the Tate the other day. I think that for sheer colouring and detail nothing is more satisfying or contentious than *The Hireling Shepherd*, and for these qualities and feeling as well Millais' *Christ in the Carpenter's Shop*.']

If this letter is rather bad, you mustn't mind as I am so chock full of happiness that having to stop still and write about past things, and think of words, is hard. I left Nettleden and the pie-bald pony on the 22nd with many regrets. The big cartoon is done now and on 15th September I go back to actually fresco it on the wall! The final days were exciting, drawing the larkspurs and snapdragons and cabbages. It was good to do. Lane took me to the top of a high hill and we watched the sun set. She talks very beautifully about things, and the country. It is good to be with a person who is so excited about the fields and the trees. One night we stole out of the house, it was Saturday, when everyone was slumbering and ran barefooted with big leaps across the fields through sleeping cows still we climbed the slope to a cornfield. The moon was new and shining. . . . Do you ever go out when everything is over at night? The cornfield was greeny-purple and poppies making dark blackened stains, and you grabbed at them, for they seemed only stains on the waving mass of wheat. Lane's nightdress shone a wonderful colour. . . .

On Monday night I travelled up here. What a journey! Everything cold and noisy, and do you know of the hardness of a carriage seat, and the fear of a cockchafer on the ceiling, and trains that pass in the night and shriek to each other? . . . Worn out, I arrived at Callander at 6.30 on Tuesday morning. . . . The excitement of these big hills and forests and lochs. Humphries is here too. The house is pink outside with slate pointed towers, and the garden has many flowers. . . . We go out every day drawing on these big mountains and one day Humphries and me swam in a big loch, the sun shining hot, and all round towering mountains, and the water very deep and clear, and nobody else to be seen. The whole world was ours. Every day is hot here. It is never ever cool. From the top of the mountains one can get a most gorgeous view of big lakes and these mountains sliding down to them, and a little river winding through coloured fields pale-green with new wheat, and reddy-yellow with hay. . . . But how hard to draw. And when we return at 8 we have astounding dinners. Are you above grub? I hate aesthetic people who pretend not to be interested. The strawberry and fruit ices are beyond all comparisons. Venison and 'pasties of the doe' (Scot.).

Brett's father is a nut [dandy] in his highland kilts and aristocratic demeanour. The picture of the 'Fresco Calamity' or 'The Girl who took the Step Backwards' caused great joy to us all. How did the drawing of the sow and family come off? Brett sends you and Paul her love. Humphries left our camp last Thursday much to our sorrow. So Brett and me now explore these mountains alone. She is a very charming person. On Tuesday I am going away, right down to Hove, Sussex with my family. Noel, the little brother, will be with me, and Pendennis his friend, who has a good head to draw. But it will seem smooth and slippery after this land. . . .

The house is beautiful inside, old furniture and panelling, and a wonderful relief plaster picture of the Jacobean period. The strain of the perfect lady is rather much as it is now almost a month since I was natural. But all day we can break out and shout and run on the hills. Brett and me are decorating a clothes-basket in red and purple, and painting the straw. It was a common fellow and as the rooms are different colours it is going in the 'red room'. I sleep in a 'flame room'. My evening dress matches it. A river with salmon and trout runs through the garden.... The flowers grow right down to the water's edge. Lovely orange lilies and loose-strife and larkspur. It is so like Japanese prints, everything pure.

Back at Nettleden with Cooee to finish their frescoes, Carrington urged John Nash to bicycle over for the day to see what they had done. She felt at ease with both her family and her friends. The Hove holiday, faintly dreaded, had turned out delightful – partly because Claude Miller happened to live nearby and had joined the party. He had driven Carrington to see some medieval wall-paintings in his 'ripping car' and had played tennis with her and Noel. They had bathed before breakfast and she had 'painted golden brown wheat and beautiful coloured fields and swelling downs. It was an astoundingly good land.' Now she and Cooee were 'working hard at our cartoons, drawing and painting them, Cooee Lane's is best. She is doing sheep shearing. She sings whilst we work, lustily with much force old ballads and folk songs, and Handel. The plastering is a joy to do. But it is mighty hard work. The lunches are gorgeous.' He must come. Paul too, and Bunty and Rupert Lee – everybody.

But John set off alone. It was the last September of the old world and he bicycled twenty miles through its harvest. He was staying with the Odehs, Paul's future in-laws, at their retirement house Elm Tree Cottage, Hillingdon, so it was quite a journey to Nettleden, a village on the edge of Berkhamsted Common. Carrington said, 'bring your drawings with you', but he couldn't manage them on the bike. Soon, she said, 'You will burst in upon the sanctuary of the Fresco brotherhood.' And she mentioned the future – 'Slade begins on 6th October.... I have another studio in Fitzroy Street.... *How is your work?*'

John's reply to this when they met was seriously at odds with the flippancy of his letters and all the stuff about being an accountant, and his 'I think we had better all go to the colonies, will you come with me?' Claughton Pellew had transformed him. Carrington observed a new purpose in John when he wrote, 'After Norfolk scenery and general landskip I have three pictures now on hand, or rather on the easil, and some ½ doz or so more in my head.' He asks her for information about the Friday Club and the English Art Club. He says that he has been taking collections of his comic drawings round the London publishers, John Lane, Elkin Matthews, Grant Richards. He seems at this point not to be a student at all, though diffident, or, rather, uncertain and confident at the same time. Here it might be mentioned that Carrington says nothing about his not studying at the Slade or any other art school. He must have told her of his practice of seeking help from older painters, etchers, and established artists whenever he wanted to know how to do something. He was in fact an atelier-haunter of the old school, the kind of youth who crouched in corners to pick up technique and watch the old hands at work. But his real professors were his Buckinghamshire ancestors, those generations who had left their mark on his country, and plantsmen like his new friend Clarence Elliott.

The bike ride back to Hillingdon was almost too much for him and he arrived done-in but cheerful. Not only had there been the twenty miles to and fro but the further journey to Ashridge to admire the frescoes on Lord Brownlow's library wall and Carrington's and Cooee's mutual exuberance. Yet he felt that he had crossed a barrier of kinds and was himself elated. He ordered some tempera paints. He even told Carrington, 'I feel I am beginning to write like you, I don't know quite why.' Less inhibitedly, perhaps. He also felt rather ill. Later, he, Bunty and her parents sat in Elm

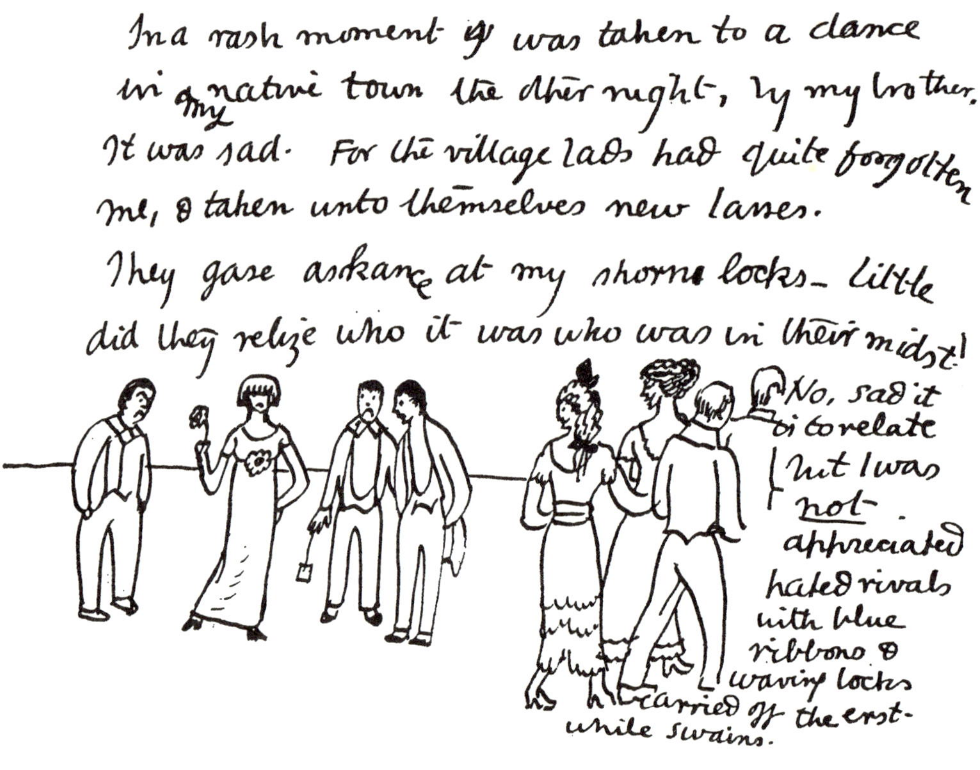

Carrington (to John Nash) finds herself forgotten at a dance.

Tree Cottage to listen to Paul reading *Man and Superman*. This was the summer when Paul found his brother 'so extraordinarily productive' that he could 'only stand by in amaze and envy'.

Soon after this, with wild notions of taking a studio together in Hampstead, the brothers decided that they now possessed enough work to hold a double exhibition. The venue was a lampshade shop in Pelham Street, Kensington run by two young men who had given it the Wildean name, the Dorien Leigh Gallery. Paul and John had gone in and enquired if they could hang their paintings and drawings on its blank walls. 'There was talk', as John put it, of Carrington joining them but she seems to have declined the invitation. The poster they designed showed dandified Paul, countrified John, a harvest field, an open road and Wittenham Clumps rising in the background as their Mount Fuji. Thanks partly to William Rothenstein's influence, the show was for the brothers a quite unbelievable success. Rothenstein had written to Michael Sadler, who had a keen eye for new work, 'If by chance you are in town, do contrive to go to it. They are both very young and extremely interesting and talented, and nobody save myself and one or two equally helpless people take any interest in them. They are badly in need of both help and encouragement and Paul's work is quite first rate. The other brother is younger and still not quite developed.' But it was John who sold the most. Roger Fry, who had admired Paul's work at the New English Club show in May, also came to the Dorien Leigh Gallery, as did Edward Marsh. The visit began a friendship between John and Eddie. It was Eddie who purchased the glowing evening *Cornfield*, now in the Tate Gallery, and who gave John a bed when he was in London. John wrote to Carrington, 'We have altered our minds and are keeping the Gallery on till Saturday next. Prof. Sadler has bought three of mine and one of Paul's, isn't he a frightfully good man. I long to see you and tell you all about it; it is so exciting. Paul and I hope to have a sort of tea party in the Gallery before it ends . . . if so you will all come, won't you. I have seen *Allotments* sold, to the New English in company with *Golden Hill* (which I believe is your favourite one). . . . When are you coming to the Gallery again? . . . Yours in coma, Jack.' Carrington would sell her first drawing the following year for £5. 8s. She had by then won a Slade scholarship, three prizes for painting and the Melville Nettleship Prize for figure composition, all her work containing elements of vision 'beyond' academic requirement, which made it especially noticeable.

Back in Bedford it was all a matter of the prophet being not without honour except

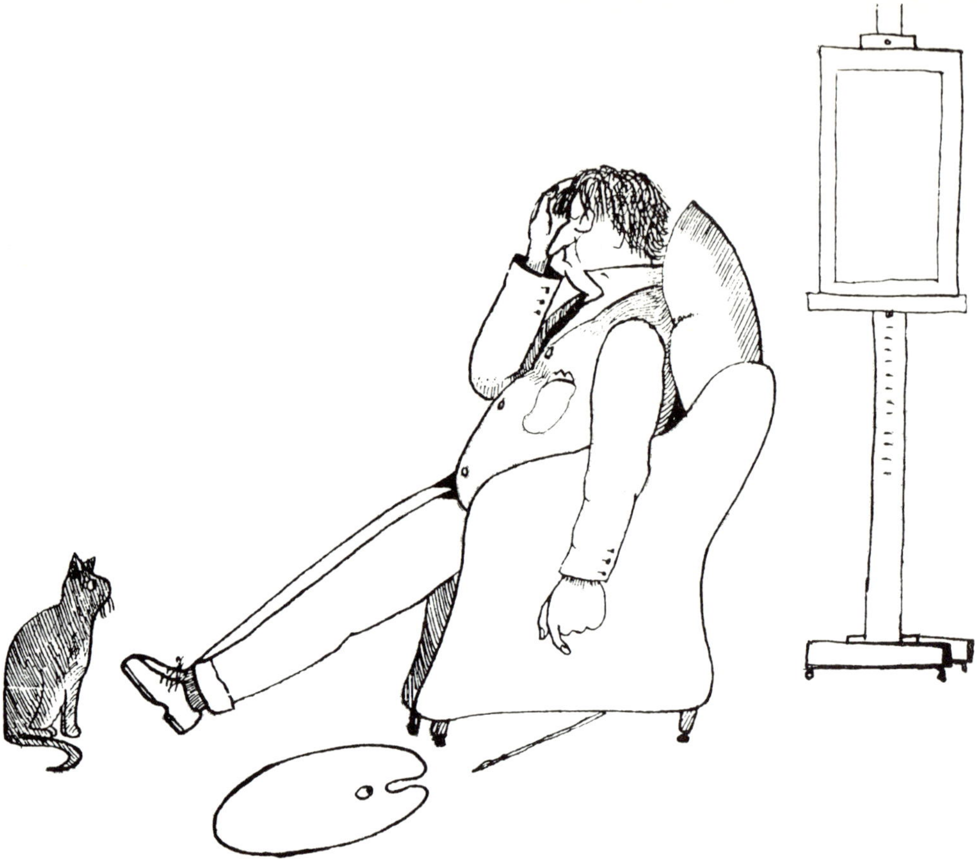

John Nash to Carrington, concerning his depression:
'I am silent. This picture tells a story better than any words of mine. The cry goes up "how long" as the hymn says. A rush of words came to his lips, he swallowed them down (to the detriment of his digestion).'

in his own country. The distinctive artist whose emergence was so marked in London was still tiresome Dora at 1 Rothsay Gardens. A letter to John from this crushing address in the spring of 1914, though lightly written, said it all.

> I have done no work these [Easter] hols of any worth as the family do not encourage my efforts and won't let me use the study to paint in.... I did a painting of my youngest brother side view which met with some approval in the family circle. But a great discussion still continues as to whether his nose is too long, or his upper lip too short. In a rash moment I was taken to a dance in my

native town the other night, by my brother. It was sad. For the village lads had quite forgotten me, and taken unto themselves new lasses. They gaze askance at my shorn locks – little did they realize who it was who was in their midst! No, sad it is to relate but I was *not* appreciated . . .

It is in the same letter that Carrington reacts to John's bombshell. 'You are going to Florence! And you announce it calmly in a word. And again you tell with a coolness only found in Strand magazines that Maresco [Pearce] has bought your *Gipsies*! Try and have a little enthusiasm about it. I know after selling so many pictures it must be hard. But surely one doesn't go to Florence every afternoon. Is Paul going too? And can you speak Italian?'

She might have added, 'And how can you afford it?' For they lived on shillings. But he had saved the Dorien Leigh money and Claughton Pellew had persuaded him to spend it thus. Claughton was quite a traveller before he withdrew from the world. He had visited the art galleries of Paris, Florence and Vienna in 1912, and was in Italy again in 1913, although now he was on a very different journey, a pilgrimage to Assisi which would last many weeks, time enough to become a lay Franciscan. If he had ever attempted to persuade John to accompany him on this route, either in Norfolk or Italy, John never mentioned it. He remained uncharacteristically vague about his first visit to the Continent, and the most important painting he did in Tuscany, a watercolour of a villa, was marked where it had been torn up and later repaired.

He was about to be left on his own when he wrote to Carrington, something which always frightened him. Behind the typical English complaining, the 'bloody foreigners' or 'give me Berkshire any day' tone, the letter reveals the dependent, slight and always-in-need-of-somebody-to-look-after-me young man who, just a couple of years later, would be on the Somme. John was what they used to describe as 'sickly', a person often laid low by 'chills', or cast down by the dreaded Black Dog, an hereditary beast. He also happened to be, as delicate folk often are, as tough as old boots. By the time he had emerged, and as some mistakenly believed without apprenticeship as an artist, and not an art student, landscape had become not only his chosen away ahead but his and Carrington's truest form of communication. A fine account of Florence and district gives a nod to the Uffizi en route to what they both really wanted to hear about and look at. To the end of his life John would be seen at exhibitions and galleries *not* immersed in what they contained. He caught sight of great art glassily from the corner of his eye. What held his attention was a plant on a sill and the warmth of the gathering. The Italian letter, written when he was twenty-one, is as much a candid confession of his own nature as an account of scenery. Carrington would have gathered much from it – more than was actually on the page. By now she knew her Jack. After the usual bantering preliminaries, he gets down to the serious business between them:

> . . . the ground is dug in brown grooves with narrow channels between each for irrigation. When the space is large bullocks (white) plough it. The most common tree is the olive of silvery grey green colour, vague shape – to the landscape painter's eye – and scarcely to be distinguished from its shadow. The most *prominent* tree is the cypress, which we in England know only from the Old Masters; it is generally absolutely regular . . . some are fatter or thinner like steeples. The willows are a bright orange yellow. Turkeys gobble to one another from countless farms, if you whistle at them they get furious. It is terrible the lack of wild birds. You may hear them a little in the early morning but I have not seen one yet of any kind. Lizards run in and out of the rocks on the banks in the sun like Metropolitan trains in and out of stations, stopping as it were for passengers and then starting off quickly, and entering a tunnel to be lost to sight. The hayricks which are few and small, there being no fields, are made round a tall pole, on the top of which is placed a small pot. The by-roads and lanes are villainously bad. Many daffodils and narcissi are about to 'burgeon forth', wild, I suppose, as they are everywhere in the grass. Irises, white, are out too, but very dwarf. There is a fine orange tree (Seville) in this courtyard covered with fruit.
>
> All the men wear black hats like mine. They are naturally idle, pleasant, talkative people, always ready to do you out of anything, but may generally be relied upon to do so in a pleasant manner. The Scouts or soldier police have little sentry-boxes at nearly every corner of the lanes. They sing lustily and play mandolins and are very nice men.
>
> A note on food would not perhaps be entirely uninteresting to you [Carrington's greedy descriptions of the meals at Cooee Lane's and Lord Esher's Scottish baronial hall had brought warnings about putting on weight]. Macaroni is largely used and a frightful amount of olive oil in 'lieu of' butter. Tongue, eggs, rolls, cheese and wine are the chief feeding matters. Italian soup is merely hot oil and macaroni. I do not care for their food very much.

I find it extremely difficult to do landscapes here owing to the entire lack of open country. The mountains are very fine, but never appear unless it is very clear. I have only seen them once so far. Michael Angelo's *David* and Benvenuto Cellini's *Perseus* and *Jupiter*, colossal statues, the first in white marble, the latter two in bronze, are very fine standing in the terrace by the Uffizi. The Ponte Vecchio is also marvellous.

When I look back to my journey out here nothing pleased me more than the country between London and Dover. The Channel was in fog. The country between Calais and Paris is monotonous. Part of Switzerland ... was marvellous, but so big. Between Milan and Bologna the country is inconceivably dull – miles and miles of perfectly square fields (grass) with broad ditches full of water and bounded by pollarded willows in endless 'sameness'....

These people talk of leaving for Rome for a month tomorrow and it ain't much fun being left alone in a largish villa with but slight knowledge of Italian. It is bad being ill out here, for it always tends to a form of homesickness, even among friends.... I shall come back earlier, I think, since Claughton Pellew has already got back to England and I long to see him again and catch him before he goes off elsewhere. Besides which.... I don't think I can do very much work in this district owing to this garden business [the over-formalised landscape] and I can't afford to go further north or south because it means putting-up.... So altogether I'm in rather a frenzy....

[The villa is so close to the city that another Florence makes itself heard, that of its hordes of workers.] The midday gun goes, followed by a deafening din of combined chorus of multi-toned and multi-noted hooters, beginning low like the noise of Underground lifts and soaring to a frightful key, and down again. The hooters cannot begin till after the gun, it is not etiquette.... I think I must have tried your patience, Carrington ... write and tell me of everything, with love yours Jack.

Safely home to the wonderful summer of 1914, with Italy no match for the Home Counties, John continued to see Claughton. Not only had the weeks at Assisi left their indelible mark on him but he had been received into the Roman Catholic Church. He was twenty-four and enormously attractive to John, who continued to take him back to Iver and to accompany him on long walks. He became for the younger man a kind of priest, someone to whom it was safe to talk intimately and whom one need follow only part of the way. All the same, Claughton's chosen path was to Paul, John and Carrington alike, frankly unbelievable. How could he *not* go where every artist they knew longed to go? It was strange to John that Claughton did not appear to want him to come with him on this turn-your-back-on-everything journey. Should it be to Cornwall, or Norfolk, as well as to somewhere in Europe? Claughton was never homesick abroad. Although he never said to John, 'Come with me', he allowed him closeness and protection, the very things essential to his well-being. John remained disturbed by Claughton all his life, by his feelings for him, by his indebtedness to him, by his genuine bewilderment at the course he set himself, which seemed to him perverse. Christine, in whom the German-Scottish work ethic was highly developed, simply found Claughton 'lazy'. His minute output – rationally accompanied by his tiny income – was all the result of 'he didn't work'. He contemplated Christ by the Norfolk sea, now and then pausing in this serious occupation to make wood-engravings and etchings in which scenes from the New Testament and pictures of East Anglian farming ran into each other, contemplatively speaking. 'It would be difficult to find another artist of his promise who deliberately appeared to seek retirement and obscurity. He seemed to possess no burning ambition and to have decided early in his life that the struggle in the arena of Art was not for him', wrote John years later. Claughton's retreat was not from 'the world' but from fellow artists. But where John was concerned he neither invited him to do likewise nor left him when he found the way he had to go. Paul Nash, in whom mysticism was far more developed than in his brother, also paid homage to Claughton after listening to him on the subject of rick-yards. 'At first I was unable to understand an almost devotional approach to a haystack and listened doubtfully to a rhapsody on the beauty of its form. Such objects and, indeed, the whole organic life of the countryside were still, for me, only the properties and scenes of my "visions". Slowly, however, the individual beauty of certain things, trees particularly, began to dawn upon me.' Claughton's visits to Iver were angelic – filled with message. He was the English gentleman with the alluring gypsy face, the setter on the right road, a traveller in time and eternity. Travellers do not toil but do just as much as is necessary. In 1919 Claughton married Carrington's friend Emma-Marie Tennent ('Kechie'), a Slade girl who asked for nothing and was prepared to sit out this life in all its fullness by the North Sea. 'And *she* didn't work either,' said Christine.

Christine

In April 1914 Carrington tells John Nash, 'I met a girl at Slade who was a great friend of Pellew Harvey [Claughton Pellew-Harvey – he dropped the second name] and showed me a drawing of his. I forget her name. I think she does awfully good work herself. She wears glasses.' And she sounds like Christine Kühlenthal, although by this date they had known each other for over a year. But young people often keep their friends in separate suitable boxes.

Christine was in her way as attention-attracting as Carrington herself, though for other reasons. Whilst not beautiful, there was something about her presence, her voice, her movements particularly, which made her memorable. She was tall and dark and the cropped hair bounced around her small-featured face as she walked or sat with what seemed to be a practised gracefulness. At first sight she looked more like someone from a ballet school than an art school. She had a slightly averted gaze which might have been mistaken for shyness or even furtiveness, but which existed for a reason which was not immediately apparent – some trouble with her eyes themselves. She was leggy and took long, yet very feminine steps, and she wore simple Dorelia John dresses which she made herself. Unlike Carrington, she was an only child and an aura of being 'special' clung about her. Although she never railed against her parents, as Carrington did against hers, or encouraged friends to come to her home as the Nashes did to theirs, she possessed a certain confidence and poise regarding her background. She gave off the aura of a girl who queened it at home and who now had to tread carefully among gifted and critical strangers in London. She spoke German, was a trained pianist and showed every sign of becoming a remarkable artist. She travelled back and forth to Gerrards Cross each day, where Mr Kühlenthal had built what might have been a woodland bower for his beloved daughter, called 'Forestholme', a pretty Edwardian cottage rather than a suburban villa, set secretly among trees. There Christine and her first important companion, Norah, a neighbour, danced in glades, dressed in cord breeches and shirts, a pair of Home Counties Rosalinds. Norah and her boyfriend Charlie modelled for Christine's Slade set pieces, *The Picnic* and *The*

Nativity, and Christine herself modelled for Carrington. Carrington saw almost at once that Christine's Gerrards Cross friends were on a par with the young people she knew in Bedford, and from whom one would move away. Emotionally Christine would never move on from what she and Norah had discovered. It was not a part of her growing up but of her maturity.

Carrington, two years Christine's senior, but still only twenty, could be open about girlfriends. 'You must not love Humphries too much as she is my, most of all people, intimate and close friend. I love her very much. I am so glad you do too as I love talking by the hour about her. Yes was not she very wonderful in that yellow dress. No don't let us "gloat" over her. It reminds one of men somehow that word, and running the eye up and down, and over. Like a gourmand and an oyster paté. Let us exchange thoughts, and praise this lady beauteous. I will be seeing her next month, as we are going to stay in Scotland with Brett, who although not so wonderful, has a most charming nature ever bestowed on woman kind. Brett really is a very worthy person. I shall insist on you liking her too!' This letter begins, comically, 'Dear Hope-Johnson' as if she had forgotten everything except 'Gerrards Cross' and it ends, 'As I perceive you love Humphries worthily I will give you a snapshot I took of her at Slade, one day when I get it printed ... but only on condition you sit for me next term again. Well goodnight, as I am so sleepy, Carrington. My letters aren't usually quite so deplorable as this.'

As with those to the Nashes, her pages to Christine are festooned with excuses for broken engagements, most of them caused, not by any sense of their not being important, but by the muddle and demands of her existence, the shifting in and out of lodgings, the need to earn money by teaching, and most of all by the severe discipline she set herself as an artist. All four friends, Paul, John, Carrington and Christine, came from orderly well-staffed houses, and having to look after themselves as students in London, and being frequently broke, made it often impossible for them to observe such strict social requirements as turning up on time. Carrington would blanch at

---

Opposite: *Carrington*, Mark Gertler, 1912. Gouache on paper, 475 × 388 mm. Edgar Astaire Collection. Over, left: *In a Garden*, Paul Nash, 1914. Ink, pencil and watercolour, 368 × 502 mm. Carlisle Museum and Art Gallery. One of the girls is Barbara Nash, Paul's sister, and the picture is based on the Nash garden at Iver Heath. Right: *Tuscan Landscape*, John Nash, 1914. Watercolour and ink, 352 × 380 mm. Private collection.

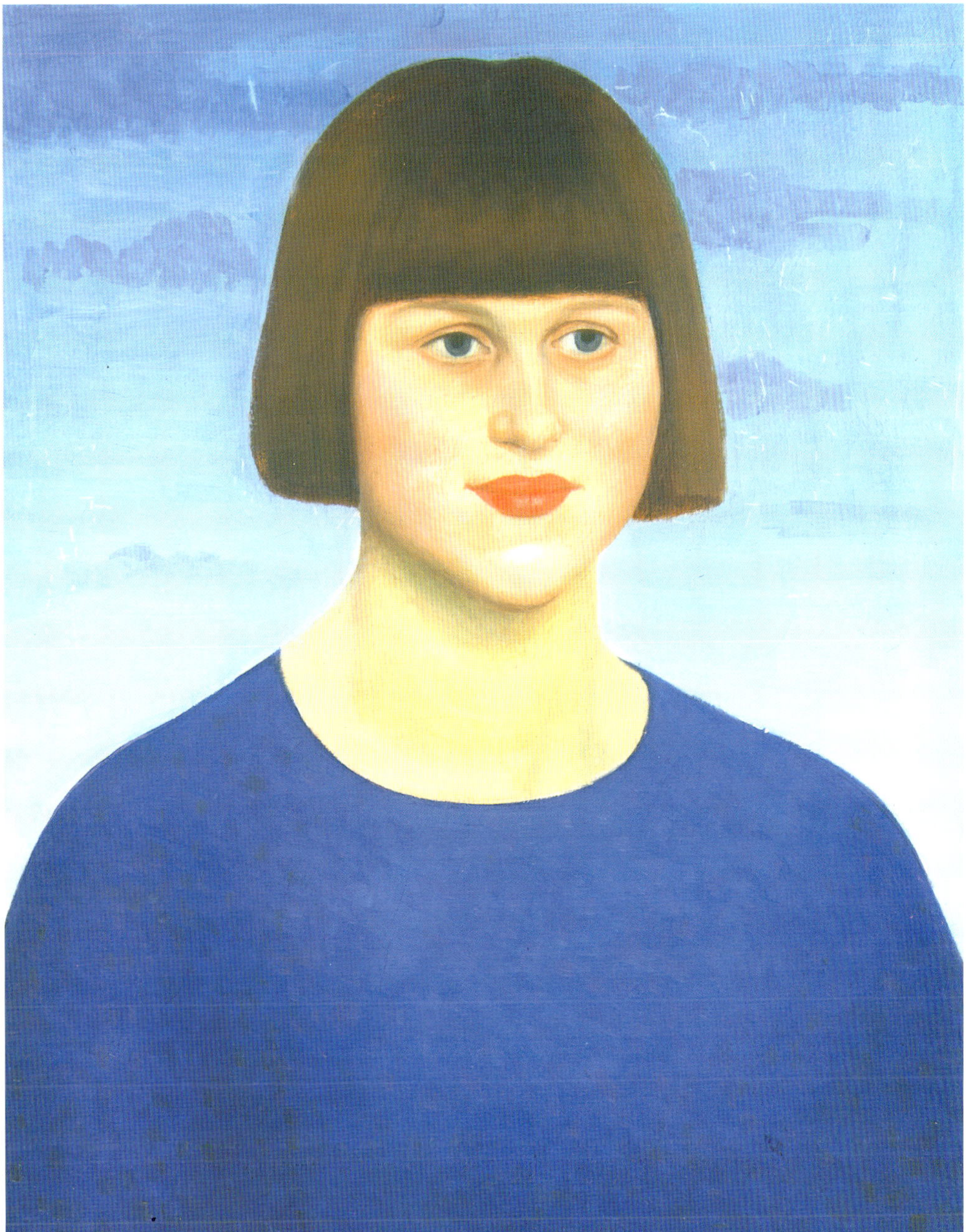

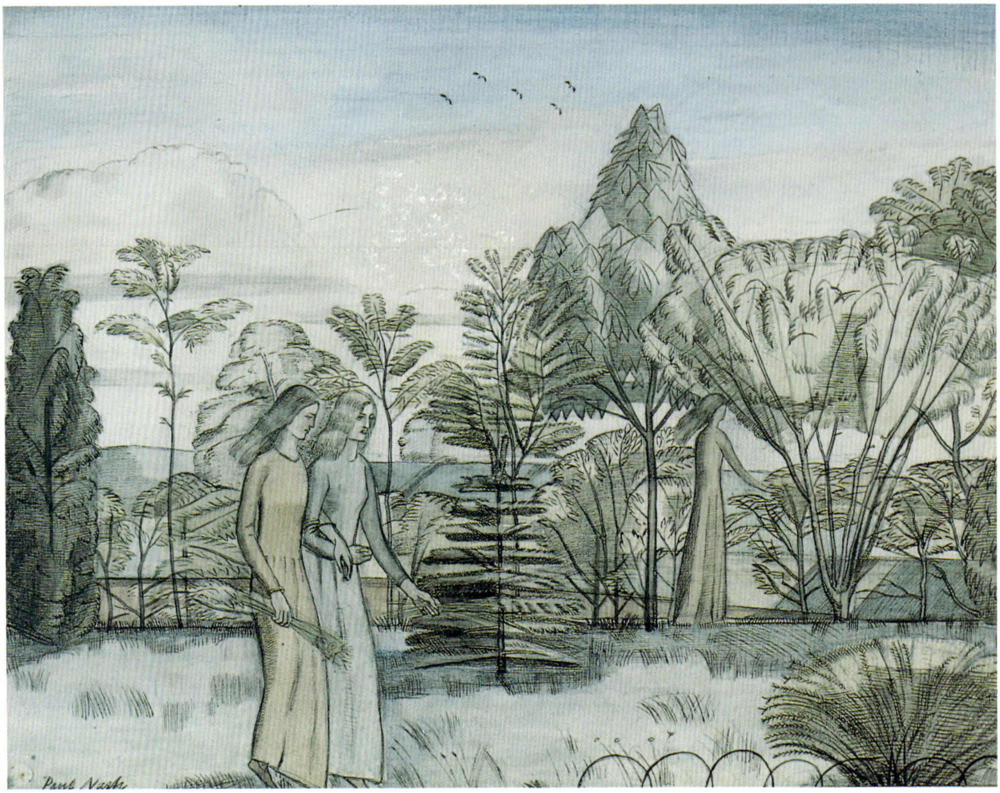
Paul Nash

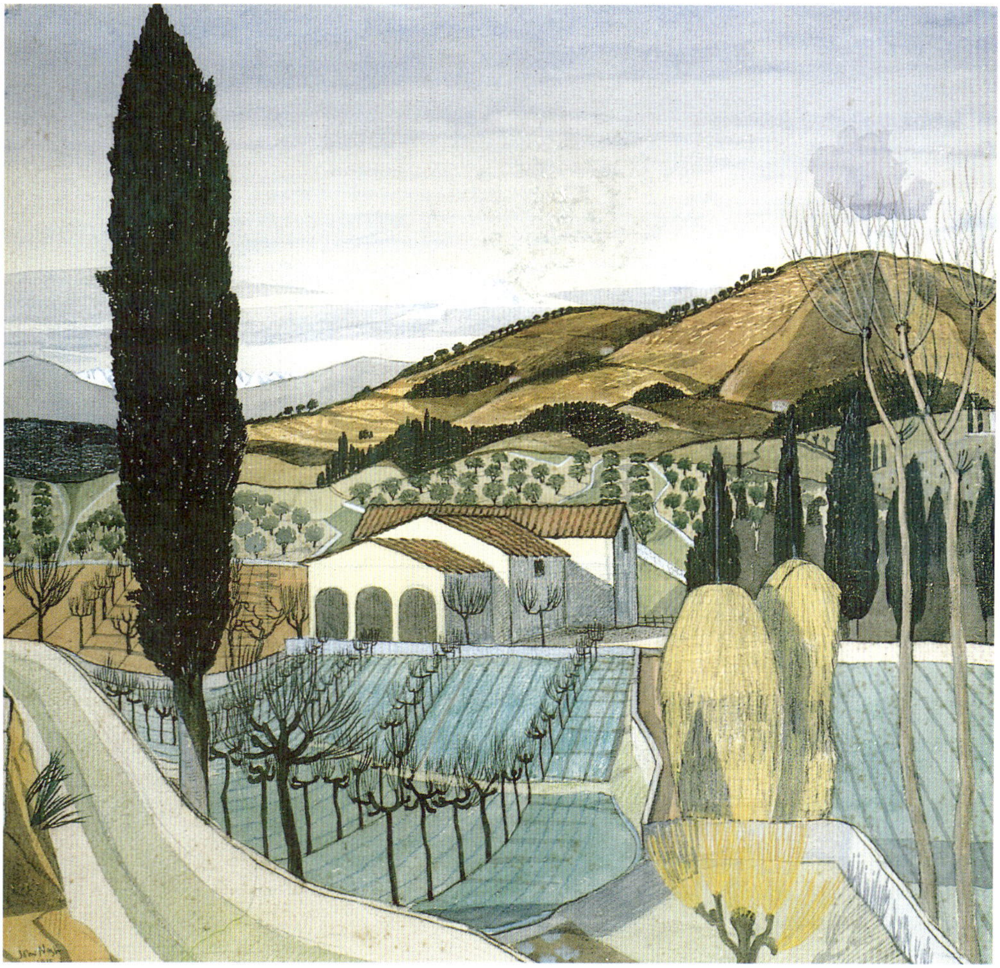

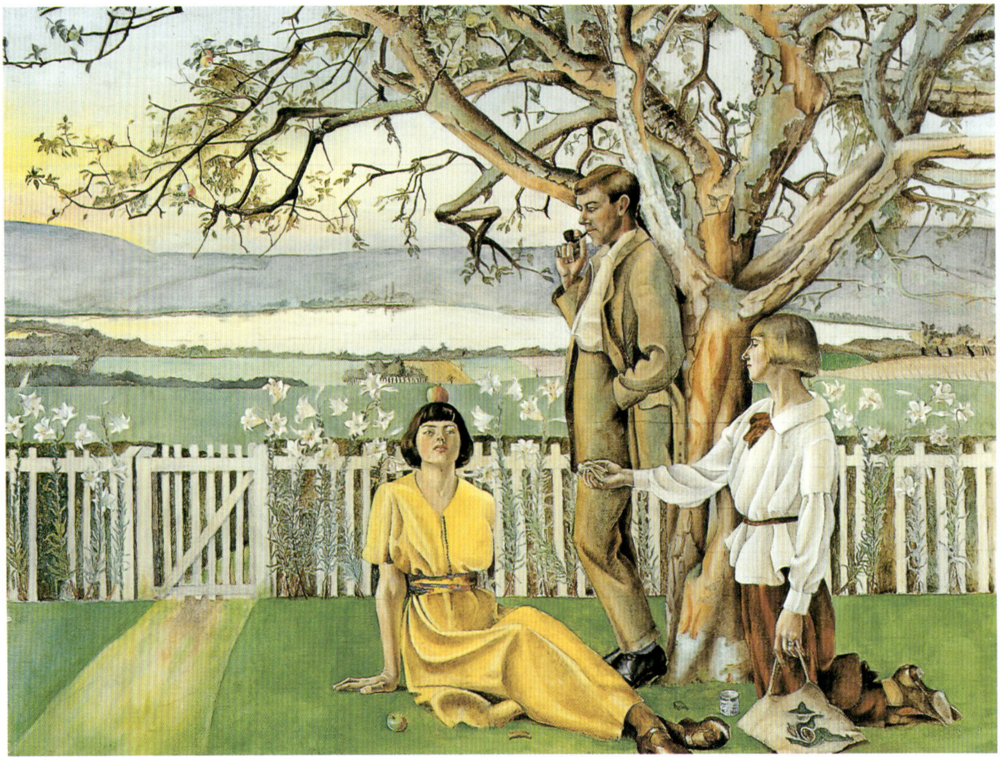

having to make yet one more excuse. 'Why I didn't tell you when you asked me at the window [to stay] for I knew then. I don't know. I am awfully frightened of you sometimes, even if I look so beefy.' Professor Tonks had that day in his equally intimidating manner told her to get on with her scholarship work. But there were countless other occasions when, unable to say no, she accepted invitations then regretted it. 'I am feeling rather unhappy – I've got to go to the Nashes today. I wish I hadn't to. Sometimes one longs to be an animal like a Fox and go and hide under the earth.... Last night it was the full moon. How lovely in your woods. I hope you are happy and will get your scholarship. My love, Carrington.' Christine, equally troubled by the confusion of student interests and the long reins, but reins all the same, of home-chaperonage, soon gave up expecting Carrington to keep appointments and appeared to settle for seeing her when she could. Her letters were neither angry nor forgiving. They simply ignored Carrington's excuses and got on with the news.

Whilst Carrington was in Scotland during the summer of 1913 staying with Brett, Christine and Norah went to Germany for a month. They were guests at Hous Nüssberg, the Kühlenthal family home near Koblenz. The Rhine flowed below the garden. The weather was grey and chilly and the girls spent part of their holiday turning some attics into a den which they christened The Bower, and Christine herself made sketches for her scholarship picture *The Picnic*. In between they played billiards and were taken on dull drives. It was so cold at times that they laid in hammocks wrapped in winter coats. Across the river a big factory puffed smoke into the sky. Behind Hous Nüssberg lay the family vineyards. But it was an apple-tree which was to enter Christine and Norah's mythology. On warm days they would lie beneath it and 'call' its fruit down. It became their Moon-Apple-Tree. In *The Picnic* the tree, and Charlie standing against it, smoking his pipe, and Christine and Norah sitting and kneeling at his feet, are arranged in the correct Slade order as well as in the pattern which suited them. Christine's self-portrait stares into the distance, Charlie looks as though he has come to terms with women, and Norah offers a sandwich like a votary, the goddess of course being Christine, who balances a moon-apple on her head, reminding the world that her first name is Dorothy. The symbol of St Dorothy is an apple. Carrington photographed Christine, dressed in her smock, at work on this

---

Opposite: *The Picnic*, Christine Kühlenthal, 1914. Oil, 915 × 1220 mm. Ronald Blythe. Christine is seated, left, with her friends Norah and Charlie.

large oil at the Slade. It, and another canvas, the *Nativity*, in which Charlie and Norah model for Joseph and Mary, and the Gerrards Cross light enters through the chinks of a barn, drew Carrington's respect. Not only the draughtsmanship and colouring of these pictures, but also a certain narrative quality in them, confirmed her interest in the tall, swaying girl with the impossible name.

Two or three years later Carrington was devastated to learn that Christine was giving up painting, that most precious and marvellous thing. She wrote to her, incredulously. An uncharacteristically unkind remark in an earlier letter might have indicated why. Although she had previously been told by Brett 'how very ill you have been' and had asked, 'Why are your eyes bad?' she wrote: 'I am all wrong and rotten. To you I am beastly. I always mean to be nicer, but fail to carry out the excellent intentions. I liked Norah, she had such lovely eyes, so alive. Yours looked like sloeberries in comparison with hers. I want to meet her again when I get to London, if ever I do. Will she come with you and me and have a winter picnic?'

Whilst making drawings at Hous Nüssberg for *The Picnic*, Christine nerved herself to make an unsparing pencil study of her poor eyes. They had glaucoma, and after the direct looking ahead stare of the girl in *The Picnic*, she would become the artist of the averted gaze. Her downcast glance would be characteristic and strangely beautiful. Eventually there would be tinted spectacles and orangey-green celluloid Suzanne Lenglen shades, painful visits to Moorfields and a steady deterioration of her sight. In 1913 both Carrington and Christine were immersed in Slade School figure studies, working from the same monumental model, Carrington in oils, Christine with pencil, and often posing herself. Mark Gertler was referring to her when he wrote to Carrington, 'That little German girl you drew nude, dances *excellently*. She has a lovely little figure to clasp.' In the drawing Christine lies on a bed, her eyes closed.

Late in 1914 the Carringtons moved from Bedford to Hurstbourne Tarrant, a village near Andover. At first Carrington herself was euphoric – moves always cheered her up – then came the reaction. She told Christine:

> I am still depressed. I cannot really make out why. Mostly because I am longing for something which I cannot have. Accentuated by the joy of spring everywhere, I hoped that this country would cheer me, but I feel so much further away now – even more unhappy. This evening Mother said, 'How the evenings are drawing out' – and I was thinking so far away. And then I realised how stupid it is to long for other things when one always comes back to one's home,

and the long dreary evenings. Everyone in a different little cage. My Father is caged and cannot be ever happy. Mother is his keeper. Do you ever read Balzac? He has a wonderful way of giving one the idea of day after day being the same, the conversation at meals....

I feel I want to expose myself to the world. Really tell everyone what I feel and what I am. Do you realise that perhaps three people love you for what you are and the rest ... love quite an imaginary character – a false idea which you give them?

I am loathing myself to such an extent because I am so selfish and hypocritical that I want to go away from everyone and start new. Yet I never will, of course. It is so difficult to change when no one expects you to, or would notice it if you did! Do you really care for me – really? Do I really like your inside? I keep on wondering all this.... All this isn't because I want to love a man, as *Home Chat* would probably tell me. I never felt less disposed. I just feel always melancholy, and hunted by the idea that I am hypocritical. But enough....

I bought a beautiful dog in London at the Battersea Dogs' Home. He would have made me happier here. But I had to leave him with a friend whilst I went to the Nashes and they lost him in London.... I distempered all the spare room grey yesterday. One frieze less now in the house! Great joy of obliterating little birds (no species) sitting on wreaths of mimosa.... The garden looks really very lovely. But I hate it almost because Mother thinks it lovely too.... Christine, I apologise for all this but I felt I must over-pour somewhere.... What would I not give to come and live in your £5 cottage.... My love, dear Fawn.

How to Paint a Church

The outbreak of the First World War apart, a major disturbance for Carrington and John in particular, and to Paul occasionally, was the possibility of their being commissioned to fresco an Uxbridge church. A Mr Eves – no doubt somebody Mr Nash knew through his advisory work as a lawyer with the Church of England – was willing, the vicar and council permitting, to pay for this. Mr Eves had been to see Cooee's and Carrington's frescoes in Lord Brownlow's library and was enthusiastic. Carrington wondered whether, as an unbeliever, she could accept. John said, 'Do you not go to church at home to please your father, as I do here, and could you not do so to please mine as I would were I with you?' Meaning, of course, conceal your agnosticism for the sake of the cause. A whole church near to London painted by them – what fame! She agreed to help but was not an easy colleague. It was a time when pre-Reformation wall-paintings were being recovered from the lime-wash of centuries, such as those which Miller had taken her to see in Sussex. Anglo-Catholic clergymen were also richly decorating their chancels and roofs, making them gaudy and pretty. Although the Uxbridge vicar was agreeable to having his church elaborately frescoed by these gifted young artists, his parish council had its doubts, and the business dragged on all through the last days of peace and into a time when there was good reason for abandoning it.

In January John has 'definitely settled to do A Nativity', even if his 'figure drawing is so queer', and he has just finished a water-colour Elisha cartoon. May she fresco some pigs, Carrington asks, there being so many of them in the New Testament? John then recognises his plight. She is in an uncommitted mood. 'Young woman, stop a moment, for, alas, Mr Eves says as how pigs may not be. The councillors, he says, would not allow it. . . . [How about] Baptism with *sheep* . . . or an Entombment? Do try . . . you might very well bring in your little lambs in a baptism.' They are to stick to New Testament subjects because the Old Testament ones are 'too romantic'. A Crucifixion is essential. They 'must begin painting by the end of February'. Worried by her playfulness, he reminds her, 'I have your promise in writing.' But the antics stir him and he tells her, 'I wish I could see you. When I write to you I realise how I miss not seeing you – do you mind my saying this?' As their project drags on he soon realises that it is not so much her unbelief which is making things difficult as her own wayward interpretation of popular religious stories and notions – she whose orthodox parent had drilled her children into Bedford parish church Sunday after Sunday for years and years. Alas, where Dora was concerned the faith was an inoculation which had failed to take. Agnostic was a very learned way of describing her. John recognised this at the start of the Uxbridge frescoing and at once took over the direction. Which was a relief to Carrington. At this stage of her career she had begun to take it for granted that she would have to do all kinds of things to make a living, so why not paint a church? And she had loved working with Cooee at Ashridge. She had also enjoyed the naivety of the medieval wall-painters. With John to keep the main business on the straight and narrow, she could fly off here and there. This was what frescoes were about.

John: 'Should angels be portrayed with real wings, or only as young men of noble and dignified aspect? Why not wings?'

Carrington: 'Angels to my idea did not always have wings because you never saw them, like aeroplanes coming from a distance. But suddenly when you turned round they stood just behind you ... and then again something like a bee buzzing, or a sound, made you turn your head, and again they disappeared. Still, why not wings too? I am sure they were very calm and dignified, and simply dressed.'

She too frequently disappeared for weeks. Letters would jocosely enquire, 'What about it? About what? Why, our church and fresco.' But every now and then remarkable religious pictures would find their way to Iver to be vetted by the young fresco director.

John: 'I think your design excellent. I should certainly not alter the three forms; shall I ever aspire to such manly drawing?... Cannot Christ have a little clothing on?'

Carrington: 'I think our subjects ought to bear relation one to another, i.e. "Daniel in the Lions' Den" and "Samson Killing the Lion" would, I feel, be tactless to lions in general.'

John himself would sometimes vanish, once with Claughton to 'Mundesley-on-C', but he remained firmly in charge of the frescoing. 'Mr Eves (of architectural fame) is going to measure spaces and find out estimates re. scaffolding which it appears will be expensive. Paul is still willing to decorate those pillar spaces....' Just before going to

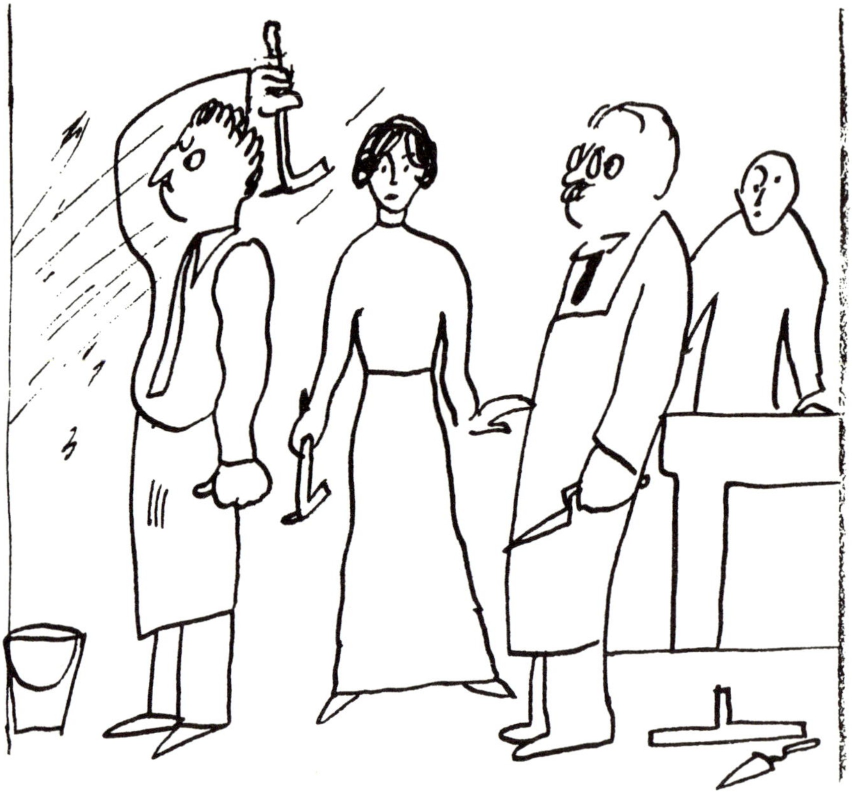

John Nash laments Carrington's failure to discuss frescoes:
'Alas! for a terrible calamity! what food you missed! what spring freshness! & flowers, chocolates, aunt, cats, & above all what disappointment to us all the aforesaid! I was so angry and went to fresco classes and pretty nigh did in the wall as above & might have murdered the "instructor" & Miss Cole (whose acquaintance I seem to have gained) without much remorse.'

Norfolk, John and the architect had waited for Carrington in the dark church to show her what they had in mind and she had failed to turn up. It was embarrassing for him but he played it lightly: 'But all disappointment. Aunt went off in tears, father had to take to [lawn] rolling to relieve his feelings.'

Carrington (piously): 'I have read my Holy Bible most of this day.'

Worse was to come.

John: 'I think your subjects good but doubt whether "Sarah Laughing" is an important enough event ... your remarks on angels are very amusing. I laugh whenever I think of it.'

Carrington: 'Yes, dear friend, patience is what you will require above all things re. these frescoes and re. getting answers [to his letters]. Well, well. I have worked hard all this evening at "Jacob meeting Rebecca [*sic*]". I am doing it in the 4 ft by 7 ft panel, so you will do the larger one, will you? ... Mine will be mostly sheep. Is yours mainly corn?'

John: 'I am doing already the meeting of Ruth and Boaz.' Cast down by her vagaries he writes, 'Will you dine with me on Wednesday [late May]? Before fresco early. Will you let me know? I hope you will, please, and then we can talk fresco work (or not). And if you are Carrington, I am Jack. Eddy Marsh is coming [to Iver] tomorrow ... another miss by you.'

The project limped on all through the summer. Drawings were laid before the church council, which viewed them without enthusiasm. The artists worked so far apart that the intended pairings of their frescoes failed to match. Carrington was much in Exmouth, looking after her sick father and sending John some of her jolliest excuses yet. 'I am sorry not to have written before. As "excuses are first cousins to lies and often near relations" (as my teacher used to tell me in my extreme youth), I will make none....' But she did. 'My small design for the Church is *really*, and I promise you, coming for your inspection, and I fear also rejection, not later than this week. Like the man who mends my shoes and says, "Saturday next Miss they'll be ready" and I find he means Saturday two weeks after.... I realise your anger must be increasing daily. Not a bright prospect for our friendship.' By August matters were reaching a peak.

John: 'Will you excuse pencil as I have much to say.... Your measurements are incorrect, young woman. I am not much of a mathematician but I perceive you are even less [masses of figures].... And now about the design itself. You have asked me to say exactly what I think, it is difficult but here goes. I think the drawing of Jacob might be improved and I think will have to be improved before the councillors, who you know are queer old boys, see it.... I don't like his face and I think Rachel must be a singularly feasible young woman to be taken in by it. I think he must have a *beard*.... One more quibble, Miss Carrington, as Ruskin says, Jacob's bathing drawers were not approved of.'

Whilst working on Jacob, Carrington had been playing with her brothers on

Exmouth beach. She sent John an enchanting picture. 'Little streams run down these huge cliffs and make tiny waterfalls. Grass growing in the niches and then the water makes little channels along the sand and joins the bellowing ocean. Me drawing brothers building castles of sand attired in a wonderful yellow coat of leather, which I am now the glorious possessor of. You wait till you see it! But it really is a wonderful place and these young striplings with long limbs and agile movements greatly excite me to draw them, especially against Indian Red Rocks. I am going to do a picture of Moses calling forth water out of the rocks. This land was made for Bible O.T. pictures.'

But the Uxbridge church council blanched a bit at being offered a lanky semi-naked Carrington boy as Jacob. And how might Moses arrive?

Carrington: 'I knew Jacob was badly drawn, but I only had my brother for about 3 mins. to look at, and his face I was aware was a failure. It was unkind of you to show it to Mr Eves.... I think probably the beginning of November will be best [to paint the frescoes] as it will take some time to do the cartoons out and get everything ready. I am awfully glad the vicar can let us do it. I was fearfully disappointed when you said he might not be able to.... PS This is a stupid letter. I am sorry. But somehow it is difficult to write just now. My eldest brother was wounded, only not very badly I think. I hope he will get well enough to fight again soon.... Thank you for being so kind about my bad design. When I get more settled in my brain I will do something better, at least I trust so.'

By November it was decided to abandon the Uxbridge frescoes until the spring of 1915 because as Carrington said 'the wet and cold affect the plaster. But the fault to whom does it lie? Nobody but my erring self, so I cannot complain.... I saw Sam, my brother, when he was in the hospital and listened to gory and sanguine accounts of the battles. It sounds so like Goya, who is a fine man withal at depicting battles and bullfighters....

'I have been in London a little while now and I am working hard on a beastly scholarship job, as we are poorer than ever now through this old war. I cannot get a model to sit for my design. I have agitated for my two models I usually have, but [Henry] Tuke has lured one to Cornwall and the other is away.... How angry you must be becoming. How I lower my sex in your estimation by my idle promises and constant backslidings, like the Bull of Bashan ... I am neither well nor happy here.... Dürer at the British Museum is sustaining, and keeps one from getting too depressed

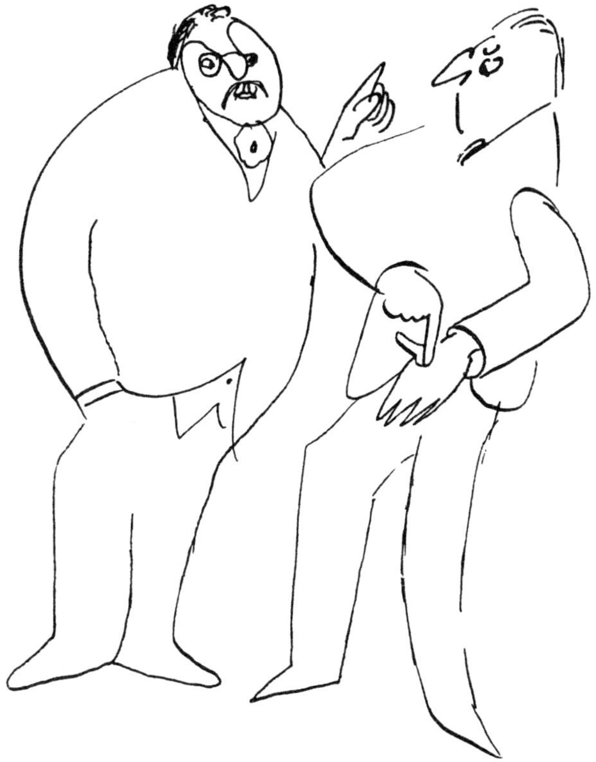

John Nash to Carrington: 'Sir, and as I've said before, I don't pretend to know much of women but I know one thing – that they are artfull Sir I say.'

amongst these people who talk so constantly of the war. Well, I shall be glad to see you again also.'

John (December 1914): '*Bad News.* Alas and alack the fresco is again off. It appears that a faculty is necessary from the Bishop which would if carried through by the whole congregation be an easy matter, but if, as is probable, some people object . . . it will be a matter of £90 or so to employ counsel in the Consistory Court. Mr Eves thinks the congregation so apathetic, and some even antagonistic, that they have postponed it till after the war. He is anxious to refund you any expense you may have incurred. . . . May bombs fall on Uxbridge and destroy it.'

Carrington was relieved. Uxbridge was a far cry from Ashridge and its joys. It came into that jobbery category which interrupted her painting, but which she was obliged to accept because she had less and less money. She once exploded to John:

I have to do the worst form of prostitution – hold on, it's all right, no need to wire Bunty – she (the client) gives me bad postcards of painted fruit or photographs of terrible eighteenth century still-lives, and then I have to compose a still-life from these and paint entirely out of my head with great detail and highlights everywhere. Significant form! Not much. Rosebuds and blue cockatoos mingle with luscious peaches and grapes. Always green grapes with highlights, and this for a shilling an hour – is it worth it – I worked from 9 till 3.30 yesterday and nearly went completely off my pegknot. She said to me, 'Of course you'll try and get the decorative spirit of the period'. May she die in the night.

I drew a hawk from a stuffed bird, almost equal to Bewick, at my drawing-lesson I give to a little girl, which was so good that the mother promptly made me come twice a week instead of once. Well, dearie, I am sorry to write you such a cheerful letter. But I want to paint so much myself and really feel inclined to let the shillings go hang.

Paul, who had loftily agreed to join in the frescoing at Uxbridge, was getting married when the whole thing was called off. Not the least upsetting part of the business was that his lawyer father, an expert on Church of England regulations, should have allowed Mr Eves, John, Carrington and himself to have gone so far ahead with drawings, cartoons and measurements, without a faculty. But all this year-long labour did achieve one important result. It provided a kind of neutral ground, a breathing space for John in his pursuit of Carrington, and for her to remain at an excusable working distance from him. Without it there might have been a painful collision, then break. Of course, had it all gone ahead there would have been no option but for them to share an Uxbridge scaffold. Weeks and weeks of proximity which, for opposite reasons, each would have found unendurable.

The direct manner in which John presented himself as a lover offended Carrington. His feelings may have been heightened by Paul and Bunty's wild courtship, or even by his father's engagement to a widow who promised to bring some comfort and warmth into his desolate life. Paul evidently thought it a good thing to speak of his brother's merits to Carrington, and several times he suggested that they should accompany each other when they invited themselves to tea at her flat. Paul's acquaintanceship with girls before he met Bunty had been graceful, Meredithian, and Carrington had come under his spell. At twenty, John's understanding of women was that it was natural for them to present 'wiles' which had to be overcome. He was the first young man to encounter her obduracy, her determination to be herself. Totally inexperienced, he at first played by the rules and disgusted her. They then by banter and wit, and a shared admiration for so many things, landscape in particular, became great friends. His desire for her and her dislike of him when he was carried away by it not only hurt, but baffled them both. It was a puzzle to them to have so much in common and to be so incompatible. Neither knew why. Where their emergent personalities were concerned they knew almost nothing. John alternately blundered on, and pleased her with his fun. He became her youthful dominie with his botany lessons and the like, and she led him towards emotional freedoms which were to her the very essence of being an artist. But he did long to have a girl.

John: 'A short letter to ask you to forgive my behaviour last Wednesday. You must have been feeling wretched enough without my providing extra trouble and will I fear think twice or five times over before coming out with me again. Yet I hope you *will* come out again.'

John: 'Thank you for your (with the exception of drawing) "mingy" and, as regards news, unwelcome letter; in fact thank you for nothing, as they say. How can I please you or ensure the pleasure of your company for more than 15 minutes at a time? Tonight it being oppressive and portentous with heavy laden air and lightning and thunder, I feel like Blake's drawing of the child and the Moon. I wish, I wish, but all this is vain, I realise, when my father breaks in upon me to ask my opinion on Asquith's last move X X X X (parenthetical markings and not what some people might think 'em).'

Carrington (July 1914): 'Thank you very much for accepting things and for seeing my point of view. You know I would like to be friends with you, and if as a friend I can ever help you, I will be happy. You cannot think what pleasure it will give me to know you better, and your work.'

The blandness with which she dealt with his feelings drew a feline response in the style of Gilbert White. It upset her greatly. 'Dear Madame, I have latterly been observant of the habits of the common cat or *feris vulgaris*. A person of curious observation assures me that they do play with their prey when caught in a most brutal manner, letting it run away and again recapturing it (Cat and Mouse Bill)* but I believe myself that this is not the case, but that they first catch and kill it and then indulge them-

* The Act by which Suffragettes were released, only to be promptly re-arrested.

selves in a game of grisly make-believe by tossing the dead body about as though it was again alive. In the same way we are told, and some no doubt have experienced it, that the fair sex will play and lacerate a man's feelings.'

Carrington's response was predictable and John's apology absolute. It marked the nadir of their youthful relationship. She was strange but she was not playing cruel games. He on the other hand was hurt and bewildered because whatever he said, whatever he did by way of courtship, met with reactions which made no sense to him. But he did now see that the spoof Gilbert White letter was tasteless and gave her a reputable excuse this time for having nothing more to do with him. So he wrote:

Dear Carrington,

> I have today received your letter which is troubling me very much. I don't know what I can say but to ask you to forgive me for being so rude. I would never have written what I did had I known, or thought, it would have seriously annoyed you, for I feel you *are* angry with me and not without a cause. As I said, I have ill-kept my promise of patience to you and though most of Gilbert White's unlucky letter was but in jest I own I was feeling angry with you because I thought you did not wish to come out with me, which may be true or not, but in any case I have no right to be angry with you, nor should I have any reason to expect you to regulate your movements to my wishes. I was therefore both presumptuous and bitter, which I now realise much to my distress of mind. I beg you will, if you can forgive me, if you cannot, forget it. And yet I cannot quite realise that I could have been angry with *you* but rather with the course of events. I do not feel I want to come to your picnic now, nor will you wish very much to see me. Also I am catching Paul's cold. I could not tell you my letter was all jest for I feel it would not have been true and you would not have believed me.
>
> I am sorry to bother you with this tiresome explanation. I hope I may never be the cause of so much trouble again. Yours, Jack.

As it became plain to him that Carrington had no intention of becoming his lover, John thought that he would have her blessing if he chose someone who would. He had mentioned Mary Lloyd – 'Little Lloyd' – another Slade student, as a possibility. Carrington did not think she was right for him and warned him off. Nevertheless, after meeting her at the Cumberland Market Group, he went ahead. 'I remembered your warnings for a little but found her pleasant and she lives close to Aunt Molly and knows a lot of people I know.' A few months later, Carrington could have told him 'I told you so' because, she now having become his confidante in all things, he had to confess:

My dear Carrington,

You must think me a beast and unworthy of the excellent friendship you have allowed me to enjoy.... I am not happier, only more unhappy if anything, though now more certain as to where I am ... Mary does not love me, only she feels a warm feeling of friendship such as I imagine you do – I hope so – she feels she is too young and thinks I am too. What could I do but submit to be friends, though I cannot for a long time meet her on that footing, so cannot see her at all. Sometimes I feel it is all not true. I can scarcely realise what we have done. How difficult and how intensely bitter it is to come to this after regarding her as a lover. At times I have felt abject even to implore her not to take this step but at last a dull unrealising sort of commonsense compelled me to give in. Perhaps it is not right to struggle so much for happiness.... How I wish I could see you and explain to you better in words.... I feel only your sympathy and Claughton's (my other real friend) are of any use to me....

If only I could get away from home and London, and factory work [at the White City, where he is punching eyelets in tents] and all. I have awful doubts also on the war; whether I am doing right, and the work is so hard that I am always tired and more or less depressed. Not one good landscape done since April and Autumn coming on quickly now.... I enjoyed your county [Hampshire] so much that the thought of it compared to my present method of existence is hardly endurable. My work consists of standing for 10 hrs hammering (no pay as yet although overdue and promised).... Please write again. I badly need letters such as your.... Ever yours Jack.

Paul Begins

Paul was 'lucky Paul' to John, and 'proud Paul' to himself. In 1914 all the main strands of his future life emerged: his marriage to Bunty, his recognition of the poet Gordon Bottomley as mentor, and of landscape as a personal metaphysical territory. He had at last broken with his early hero Rossetti and he had found – in the grounds of his father's new suburban house of all places – his own visionary countryside, a realm where elms, its most ordinary trees, reached from the earth with an aerial lightness, or out of the night like monoliths. His Iver Heath parkland was wired in and caged, yet unimprisoned, allowing the viewer access to ordinary sights made strange, yet beckoning. Remote women (sister Barbara and Bunty) are sometimes caught strolling and conversing in Mr Nash's Bird Garden. At midnight there are falling stars and a staring moon, each common enough, but unusual when Paul had done with them, and often the hill he had claimed – Wittenham Clumps. All these surprising pictures were in pen, wash and chalk, or pen and watercolour, and they had titles rather like those of poems: *A Lane in Blue*; *Their Hill*; *The Three in the Night*.

Paul's first exhibition at the Carfax Gallery in November 1912 had been excusably mannered for such a young artist, but in the shared exhibition with John at the Dorien Leigh Gallery a year later, manner had deepened into originality and meaning. It was after this show that both Paul and John felt the first slight irritation of the critics' 'the brothers Nash', and subsequently the first conviction of how unalike they were. John too had journeyed no further than Iver Heath, except that his trees and plants grew naturally from the chalky ground. The first half of this momentous year found them both hard-working and buoyant. Paul was orderly and imposed discipline. They must sell their work and make a living. He purchased a football and they kicked it about before breakfast to keep themselves fit. John was never entirely well. He would also disappear for an hour's fishing or afternoon's gardening. Each went up to London frequently, Paul to be with Bunty. Lance Sieveking, a young friend, summed up her fascination in *The Eye of the Beholder*, his autobiography (1957):

One evening, a day or two after our first meeting, Paul said to me, 'I want you

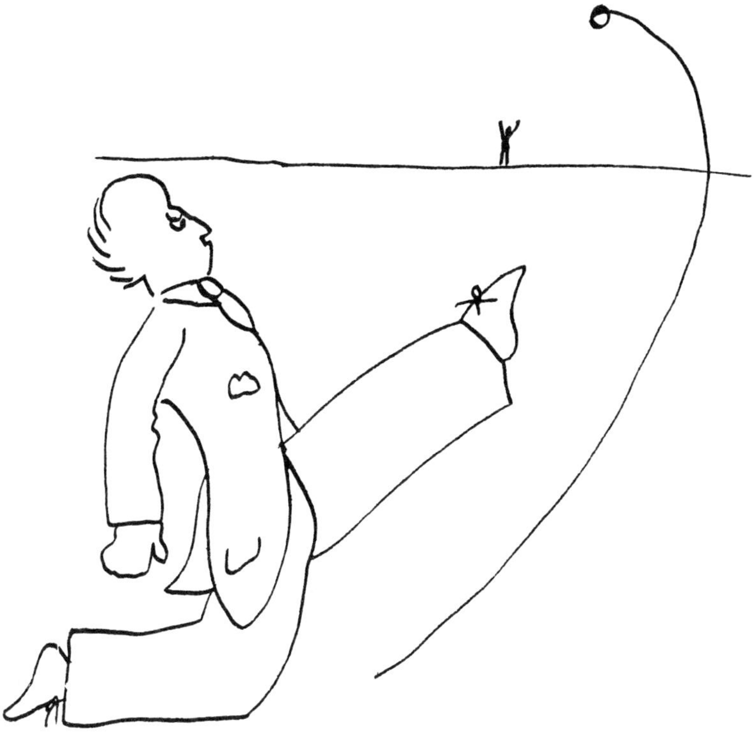

John Nash to Carrington: 'Paul & I, in order to sufficiently exercise ourselves before sitting down to painting, in the least amount of time, have purchased a small football which we kick colossal distances so –'

to meet my girl'. Bunty was living in a block of flats called Queen Alexandra Mansions, in Judd Street. This was only five or six minutes' walk from Russell Square. It was an enormous red-brick warren of inexpensive flats. I was at Number 33 with my father and Paul's girl had Number 176, which looked out over a vacant space and commanded a magnificent view of St Pancras Station, which several years later Paul used as the subject of a number of paintings and drawings.

We mounted a great many narrow concrete stairs, and the little blue door was opened by a small, plump, rather Oriental-looking girl with black hair, enormous black eyes, and a voluptuous mouth. She greeted us in a deep musical voice: 'Come in, dears. I've got a delicious supper for you.' The flat consisted of two small oblong rooms and a tiny kitchen in which there was a bath.... There was a little watercolour drawing of a nude by Albert Rutherston on the mantelpiece in the sitting-room, and also several unfinished canvases leaning against the wall. There was also a clavichord. . . . On one wall was a fair-sized drawing in watercolour and ink of a group of elm trees in a field with lots of birds flying about.

Margaret Theodosia Odeh was, as all of them soon discovered, both eminently practical and hazily clairvoyant at the same time. She mesmerised Paul – swept him along. He was her handsome cub genius and she intended to roar for him. Her Oxford degree itself, let alone the Arab streak, made it impossible for his family and his friends to regard her as they usually regarded women, and the pair of them soon found themselves in some ways rather isolated. Rupert Lee prophesied trouble to come, and he was right. Yet, equally, there would be Margaret's utter devotion to come. It would ride the storms and Paul's bouts of faithlessness. Dreadful squalls and safe harbours would alternate. Bunty made Carrington feel that it was best to keep out of her way, and John that he longed to have a girl who would love *him* to distraction. Although not a Bunty. Whenever she appeared among them, she seemed like a grown-up among gifted children.

During the latter part of May 1914, Paul told Carrington how he and Bunty intended to travel to the Lake District and back without letting their families know. 'We mean to go up by train in the ordinary way but returning we shall come by easy walking stages, putting up at odd inns, or sleeping under hedges, and just catching a train when we're tired. I think this is the better plan on the whole and we shall have all the same sort of gypsy fun.' In *Outline* an earlier plan reveals the strength of the social conventions which still bound them, those of Bunty's clergyman father and those of Iver Heath. Especially where the latter was concerned now that Mr Nash, after years of marital suffering, was about to find happiness with the Hon. Audrey Handcock. Keeping a welcoming house for his sons' artist friends was one thing, taking into it the peculiar Miss Odeh as a prospective daughter-in-law quite another. He did not like her at first because he could not understand her. Where did she

---

Opposite: *Standing Nude*, Christine Kühlenthal, 1913. Pencil, 530 x 280 mm. Ronald Blythe.
Over, left: *Hill in Snow, Hurstbourne Tarrant*, Dora Carrington, 1916. Watercolour, 539 x 641 mm. Private collection. Painted from Carrington's bedroom window.
Right: *Uplands around Hurstbourne Tarrant*, Dora Carrington, *c.*1916. Oil, 620 x 512 mm.

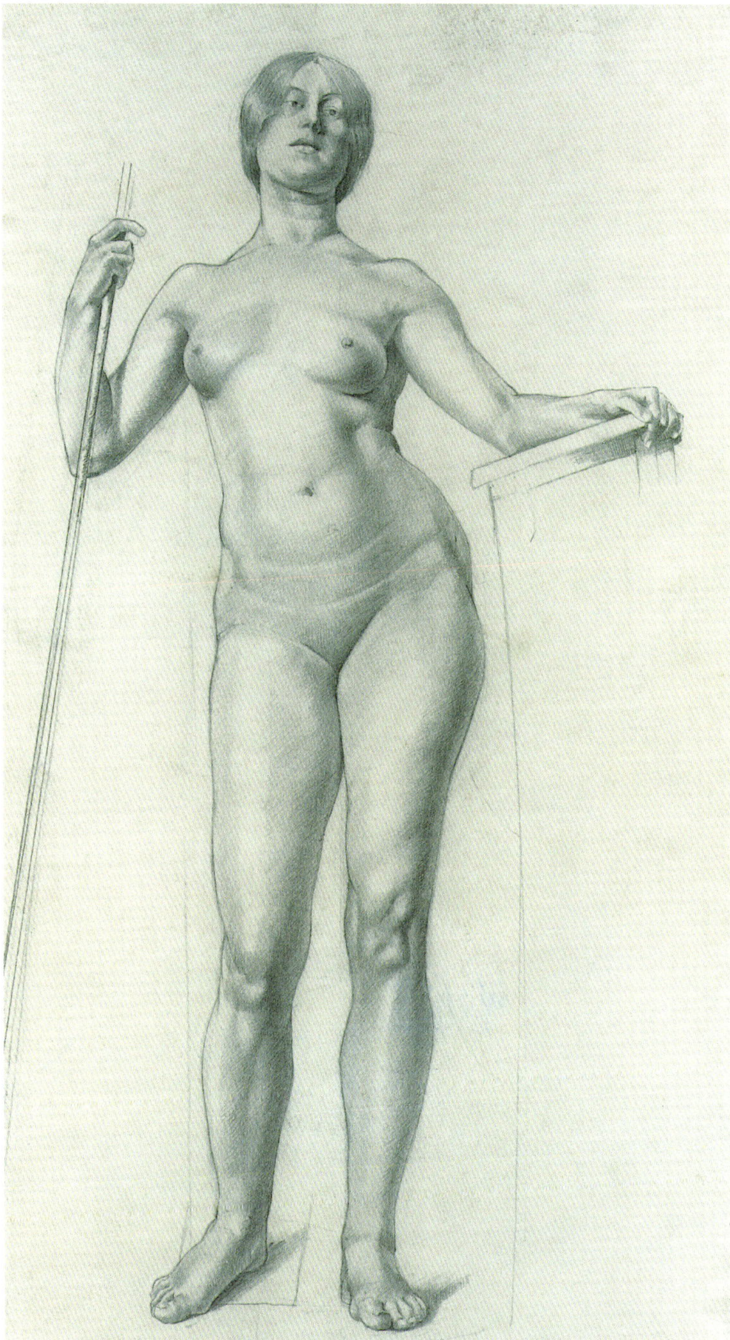

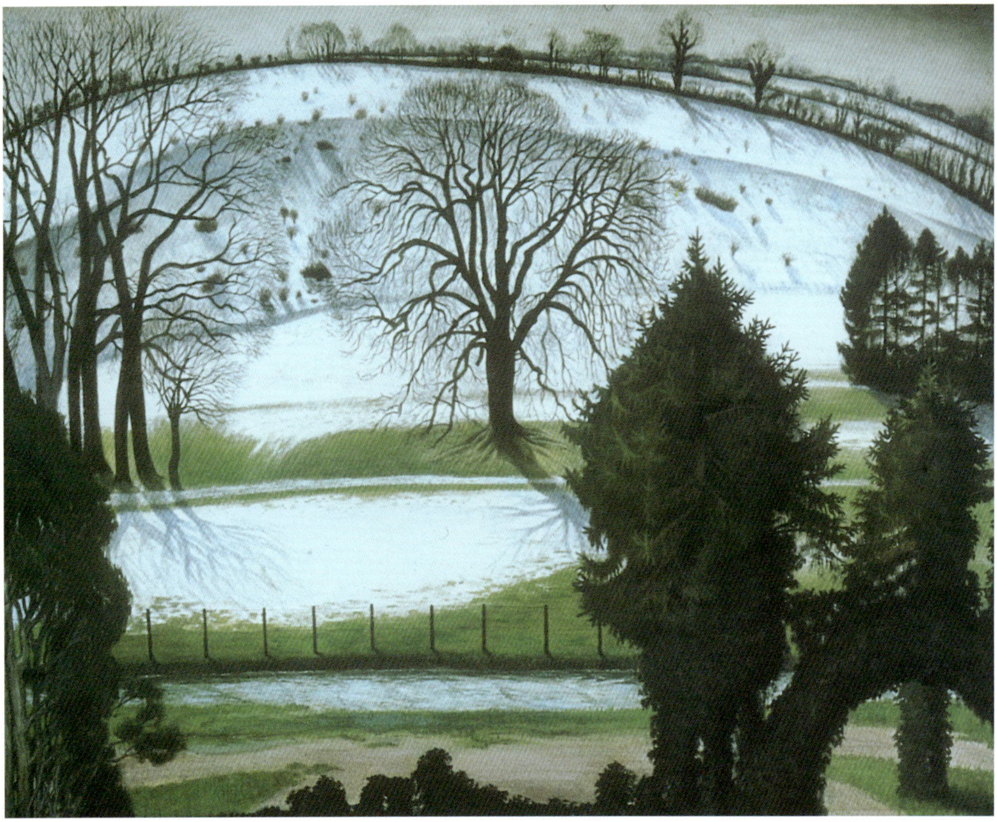

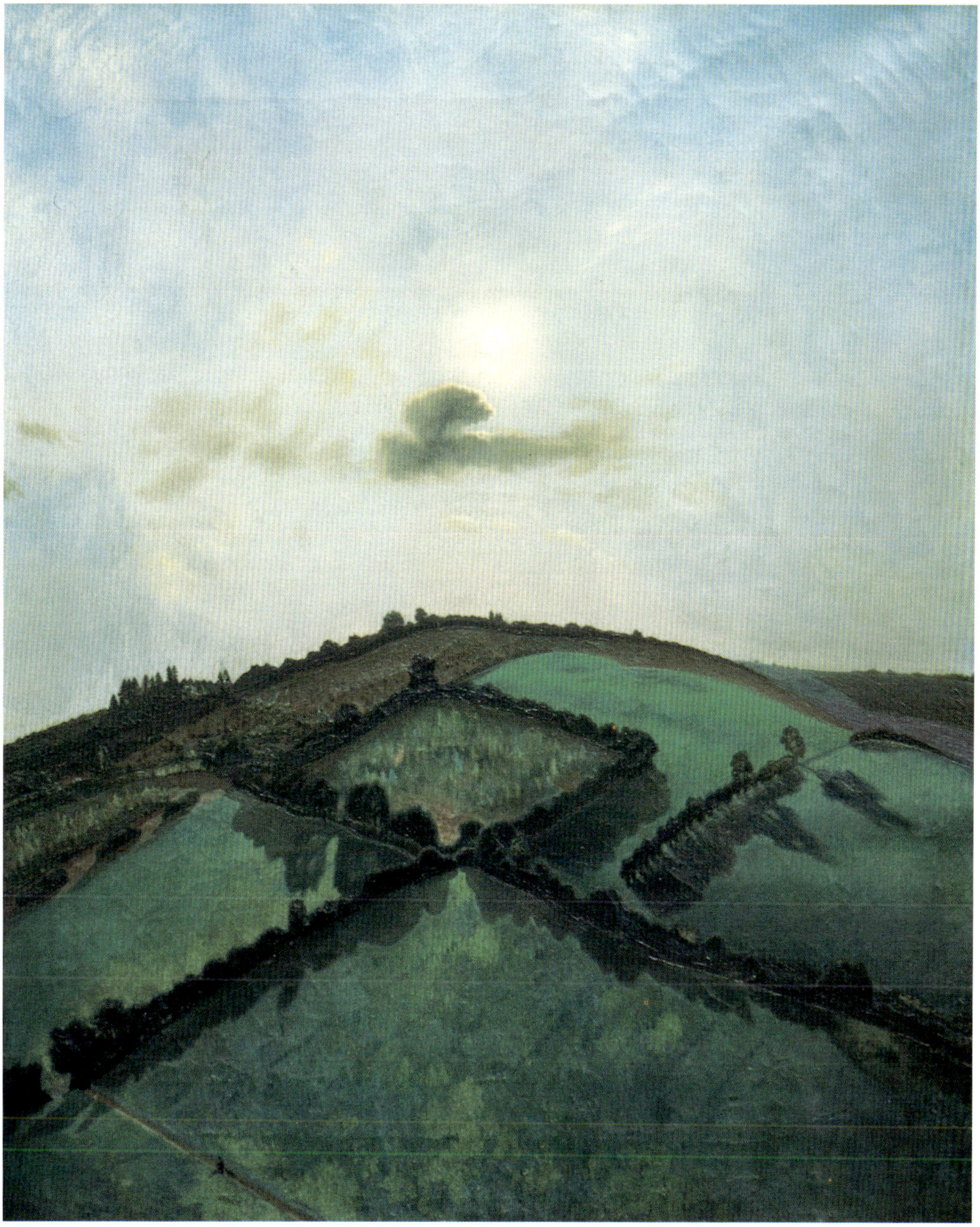

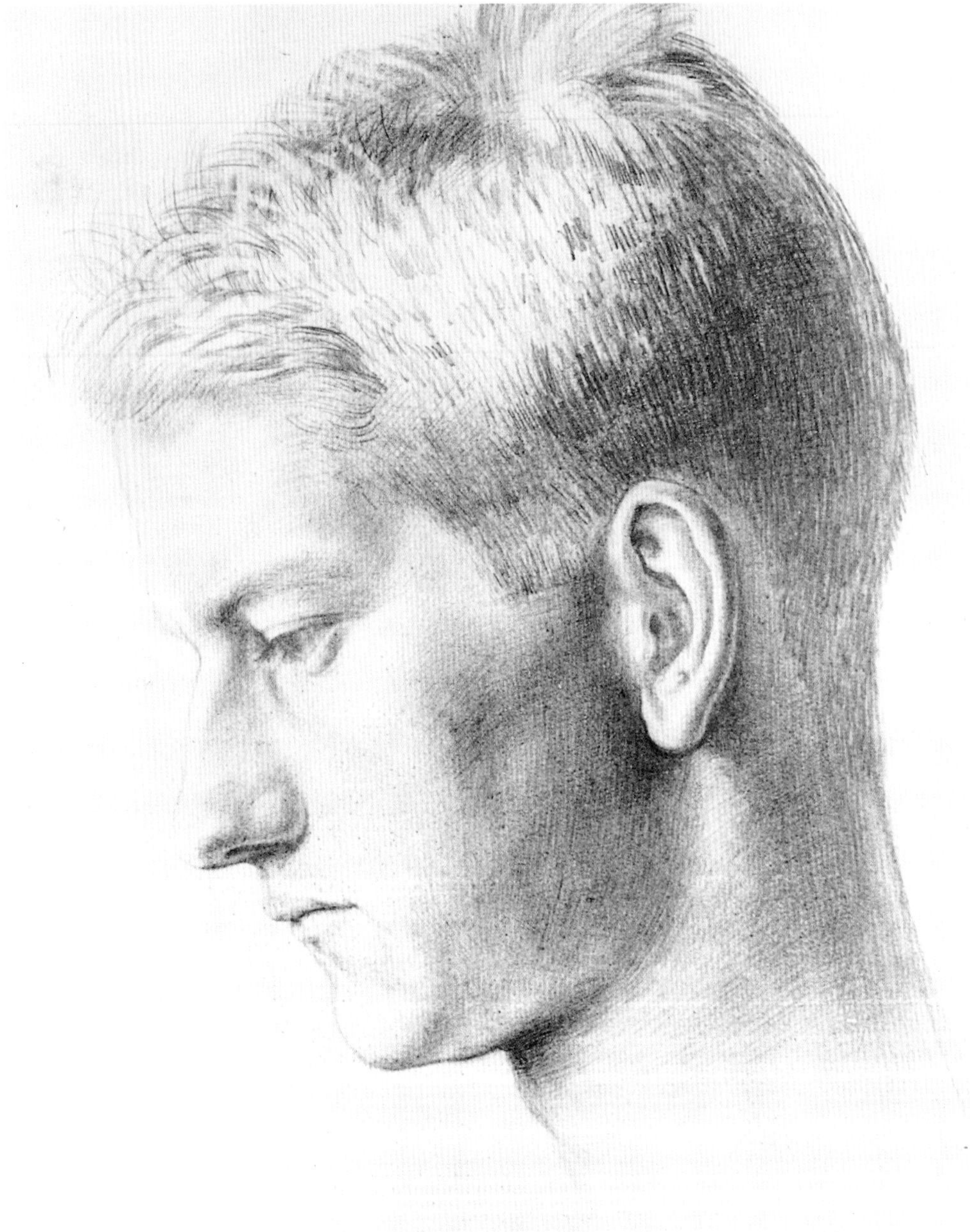

belong? In what category? There were rows with Paul. Hence the secretiveness of their original journey to Lancashire to meet Bottomley. Paul made it sound like the reputation-threatening trip to London from Cornwall of the young lovers in Thomas Hardy's *A Pair of Blue Eyes*. He warned Gordon and Emily Bottomley, tongue in cheek though deadly serious all the same: 'Bunty and I agree that to travel in a train thro England would not only be dull but a sinful thing. So we mean to go in a cart or buggy of some sort and creep gradually up to see you, and see everything upon the way. *But* it must be a secret journey. For to publish such a idea would be to electrify the family – I mean fathers, aunts and uncles.'

Paul had first heard of Gordon Bottomley when Ida Goldsworthy, a neighbour in Iver Heath, had lent him a book called *The Crier by Night*. It overwhelmed him. 'The mood, the nocturnal scene, the mysterious, horrific nature of the Crier, and the extravagant poetic language seemed to accord with my own imaginative experience.' Which is why Mrs Goldsworthy drew it to the brilliant youth's attention. He illustrated it before handing it back and she sent it to its author, whom she knew slightly. Thus began the huge correspondence between the painter and the poet. Bottomley was a sick man who, after a brief spell as a bank clerk, had retired to Silverdale, a village on the upper coast of Morecambe Bay and only a few miles from Wordsworth country. There was in his and his wife's seclusion something which foretold that of Claughton and Kechie's retreat to Overstrand. When Paul met Bottomley, however, sickly looking he was not. This was two years before the Silverdale expedition. Eddie Marsh had chosen work from – for Paul – Bottomley's significantly titled *Chambers of Imagery* for inclusion in his *Georgian Poetry* (1912) and it may have been because of this that the Silverdale hermit had come south. Paul had a sad vision of him as a sick, racked figure but was met by an apparently healthy giant whose head 'seemed moulded like his own undulating hills. His slightly flattened, black crest, roofing his broad sloping brows, together with the longer sweep of his great red beard, all suggested rather the flow of polished, sculptured planes. . . . [He was] a Northern God who in happier times might have lived in a grove and dispensed oracles.' The great man was 38. Paul was awed. So in a sense was Bottomley. Both of them instinctively knew that they possessed a similar understanding of landscape and humanity's brief

---

Opposite: *Noel Carrington, c.*1910. Pencil, 310 × 250 mm. Private collection.
Photograph courtesy of Tate Gallery Archive.

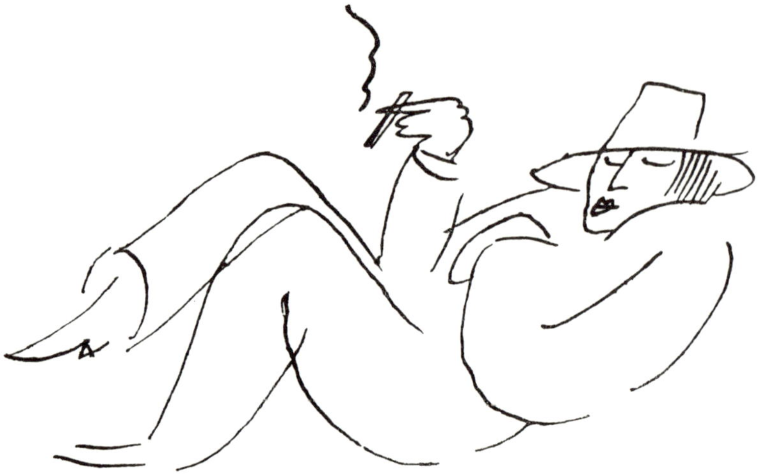

Paul Nash to Carrington: 'and then great peace – the artist's vacation and rest cure.'
Above: 'What may be the idea of the Artist's Rest Cure.' Below: 'What it is.'

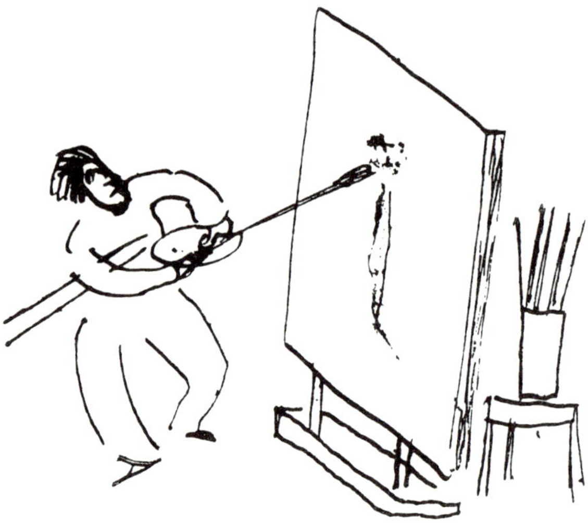

tenure of it, that they shared a common set of symbols and caught the same note in poetry. Bottomley was a considerable poet-dramatist who had studied the Japanese Nōh plays. He was also capable of sending rather frightening flashes of his own into the wistful drama of the Celtic Twilight. Like Bunty, only differently, he was occult. What with her and Gordon, Paul had stepped right into the enchanters' den. He was intensely happy. In his going-to-the-Lakes letter to Carrington, he wrote:

I found it quite impossible to write last night so have risen early this morning and met the sun upon the upland lawn. For half an hour I have stood about in the garden watching the birds and the trees and flowers. What a charming business it is on these spring mornings. The sun seems shining with all his might, almost with agitation – I seem to see and to hear and to smell him shine. And the birds keep up an incessant singing, like egging on the sun and shouting to him to keep it up! The grass and the flowers glancing in the light and touched with dew....

Jack has a new hat in which he looks a new man. Bunty has a new hat in which she looks very naughty. I have a new black coat in which I look as slim as a swallow.... We had a great friend of yours down here [Iver Heath] the other day, Mr Gertler. We like him upon acquaintance. Especially I like his outlook. I have always been rather repulsed by his manner hitherto but I think he is really nice and rather amusing often. I hope to know him better. It is curious you have never talked of him to us – but I suppose not – everything hath some reason.... Gertler tells me you did a very good head of him. I have finished the landscape with the pink hedges and a gate across, and nearly the orchard one, and am having rather fun with two smaller drawings of wood ladies among trees. No I did not say I was having fun with the ladies. Jack and I have both sold at Leeds, and the new pictures go to Whitechapel. Then comes the funny old New English and then great peace – the artist's vacation and rest cure.

I began to try and draw my impression of the opening night of the Crab Tree Club – a very diverting affair. John [Augustus John] was most painfully drunk but alone in his glory, everyone else very sober and bored. The only woman in the place when I got there about 11 o'clock was nice Miss Tapp and even later the club only raised three old girls verging on 40 and one very fat female on the right side of 30. I did not stay long. Gertler says things livened up about 2 o'clock and at 4 John expressed a desire to be married then and there to all the women present....

I am sorry this is not a successful letter. I feel it. But it is a noble effort in scale and conception. [It is written on huge sheets of drawing-paper.] One cannot always write good letters or even do good drawings in bad letters. We send you our love and blessings. May you spend happy days. Ever yours, Paul.

The Great War

Carrington was on holiday with her family in Exmouth when England declared war on Germany on August 4th 1914. Christine was in Dunwich with Norah, the two girls travelling to the drowned city in a cart. John had just returned from Norfolk. Paul and Bunty were with Gordon and Emily Bottomley in Silverdale. As soon as he got back home to Iver, Paul wrote to Carrington telling her all about their wonderful gypsyish trip north.

> ... I did so many drawings – 26 in all in the North and am so excited over 'em that I spend all day working them out or thinking about them. We had a gorgeous time. Travelling by the midnight train we saw the dawn break over the North country – very grey it all looked. Great horrific factories loomed out, the landscape bristled with chimneys, furnaces flamed suddenly, and as we ran on into the country the light strengthened and we saw the Trees. We reached Leeds at a quarter to six and from that moment spent an adventurous day indeed, and towards evening a devilish wet one about the lovely neighbourhood of Bolton, until at last at ten o'clock we reached Silverdale and our dear friends' house. This proved a charming place, the poet's ideal. Imagine an irregular wide-windowed little house hidden in a covering of creeping roses, clematis, honeysuckle and ivy situated upon a hill and surrounded by a Lake-country jungle – that is a close tangle of small oak trees, nuts, wild apples, hornbeam, blackberry, wild raspberry, grey rocks and numberless ferns. A fairy place, my dear Lady, incredible to behold and really – I never got over it.
>
> From the windows you looked from one side out over the tree tops to the bay with its 'dove-grey sands' (as Yeats would say). From another across a stony, bushy, ferny, rabbity hill and a valley, and more hillocks and valleys to the MOUNTAINS....... The great joy of the place was the combination of countryside and seashore, so that there was all that the heart of man could reasonably desire, sea, rocks, shells, seagulls, cliffs, stony hills, quarries, trees, wild woods, wild raspberries, rabbits, black cattle, black sheep with horns, star-fish, dotterels,

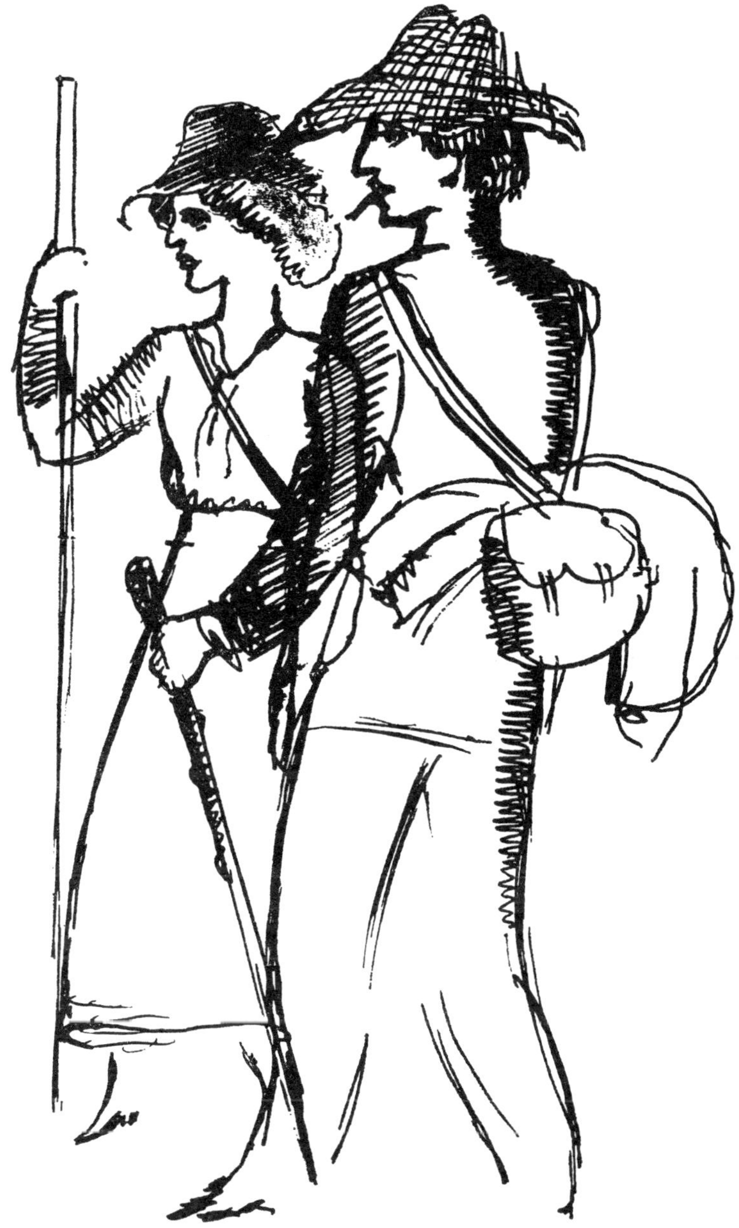

Paul Nash to Carrington showing the 'two travellers' – himself and Bunty – visiting Gordon Bottomley in the Lake District.

curlews, stormy petrels and yellow thistles. Bunty and I revelled and wallowed in it all. We went for long walks and ate preposterous teas. We paddled – all the time we were at Silverdale it was too cold to bathe – and of course I made some drawings.

The poet's house within was a treasure store of all the books one wants to read or look at, great books of drawings, or reproductions of Max caricatures, of Beardsley drawings, Blake, Samuel Palmer, Calvert, Girtin, Ricketts, Conder and Botticelli drawings, and Frederick Sands woodcuts, Rossetti letters and pictures – everyone and everything jolly – you would have stood on your head!

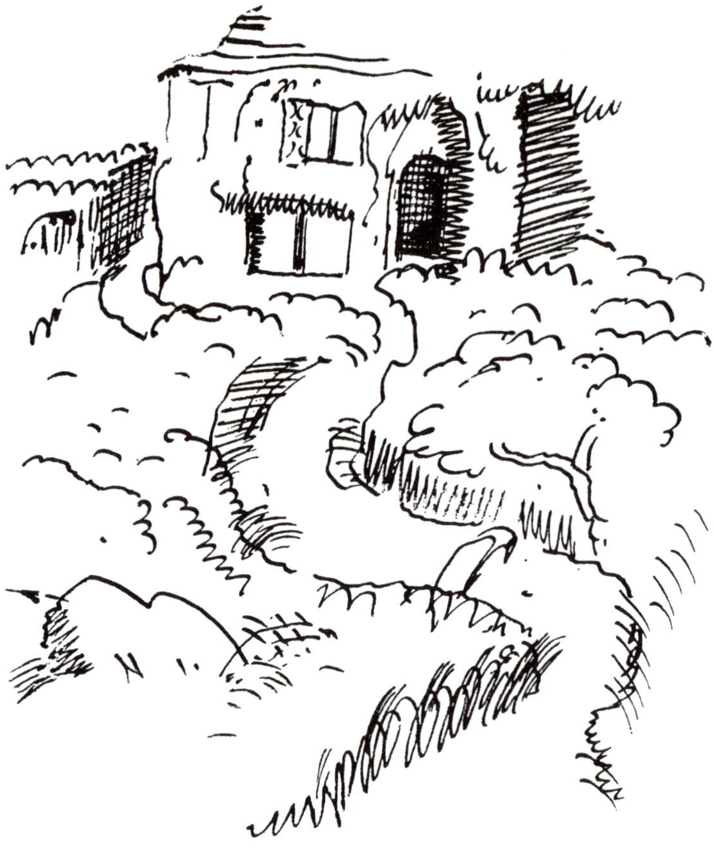

Paul Nash to Carrington, of Gordon and Emily Bottomley's house: 'a charming place, the poet's ideal'.

After the delights of Silverdale we adventured further North and saw most of the Lake District. . . . I must tell all our adventures when we meet. . . . Here is a drawing of the two travellers. Yes isn't this an abominable business this war. I am so sorry to hear about your brothers. I do indeed pity all poor folk whose brothers and sons go to the Front. Jack and I are not rushing off as yet. Personally I am more in favour of mending men than killing them and think I should be more use at it. We are learning Ambulance and First Aid business and playing at Special Constables, and taking in the harvest and all that. But later if the country gets invaded I suppose we shall get a gun and do our worst. . . .

Well adieu my dear Carrington. I was very touched by your nice remarks about my funny old work – thank you – you are a dear, if I may say so. Bunty sends you much love and so do I. God bless you, ever your friend Paul.

But the patriotic uproar became irresistible and Paul along with a million other young men was swept off to the recruiting centre. John told Carrington about life at Iver:

I hope you are well and as happy as the present circumstances allow you to be. Paul has tried to enlist and has been turned off after fruitless waiting. I have not tried and don't think I should pass the medical. I have been doing work for the Board of Trade re. unemployment, but they don't need me any more. We are so sick of trying to make ourselves useful and being turned off that we are now waiting a bit and attending once more to our work. I suppose Art will be needed again one day soon. May the time not be long.

I am going to Cheltenham to take care of Father one day next week. I suppose there is no chance of seeing you from there? Rupert [Lee] is staying here with us as all artists are down on their luck now. Albert [Rutherston] was also turned off from enlisting, so has returned to *Art*. I am going to try and pass a first aid exam.

. . . [the so-called philosophy of Nietzsche has made the war party] a truly atheistical crew which seems to make the Allies' cause almost a Holy one; certainly civilization cannot advance until it is wiped out. I hope you are feeling fairly calm. I found it almost impossible to doubt the good issue of this war.

Whilst looking after 'the Dad', who was on legal business for the Church of England in Gloucestershire, John was at work painting a 'so' or 'soish' oil of sun-rays descending from behind clouds to behind a great tree. It was a painting of an

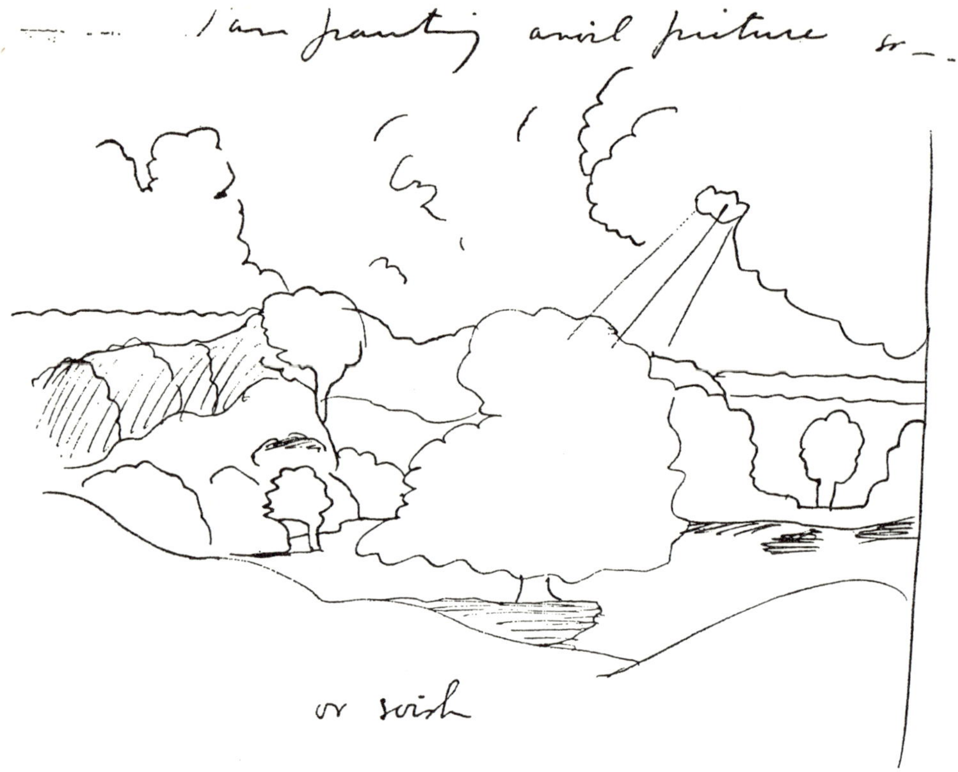

John Nash to Carrington: 'I am painting an oil picture so – or soish.' This is the oil painting *Gloucestershire Landscape* (1914) which hung over the piano at Bottengoms Farm until John Nash died, now at the Ashmolean Museum, Oxford.

intentional substance. After the Dorien Leigh Gallery exhibition he had had his first bitter taste of the critics. He complained to Carrington, 'The papers have been extending their wit (?) ... on my pictures. I am "always trivial and conventional". Unutterable madness. What can they know of the beauties of the country and does Nature show her treasures to such complicated phrase utterers as they are? (She does show them to us, doesn't she?) However, I suppose it is better to be mentioned disapprobatorily than not at all. Middleton Murry says that the sale of my two pictures is "success too cheaply attained". One of them is that landscape from Paul's window, the last you saw.... For some weeks I have been doing, and have now almost done, a picture that I hope you will like, a painted study, so to speak, of two elm trees. I had a canvas 30″ × 40″ restretched and gessoed. You remember we talked once of "tree portraits"? I have now to go on duty.'

Paul applied to join the Artists' Rifles early in September 1914 and was accepted. Lance Sieveking, his comrade in 'D' Company, the Second Battalion, recalled them drilling in the gardens of Russell Square. They were both still in civvy clothes and had to bring their lunches along in paper bags. There was a heatwave. There were flags and bands and cries and everywhere the sound of young men marching. London was intoxicated by the war. Well-dressed women were out in their thousands, urging the men on. Recruiting offices had queues a mile long. Those who could not get into their favourite regiments wept in the streets. Resting under the Russell Square trees, Paul and Lance smoked Snake Charmer cigarettes. Paul, said Lance, 'was small, neatly made, a closely-knit young man who held himself well. He was always alert, standing very straight. Also he was very dexterous in all his movements, managing his rifle and all the drill with a smart accuracy.... His black hair was brushed back off his collar in a thick gleaming mass.... His collar was very low and he wore an enormous tie neatly knotted.' He was twenty-four and already had that air of quiet assurance, almost of authority, which was one of his chief characteristics all his life.

In October Carrington, still at Exmouth, wrote to John, 'Thank you, I am quite happy. I only get sad intervals over the war, as I am sorry to admit it but I forget it often. Yesterday at 6.30 I went for a fine swim in the sea by myself, as my youngest brother [Noel] has gone back to London, to enlist. I hope you are well and able to do some work. I have done practically nothing this summer. For most of the day I seem to spend picking apples and storing them, and picking beans, and making large pots full of blackberry jam. The blackberries here are the best in any land, the like of which I have not seen before. I want to see your work badly, so I hope you have done some. But who will buy?'

Less than two months after its heady declaration, John's tune about the war had markedly altered. He told Carrington that everyone would be the poorer for it, especially artists:

> You suffer too by this awful calamity and I would do all I could to comfort you but I know not how. For myself at first I felt how trivial all my work was compared to the great doings, but I have now calmed down and am doing my best to work again, also to learn first-aid and be a special constable.... We are still here [Wood Lane House, Iver], sitting tight and economising. I too have

just planted turnips over my nursery garden. The amount of various fruits this year is hardly to be conceived.

I will not talk of the war. I am sick of it and of hearing people who must naturally know nothing about it, talk of it. . . . I get so restless over my work and all the time there is in the background this war. . . . I would like to go to Wales or some wild remote spot and forget about it all – not that one wishes to fly from any duties that may arise, or could despise and think it trivial, but anything for peace. I wish it were a day of miracles and that God would strike down all peace-breakers.

Back in Gloucestershire with 'the Dad', he tells Carrington: 'There are sheep here the colour of a fried sole, a fine reddish brown. . . . I have passed my first-aid exam and shall therefore receive a certificate. I am bringing back with me nigh on 8lbs of sloes to make sloe gin. . . . The farmyards here are so good: I think I shall do farmyard scenes for the rest of my natural. I am convinced now even more than formerly that a strict adherence to nature is the only thing worth doing. "Even at the risk of being dull?" . . . someone may say. But how can nature be dull? What is Cubism or anything else to nature? War also makes an immense revulsion to natural observation and simple objects. Forgive this lecture.'

It had not been expected that so many would die so soon. There was grief, bewilderment and consternation. Germany had to be 'hated' and so the crazy hate campaign began. It immediately engulfed poor Mr Kühlenthal, who had lived in England all his life, but was still non-naturalized. Poets then began to elevate the war and its victims, one of the first being Laurence Binyon, a librarian at the British Museum who, in September 1914, published an elegy called *For the Fallen* in *The Times*. Its fourth verse would eventually become the nation's last word on the dead:

They shall grow not old, as we that are left grow old:
Age shall not weary them, nor the years condemn.
At the going down of the sun and in the morning
We will remember them.

Slaughter called for poetry. Appalled by what was happening – by what he saw would happen for a long time to come – Paul's friend Gordon Bottomley wrote in *All Souls, 1914*:

To-night the young uneasy dead
Obscure the moonless night;
Their energies of hope and dread,
Of passion and delight,
Are still unspent; their hearts unread
Surge mutinous in flight.

The life of earth beats in them yet,
Their pulses are not done;
They suffer by their nerves that fret
To feel no wind nor sun;
They fade, but cannot yet forget
Their conflicts are not won.

Much has been said about the innocence of the generation which rushed to join the colours in 1914, but less of its ignorance. Paul and John had little or no idea of what was happening. The chief enquiry at Wood Lane House was when Mr Nash interrupted his sons with 'What is your opinion of Mr Asquith?' Life there was a matter of surface order, future plans – Paul was to be married in December and his father the following July. Where and how were they all to live?

Although Paul's second attempt to join up had succeeded and he had been accepted as a private soldier in the Artists' Rifles in September, and although John had begun to do his wartime bit, both their minds were far more concentrated on their painting than on the conflict. The latter, it was said, would be brief anyway. All over by Christmas. So where would they work now that a step-mother was on the way? Their father had been extraordinarily tolerant of their, for him, scarcely understandable careers, and of their unorthodox friends, but now that their pictures were beginning to sell, and Audrey would soon be the new mistress of Wood Lane House, both Paul and John realised that they would have to move out, if not during the war, very soon afterwards. During the spring of 1915, perhaps. They entertained the notion of a shared studio in Hampstead. Mr Nash too was looking forward to a happy marriage after a disastrous one. Instead of interrupting the young artists for their opinion on the government, he would say things like, 'There is a mouse loose in the drawing-room. Send in the cat.'

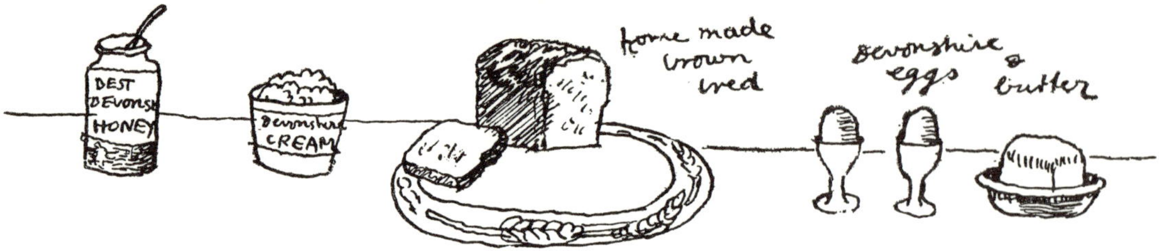

Carrington to John Nash, from Exmouth: 'Shall I send you some cream one day? As for your fried eggs and good food in Norfolk! Why it could be nothing to the food here. Now what about your Norfolk teas! So I eat enormously, & will soon be very fat.'

The early phases of the war caused little comment. Nor in what the brothers painted or wrote was there the least sign of those attitudes which would cause their 1918 paintings to be amongst the most powerful indictments of the Western Front. During the autumn of 1914 the so-called Battle of the Frontiers had led to the deaths of a quarter of a million French soldiers but this disaster was so successfully censored that few people in Britain knew of it. Similarly, the first battles of the Marne and of Ypres were so carefully under-reported that not even their casualty lists, though awful, awakened society to what must occur if these vast, unwieldly and ill-led armies continued to fight. As the end of 1914 approached, Britain was far more worried by the effect of the conflict on its economy than by the inevitability of battlefield losses on a previously unknown scale. The government, having so magnificently declared war on Germany, now had its work cut out convincing the electorate that its money was in safe hands. The First Lord of the Admiralty, Winston Churchill, declared that 'the maxim of the British people is "business as usual".' But nothing was as usual and the patriotic din could not drown out the rumblings of uncertainty.

But some young men were joyous. They felt they were Homeric and it all went to their heads. A week or two after joining up, Paul met Rupert Brooke, his beautiful face all smiles. They used to see each other at Eddie Marsh's flat in Raymond Buildings, Gray's Inn, where John Nash too would often be given a bed for the night. Rupert would have given Eddie an Homeric account of the 3,000 men Winston had sent to Antwerp to hold up the German advance. Rupert described it to Paul in the street. It was 'Marvellous'. Paul's reply was cautiously Homeric: 'I expect I should hate the slaughter – I know I should, but I'd like to be among it all.'

Private Paul Nash went to Gamages, Holborn, for his uniform, making a great fuss over the fittings. On December 17th he and Bunty were married in St Martin-in-the-Fields by the young pacifist vicar the Reverend Dick Sheppard. Private Lance Sieveking noted that the church was full of Bunty's prostitutes, who 'doted on her'. Carrington's mother would not let her come. When Paul received her present, two prints, he wrote:

Dearest Carrington,

Thank you very, very much indeed for your delightful and considerate present to Bunty and me.... On Monday we go into barracks at Roehampton, outside London. So all my dear anticipated joys are but dangled before my eyes to be snatched away just as I go to grasp them. You with your kind heart must pity us, I know. Oh, it's absolutely, undiluted Hell! Well, well, it must be seen through. It is something wonderful to cherish such a hope and longing as I store somewhere inside me for the day when Peace and Liberty come again.

We had the jolliest wedding – it was a sorrow you were not there. I shall not forgive your parents for that. All kinds of absurd things happened at the actual ceremony not at all consistent with the dull, decent conventional 'do' so dear to the heart of all Englishmen. In fact it was an absolute farce and frightfully amusing and friendly. Lots of good folk were there and afterwards we repaired to Bunty's club [the International Franchise Club in Grafton Street] – you remember that beautiful large drawing-room – it was prepared and reserved for us and filled with good food, flowers and Fiz. And there we did make merry indeed. Everyone went away eventually with a wide smile and a revolving eye.... It was on Saturday Bunty and I fled away far down into the country, to Shepherd's Rest, an old, old house overlooking a gorgeous valley.... The enclosing hills sheltered ancient farms, and about here and there strange orchards composed of the oddest trees. All was most remote from the world, most stirring somehow to me; full of a Spirit old as the hills themselves, and still alive and stimulating the imagination the more I gazed on this wonderful landscape. I made three drawings which may give you some idea of my emotions when you see them.

Dear Carrington, forgive me not writing more – tho' I have much to say – I am uncomfortable – without rest. At 8 a.m. tomorrow we march for 'prison'. I will write out of there one day more happily I hope. God bless you.... Ever your devoted friend Paul.

Between his honeymoon and his marching off to the Roehampton Barracks, Paul had taken Bunty to Iver for her first Nash family Christmas, always a momentous event. With John and Barbara and Rupert Lee, the only other guest, they had gone round the village carol-singing and had made fifteen shillings for the Soldiers' Tobacco Fund. In the trenches that same Christmas British and German soldiers had sung to each other across no man's land, and on Christmas morning had actually clambered out to give each other cigarettes and to play football. In the New Year there began the series of tiny advances at vast cost, in February Churchill's plan to storm the Dardanelles, and in April the Germans' first use of poison gas. In January 1915 70,000 Turks were killed fighting the Russians in the Caucasus, in one of the ghastliest campaigns of the war. 'Aren't you glad the Turks have got it in the neck?' John asked Carrington, his next sentence being, 'I am going to have organ lessons.' She now unconsciously began to ignore the war so far as it could be ignored, somehow recognising its shocking irrelevance. She wanted nothing but art and the countryside – and somewhere to go. Only a few months after her parents had moved to Ibthorpe House, Hurstbourne Tarrant, there came Carrington's desolating feeling that she herself was homeless. And penniless. From this moment, and again subconsciously, she began to search for shelter. The ferocious anti-German propaganda now sweeping the country made her feel protective to 'Küthenthel' albeit that she was half-Scots. It was not only Christine's suffering on this account which made her interesting to Carrington but also her possessing some kind of emotional experience which was apparent but not defined. While neither beautiful nor brilliant, she was exceptional – distinguished even. She spoke fluent German, of course, until this stupid war the language of European high culture, and she was a good pianist. Her speaking voice was singularly attractive. Moreover, she was for Carrington the only student she knew who could be relied upon to keep her properly in touch with 'Slade'. Her feelings for her were overlaid with older-girl bossiness. Of one thing she was certain – that Christine was beginning to share her own sense of homelessness. Where was she to go? On St Valentine's Day 1915 she wrote to Christine from far too distant Hurstbourne Tarrant:

> I loved your description of Slade, it told me so much. But I am not jealous! Lady Ottoline [Morrell] has often kissed me, I am sure really she likes me better than Barbara [Hiles]. Yes, dear Christine, I will write you a poem. But the inspiration has not yet arrived. Generally it comes in the bath – awful – since I

have no paper or pencil at hand . . . but soon I will write you one and illustrate it. Heathcliff's [a Hurstbourne Tarrant village friend] was better than Brett's, only I didn't draw him pictures. But he is too dour to appreciate it. I still hate him.

. . . Yes, yes, I will come and live in a cottage. Only do let us keep it a secret. Let us pretend we ought not to go. Like a 'liaison' in a book. We will stay a week in a cottage. I have thought already of heaps of things we will do – again would you be frightened to sleep in an empty ruined cottage [in which] two rooms remain in a wonderful bleak mountainous valley near here? Do come and live with me there a week in the summer. I discovered it by accident the other day – Wednesday – when I was on a walk about four miles from here. It was all in ruins except for two rooms, and it had the remains of an old garden, and was quite alone on the side of a big bare hill. Christine, be brave and live with me there. Nobody would ever see us, or discover us. You must come. Even if the remaining roof falls in on us, we shall at least die together! And do not thousands of men die every day?

How pleased I was with your second letter. I was so happy you really liked my poetry. (Heathcliff was so unappreciative over his). And also glad you do not like Barbara as much as me. She *is* friendly and kind. But don't you wish she had just one vice? If only she wasn't quite so smiling and cheerful. I also ward her off with my hand, I don't know why. It is just because she is so easy and never unhappy. I feel she doesn't play fair. It is not human to be continually bright and cheery.

But when I come up to London you must come and dance with me. I like best to dance out of doors. Then one doesn't run into the walls and easel. Our garden will be great, lovely yew hedges, very thick, and then green mossy grass. Just behind my studio I am making a wild garden, all grass and wild plants, under the tall fir trees. On Friday it was like a summer's day. . . . So I walked to Inkpen Hill eight miles away, where the country is as wonderful as you could wish for, and where I can sit in the deserted garden of the old empty house. . . . A house which I dream of all day and live in terror lest someone should take it before I can live there. You will I am sure love it as much as I do.

In a field in the sunshine I saw such a pretty sight – two hares fighting. It was really the tragedy of an over-ardent suitor and the reluctant lady hare, but it was a fine sight to see them wrestling on hind legs, twisting and turning somersaults, up again, and tearing in pursuit through the short dry stubble.... I am indeed so happy that I feel it cannot last long. Brett can say as much as she likes that the country makes one stodgy, but she is wrong.... Does one ever see two hares fight in London?

... I like Jack Nash so much. He passes the examination almost above anyone. Tell me about Slade again. Who stands at the window? I wouldn't go back to Slade for anything. Oh, this freedom is wonderful! And nobody who cares whether I work or not, or if I do whether it is good or bad.... I wear great thick woolly stockings. Heather mixture. Does this repulse you?... I sold my New English picture. Oh, I was so happy. What a good thing money is to be sure! I shall give you a big party in Brett's studio when I come up.

Goodbye now. Love from Carrington.

This is a stupid letter.... Really I wanted to tell you what I was doing and also that I am glad we are friends.

Despite these rural joys, Carrington needed to be in London. That early wartime spring often found her sharing lodgings with Christine at 16, Yeoman's Row, Brompton Road. 'Sleep in the box bed that lets down as the other bedroom is still damp.... Don't get fined by the police for too bright lights! The key which turns on all the gas-jets has a pink string on it.... The bed keeps up by a long piece of wood which you put under the end instead of legs, comme ça. I think that's about all. You can go and fetch your milk the night before or else get it from a boy in the street in the morning.' The 'other bedroom' was damp from recent distempering, no doubt. Distemper was wonderfully cheap and there was nothing like it for obliterating much-loathed Victorian wallpapers. It was made by mixing a gluey coloured powder with tap water. Carrington preferred a creamy-white distemper which set off blue paintwork, and Christine one called 'stone'. Both girls were swift transformers of dull formal interiors and liked their walls bared for paintings and drawings.

No more an art student and now an artist, Carrington found herself in limbo. Life at home or in London wasn't easy or what she wanted. Increasingly, she felt out of things and belonging nowhere. She told Christine:

Every time I come to London I always resolve it will be the last. I always imagine before I come that I will enjoy it. But I never really do. Not compared to other times. To begin with one always sees the people one wants to see least. . . . Really I should enjoy it much more if I could go and see Madame Tussaud's and Islington Market. But no. The drug of Slade routine besets all one's friends. One goes to Brett's studio – not that I dislike Brett's studio more than any other place – but it seems annoying afterwards. Then I am sorry about you, and I never said so once properly. Christine, I am very sorry.

My youngest brother [Noel] is wounded and may come home any time. Therefore I cannot even tell you when I shall go to Dorset. In fact I cannot decide to do anything as I must be home here when he is sent home. It is really love – not because my mother's sense of duty says it. But he really deserves it and I hope he loves me too. . . .

Christine, what are you going to do this summer – What has been arranged about your Father and Mother? Why not earn 10/- a day painting phosphorous on compasses, 5/- a compass like Sylvia Meyer and Barron?

Tell me minutely what happened at Jack Nash's on Wednesday evening. Did you like Rupert [Lee] and Rosalind, and did Rupert play well? Of course I am grieved about Jack and Little Lloyd. But in a way I am relieved – if I was talking to you a full confession might now burst out. But no, at a distance one is discreet. Which reminds me I was exactly the reverse with Brett and Barbara (!!!) of all people when I was in London, and yet down here I am so determined, and resolve to be so strong. But it's the joy of talking! That's the difficulty to contend with. Still, probably Little Lloyd is just as intelligent as I am. And if I was pretty I should flirt just as much. You never knew me in my successful period. Oh, yes, I had one. Rather like Little Lloyd. And I probably behaved just as repulsively thinking I was being fascinating! You would hardly believe it, seeing the stodgy and rustic cabbage I've grown into. But once I was gay like a kitten! What admissions!

I used to think Barbara was empty-headed and stupid. Now I don't. So how can one tell anything? If Little Lloyd lived with me a week she would probably talk just as interestingly about the night sky, and country, and wheatfields! But all the same she reminds me of a cigarette girl behind a counter. So let her live.

What did you mean in your last letter about Miss A and B and the truth? You meant something. Do you wish me to be more truthful? The great thing is to believe not all that everyone tells you. It's sad. But unless you live with truthful people you suffer afterwards. And do not let your life depend on people. I find books a good substitute, books on travels and roads and country. So that when I am neglected the thought of the road between me and Marlborough still excites me. (This of course does not really act as a plan! Unless one is happy, as truth to tell when I was miserable, I hadn't thought out this happy plan. So it is as yet unproved.) My only proof whether my work is most important to me is whether I can resist running at three o'clock into the house in the middle of my picture to see if a letter has come! Need I add that I almost always fail. Christine, write soon about yourself.... I am steeped in debt. I feel more and more convinced the happiest people are gypsies without reputation or possessions, and no houses to live in. I hope you will soon be happier. I grouse about nothing, whilst you have a terrible thing in England – a German father!

This same week Carrington poured out her heart to Mark Gertler. Having made it plain to him that her 'friendship and company' would always be waiting for him, but not her body, she felt that she need not check her warmth even if 'I *cannot* love you as you want me to.' Several weeks later she wrote again: 'It makes it much worse for me now, coming up to London. I long, and long for you to talk to.... You will write again soon, will you not please! I am glad you like Strachey so much. Does he talk more when you get him alone?... It's just like being in a bird cage here, one can see everything which one would love to enjoy and yet one cannot. My father is in another cage also, which my mother put him in, and he is too old to even chirp or sing. I am sorry to give you such an outburst of self-pity but I didn't quite realise until I saw you again how much I miss not being with you more. The little green stream still flows swiftly through the meadows.'

Nothing that the young artists wrote to each other during the fatal spring of 1915, when the war entered a disastrous stage which would only be concluded by an armistice nearly four years away, revealed the remotest understanding of what was going on, or any real interest in it. They were not alone. Disasters, confusions, official lies and dreadful innovations tumbled over each other by the week. The press and posters raged, the bands played, the troops sang and the bereaved wept, often as much from pride as from grief. As a national experience, the war was unique. The politicians and militarists were at loggerheads as to how to proceed. Some were for destroying Germany by a mighty army, some by the legendary British Navy. Churchill's unfortunate wheeze, ill thought out, ignorantly executed, was to enter Europe by the back door via Gallipoli. Thousands were killed and Rupert Brooke died from a mosquito sting on his way to the adventure. Just after Easter, the Germans used poison gas for the first time – at Ypres. Zeppelins began to float over London, dropping bombs, and there was the novelty of a black-out. Then Germany declared a blockade by U-boats. These wicked, sneaky submarines starved women and children and sank liners. So many peculiar tactics, all of them rushing together, could only bring one conclusion – that the Kaiser's people, now known as the Hun, although these were actually Attila's people, were civilisation's outcasts. Poor Mr Kühlenthal, the merchant chemist who had lived in England all his life but who was still German, found himself in a terrible position.

Carrington was always ashamed of herself when she compared her worries with Christine's. To have a father who was watched by the police, who might be interned, who was shouted at in the street! His persecution and the hideous clamour generally were among the factors which caused her early on to see the war with contempt. At this moment the Nash brothers could only regard it helplessly. Their strong condemnation of it was to come. 1915 marked the height of Carrington's and Christine's relationship. Its development was rapid and for Carrington it lay outside, or on the periphery of, her other commitments. She went to stay at Gerrards Cross, where the two girls danced à la Cecil Sharp in the woodland garden, sometimes naked. They visited Jordans, the Quaker Meeting House where William Penn's family was buried. It was exquisite and filled with the desired quiet, and it became for them one of their personal places. It may have inspired 'Miss Penn', Carrington's name for Christine when she came to Hurstbourne Tarrant in lieu of the unspeakable 'Miss Kühlenthal'. Or this could have been suggested by Thackeray's *Pendennis*, which Carrington was reading at the time. They were inventing a kind of 'residency' as well as growing into feelings which they needed to explore and comprehend. The privacy of these tentative explorations was important:

Hurstbourne.
Sunday.

Dear Fawn,

... You were quite right last Sunday at 5 mins to 11 I *was* going to church in my blue coat with the buttons and seal skin, with my brother. All right I will meet you in the wood, only I fear I shall have to give you some warning lest I spend a lonely day sitting there whilst you are drawing at Slade. I believe a good deal in the power of thought and telepathy, but I would never trust it if I wanted to meet anyone! ... Have you heard about the Slade scholarship yet? Do you know who went in for it besides yourself? Do tell me directly you know.

... I am glad you like maps so much. At present I have great joy marking all the places I know in Hampshire and finding out how far one is from everyone. It is such a joy to think eight miles a long way to walk, and forget you can go to London in a train in 1½ hrs from here. Think! inbetween two rests of work at Slade you could get down here and see me, and all this country. I am reading *Pendennis* and loving it more than anything I have read for a long time. He, Thackeray, is so delightfully humorous – very like Jack Nash is when he is at his best.

Oh such excitement this week! On Wednesday 2,000 soldiers arrived on manoeuvres from Salisbury Plain, and were billeted in our village! We had four officers lumped on us. Only one was interesting. He was Irish, the son of a linen manufacturer in Ulster, with a plain red face and greenish moustache, and hair like stubble after the wheat is cut, only greenish-brown stubble. But he played the piano marvellously. Everything I asked him to play, good Bach and Beethoven, Chopin and the Hungarian Dances by Brahms, and the Appassionata Sonata which nearly made me weep because I loved Brett's studio, and Gertler thundering away on the pianola so much. And it seems such a long time ago, and I know it will never be again. He [the Irish officer] played all one evening and the next day. Mother got so cheerful – 'At last I am going to get Dora married' – and she encouraged the young man and hoped he would come over again, and would I take him round the garden. She didn't know that it was Brett's studio, the windmill and the Cannans [the novelist Gilbert Cannan and his wife Mary], and so many other things which made me happy. Why should she know?

They all went away on Friday evening. In the dust, over the little bridge, the evening sun shining on their hot red faces, the big wagons and gun carriages lumbering along. The soldiers jeering and singing. They have all gone further on to another village and forgotten all this, and we are all stationary behind. It seemed so strange to have sleeping on my little landing upstairs two men in the attic opposite my small bedroom, men who had never seen me, or me them before. Whereas people I have known for so long, and love so much, I am not allowed to ask here to stay. It seems so curious, so incomprehensible. Mother doesn't actually say I cannot ask people here – men of course would be barred – but she always dislikes them, and then makes it so hateful that I long for them to leave me. Ruth [Clark] came last week and stayed, and Mother was more aggravating than I have ever known before.

One day John [Nash] came over just for the day, and he and Ruth were going to spend the whole day at Coombe looking at the house, and just because a stodgy old vicar and his wife were coming to tea I was obliged to stay at home and entertain them and not go for a picnic with Ruth and John. They both loved my house and want to live there. They would be beautiful in it. Even though I feel my heart will break when it no longer belongs to me. Already they talk about it as if it was theirs and seem to forget it was mine ever. Ruth looked so beautiful and talks of nobody but John. It must be contentment to so arrange your life that only one person matters. John had to leave in the evening.... I keep on waiting for something and letting the year slip by, yet I do not know what I wait for. I suppose it's the war. It is such a surprise to suddenly see a rose out on the side of the house, and realise it is nearly June. Do you feel like this often? I wish I could wake up and be more alive. Write again soon to me please.... Carrington.

Either not knowing of or not fully comprehending the deterioration of Christine's sight, Carrington began to scold her for her lack of enthusiasm as an artist. 'Do a good picture! I sometimes feel angry with you for your lack of energy about painting. It is an insult to go back to painting as a last resort. That isn't painting. But then I don't think you are an artist in the painting way. Excuse me being so frank. Because if you were you couldn't go back to it at odd times. You would have to live for it. No, I am not talking rot. I mean this.' She herself had completed two fine oils since the move to Hurstbourne Tarrant, one of her father in his armchair, his 'huge helpless body' thickly clad and emerging from a rug chrysalis, which seemed to prophesy two grandly chair-bound figures of the future, Lytton and his mother, and an arching snow landscape. 'Here's a rotten photo of a picture I did from my window in the spring with the snow on the ground and the ash-tree in the middle of the hill,' she told Christine.

Plans for their Dorset holiday fell through. Wounded, Noel was coming home from Rouen, his arm all stiff. Carrington's excuses and apologies for altering the arrangements rambled on as usual. Although 'Brett's studio' called, she was often more happily involved in village life than she could at this moment admit. She took first prize at the flower-show for her sweetpeas – and made the poster for it. She walked miles and got on well with the farm boys and, as his life ebbed, she became ever more deeply attached to her father. Hampshire itself she found perfect. All her letters now to Christine combined tenderness with reproach. 'I am working very hard now. It seems the only thing somehow. Tonight I sat in the garden after supper and watched the big fir trees against the sky. But the owls and bats rushed through the air, and became more and more until I could bear it no longer.... Well, Christine, cheer up, do not be miserable. Most of us are miserable. How few of us seem happy. Perhaps Brett is the happiest person I know.'

Carrington made her customary clumsy business of withdrawing an invitation. She had urged Christine to join her for a holiday at Mr Hooper's Tonerspuddle farmhouse, in Dorset, then said no. 'Yes, I am rather glad you didn't come. Is this brutal?' And she goes on to describe the lack of accommodation. Yet there was room for John Nash – 'We had some happy days, and an almost equal number of depressing ones.' She is puzzled by her attitude toward Christine. 'To you I am beastly. I always mean to be nicer.' But the truth was that she was worried about the future. Now that she had left the Slade, the freedom she had enjoyed as an art student was being curtailed. Mrs Carrington, with a sick husband, and sons in the army, and with no great belief in her daughter as an artist, clearly saw Dora as part of the household until her marriage. It was this dull acceptance of her future which Carrington fretted against. She must also, and without conceit, have recognised that while she was simply difficult Dora at home, she was quite somebody else in the eyes of her friends. Dorothy Brett saw her dilemma and set about rescuing her, though not to Carrington's enthusiastic approval – 'It's bad enough trying to lead a life you want to, and failing, but to have to try and lead a life designed by others which you don't want to, is even harder.' This to Christine.

Having fumbled her excuses for not taking Christine with her to Dorset, Carrington's own relief at having got free from stifling Ibthorpe House for a week or two burst on the page. Her genius for giving first impressions of a place was given full rein. John Nash was with her, and nice young Mr Gill, the estate architect, who also lodged at the farm, took her rabbit-shooting.

Shall I be really kind and not tell you what this place is like? Or frank and say just how wonderful it is? My days are always different in detail.... I swim at 7 in a weir near the house by myself. It is lovely as the water rushes out through the weir so one can swim against the current without moving an inch. Then I have breakfast with the farmer's family and Mr Gill at eight. Draw all the morning. Binding machines, barns, houses, thatchers, landscapes, cows, anything in fact, till one. Good foody dinner – work again till 5 o'clock tea. Generally go out rabbit-shooting and a long walk with Gill till 8 o'clock, or if he's away I go on top of Black Hill and draw. 8 o'clock supper, lettuce, onions, cheese, bread and butter. The former diet gives me awful dreams, hateful dreams, the harvest pigs having eaten themselves till they could eat no more off my stomach and body in general. At night I wake up every half hour and apply a cold sponge, a rotten method of allaying pain as the pyjamas generally get wet. I sleep in a wonderful feather bed which I make myself....

Old Mr Hooper is paralysed and always wears two hats on his head in the evening as he thinks the light gives him a headache! He wears during the day one hat at all meals! [This was a curiously prophetic idiosyncrasy, because the days would come when Christine would wear all kinds of light-subduing head-gear as she cooked the dinner.] He really is extraordinarly interesting, a great wit in the heavy style, and tells me much information about the ways of farming, and prices of wheat, etc. Mrs Hooper is rather tedious. They were very wealthy once and then lost their money, so she bears the world a grudge. One daughter is quite pleasant, the other laughs like an engine whistle....

... Tonerspuddle, by the way, only consists of this farm and 5 cottages, so in reality it is no village at all! The country here is most beautiful, almost – though I dread to countenance it as a fact – as wonderful as Hampshire. The moors are very high and wild and covered with bracken and heather, and woods. Bogs and streams everywhere, and the sundew plant in abundance! In the valleys are many little cottages, thatched, and barns, and streams with trout. And very large ash-trees, the hedges full of beautiful flowers, and red Guelder Rose berries. It is 10 miles from Dorchester. Read *Lavengro* and *Romany Rye* by Borrow.... Mr Gill went away on Thursday evening so I have his little workroom to myself in the evenings. It is rather good to sit in. So un-Sladey and un-arty. Just many books on shelves, two kestrel hawks stuffed in a glass case, some maps, one very old of

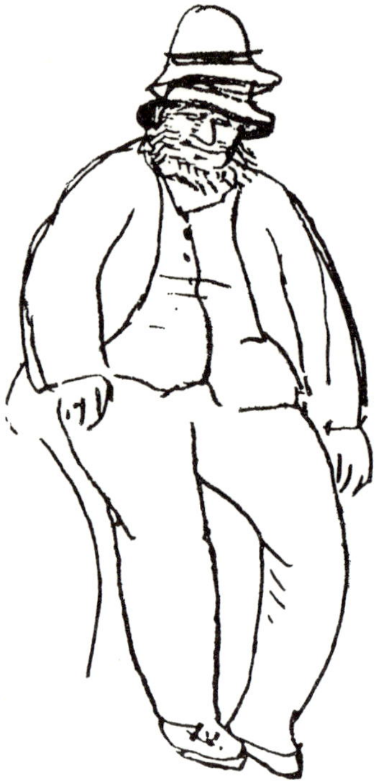

Carrington to Christine Kühlenthal:
the multi-hatted Mr Hooper of Tonerspuddle.

Dorset, on the wall. Dahlias and daisies in a jug. Architect's tools and T-squares, and bottles of inks and acids ... and a William Morris curtain. ...

What has happened to your Father? Noel is still over in Rouen Hospital. They keep on operating. ...

Miss Debenham ... runs a huge farm on very hygienic and modern principles. She has 18 girl volunteer war workers from a Campden Hill school here. They are the worst type of High School girls and go out hoeing armed with Brownie cameras, and shriek, 'Molly', 'Mar-jorie', 'Oh, Ellen!' every five minutes at each other. ...

Mr Gill is getting married next week. He is awfully companionable and more clever than anyone I have ever met all round. He plays the violin, and good old Italian music on the piano. [He is] a good architect and painter generally, prints well. Does carpentry, is well-read, rides and swims, and shoots rabbits, and is virtuous withal, and is even happy to all appearances! ... Cheer up, and work at your picture.

Things declined at Tonerspuddle Farm after Mr Gill went off to his wedding, and Carrington and John were the only guests. John sang Bach at the piano and the Hoopers 'were impossible'. He sang a song about a crocodile, and they reduced bed and board to 21/- a week, and the meals accordingly.

Poor Jack hated them and we used to spend most of the day 'strafing' Mrs Hooper. She groused from morning until eventide ... so we bought a cooking-pot and two mugs and much good fodder at Bere Regis, the village over the moor, and took possession of Spring Barn, and used to have wonderful tea-parties there. And then it grew dark, and we piled up the logs and had a merry blaze. All this was unbeknownst to the Hoopers. It was such fun coming in and pretending we hadn't been so happy. Jasper [her beloved dog, brought from Ibthorpe House] caught three rabbits. ... I did quite a lot of painting in ten days. Jack stayed on longer.... Jack is living at Iver Heath now. *Ask him to come and have a picnic* in your barn by the water and he will tell you about the Hoopers, and the sergeant who came to supper with his friend the quartermaster.

I don't know in the least what I am going to do. It all depends on where my brother goes to convalesce, and what my parents do for the winter.... Lady Ottoline has asked me five times to go for her weekend gatherings and I have refused each time. Mainly because I hadn't a cent to go with.... I get torrents of abuse from everyone, Brett particularly – and Lady O. seems injured. I have promised to go next weekend.

Dear Friend, Mentor – but not Lover

It needed all Carrington's often devastating directness to make it clear to John that she could not be wooed, or persuaded, or seduced, or whatever he liked to call it. In this respect she would always beat him off like a tiresome dog. He found it painful, frustrating, and also incomprehensible. Then why did she *like* him so much? This she could not say. His brother once called him 'scholarly'. At twenty-two he possessed the slow, exact diction of a don twice his age, also a dry wit. Carrington's education was so woeful that it required the utmost self-restraint of her friends not to 'correct' her now and then. Yet she had style and taste and culture to a remarkable degree when stood alongside so many of the middle-class women of her age who were training for some kind of independence in London. Dorothy Brett believed that some form of open-ended chaperonage would be the best way to help her. John found her difficulties commonplace – the kind an artist-daughter would naturally experience with a conventional parent. His own experience had been far ghastlier. But there was music, there were plants, there were the English counties, each one a paradise, there was painting, and there was the bloody war. Having got over what he imagined was her distaste for him physically, and her preference for Mark Gertler, he began to teach her botany. His own master was Clarence Elliott the great plant-hunter, a convivial young man much John's senior who in 1907 had established the Six Hills Nursery at Stevenage. He told Carrington about Clarence's travels in Chile, and about the physic gardens in Chelsea and Oxford, and as he did so, a whole new 'Jack' came into view. Carrington liked men to tell her things, and women to reveal their emotions.

While Paul was being measured at Gamages for his private's uniform, John was telling Carrington, 'Items: *Alstromeria ligtu* from Chili (direct) I believe is not too hardy but wd come up in your greenhouse. I may demand some later if they survive. The Lily is *most choice* and still rare in England; it is said to bloom within 18 months from seed. Later I will try and send you some seedling bulbs of a very nice blue flower called *Ixiolirion Pallasi* and will try and get you some other oddments. Elliott has just returned from Chile but I have not seen him yet – when I do I will try and rob him. ... Three prodigious large poppies [are] now out, having tried in vain to outrival each other in size (for they are all the same).'

Less delightful to Carrington, John's affair with Little Lloyd teetered on. Although they had seen each other 'nearly every day for two months' that strange 1915 summer, she had refused to sleep with him, saying 'We are too young' – which was exactly what they were not. The whole business disgusted Carrington. On July 8th his father married again. Soon afterwards John's half-imagined passion for Mary Lloyd was over, and Carrington heard with enormous interest, 'I spent a day (it being wet) with Christine at Gerrards X. She is nice and plays [the piano] well, also skips about one in quite a bewildering manner while I who you know cannot act the "light fantastic", turn slowly on my axis (rather good word) to find where exactly she is. I intend to go and draw the viaduct near their house soon.' His war work as rope-hole puncher at the tent manufactory at the White City, Shepherd's Bush threw him into a violent milieu which a young man from his background could not have imagined. Ruthless Londoners of both sexes scrambled for the high wages which the war promised and John found himself in a kind of hell. The contrast between the White City and the little bedroom where Eddie Marsh let him spend the night so that he could go to the theatre, or meet friends, could scarcely have been greater. Eddie was in mourning for his beloved Rupert Brooke, who had died on April 23rd – St George's Day – on his way to Salonika, and his grief expressed itself in helping more than ever young artists like the Nash brothers and Mark Gertler, and poets such as Isaac Rosenberg. As well as devoting all the income he received from an ancient state pension granted to an ancestor related to Spencer Perceval, the prime minister who was assassinated by a madman in 1812, Eddie used monies from the Rupert Brooke Fund to support writers and painters. In old age John Nash provided a vivid sketch of Eddie's hospitality: 'It chiefly consisted in putting one up for the night or asking one to breakfast. I used to sleep in a narrow bed in one of the smaller rooms of his quarters at Raymond Buildings, and just above me and threatening, as I thought, to fall on me was Stanley Spencer's large painting of *The Apple Gatherers*. The walls everywhere were plastered with pictures and even the doors had to share in supporting his collection. As one was leisurely breakfasting E. M. would be preparing to leave for the then Colonial Office and on his way downstairs would shout or scream in his high-pitched voice a series of instructions to his housekeeper Mrs Elgy. He placed great trust in this valued factotum. "Mrs E." he would say, "ring the Prime Minister's Secretary and tell him etc. etc." To all this, as he clattered downstairs, came the calm reply, "Yes, Mr Marsh, yes, Mr Marsh." Later one heard her carrying out his numerous orders which, considering she was rather deaf, seemed quite an achievement. He purchased my painting of *The Cornfield* which he left in his will to his friend Ivor Novello little thinking Ivor would pre-decease him.' This was the tranquil study of a Buckinghamshire harvest done in the evening light after toiling all day as an official war artist. John said that he painted *The Cornfield* as a thank-offering for having survived the Western Front. It is now in the Tate Gallery.

Eddie's patronage was not easy for some young men – Mark Gertler, for example. They had been introduced by the tragic John Currie and his friend Gaudier-Brzeska. Eddie was captivated by Gertler and told Rupert Brooke that 'he is rather beautiful, and has a funny little shiny black fringe, his mind is deep and simple and I think he's got the *feu sacré*'. Gertler took him to his Whitechapel home and Eddie took Mark to Cambridge, where his father was Master of Downing College. When the artist became ill in 1915 Eddie sent him to Winston Churchill's doctor. But the more Marsh did for him, the more distressed Gertler became, despite the kindness of what Marsh offered: 'Your birth-pains over your pictures are quite torture enough for you. Don't worry yourself additionally about how you are to live, so long as you can manage on what I can do for you.' On 19th October 1915 Gertler, embarrassed, broke it off. 'I have come to the conclusion that we two are too fundamentally different to continue to be friends. Since the war, you have gone in one direction and I in another. All the time I have been stifling my feelings. Firstly because of your kindness to me and secondly I did not want to hurt you. I am I believe what you call a "Passivist". I don't know exactly what that means, but I just hate the War and should really loathe to help in it. I wanted to do some war-work simply because the hateful atmosphere had got into me and it seemed difficult to create at such a time. But now I've changed my mind I shall paint as long as I can. Forgive me for having been dishonest with you and for having under such conditions accepted your money.... Your kindness has been an extraordinary help to me. Since your help I have done work far, far better than before. I shall therefore never cease to be thankful to you.' Marsh had been Churchill's private secretary since 1905 and had seen him inspire the catastrophic Gallipoli expedition. He was twenty years older than Gertler and, emotionally, possessive of him. But, as the tense Jewish boy knew, they were in every respect poles apart. No longer able to support him. Marsh continued to buy his paintings, and to love him.

Having joined up in September 1914, Paul, with his regiment, was still marking time in Hampshire a year later. He had a minor operation on his nose and wrote to Carrington from Cosham Hospital:

> Carrington, *darling* – is that the right word to apply to you? I think so as I mean to be particularly nice to you. What are these gross insinuations you make? Listen not to idle tongues, especially feminine ones, for they seek to spread mischief – 'Your fair form' – indeed! When have I ever ceased to admire it, from the first moment when I, a bashful student sitting among the plaster casts of the Antique Room, stole covert glances at you, an attractive chattering flapper in a check over-all, and became inflamed with a wish to know you; down to the present hour when I sit here, a considerably married man, but still retaining those tender feelings cherished for you all these years and an unabated admiration for your charms from your turned-in toes to the crown of your golden head. It is not kind, Carrington, it is not indeed. As for my nose, tho' it may seem a subject for amusement, yet even now am I not cast back into hospital on its account? And languish in this poisonous prison Cosham Hospital outside the perishing slums of Portsmouth. However I hope daily to be transferred to London.... Do not think I minded your boisterous behaviour, I thought it particularly stimulating and refreshing – sorry to have trod on your pacifist corns, don't get narrow minded, you might be able to look at drawings in a paper without becoming contaminated by the tone of the other contents. My wife and wives are well, I thank you, and I think, by the way, you might count yourself a wife by now, seeing as how we have now both confessed to continuous and undiminished affection. I will send you a book of Rules anon. You will not find the duties difficult, the only strict law being – No 18 (a) 'That I will always endeavour, to the best of my ability, and without making tiresome excuses, to accept invitations to lunch, tea or dinner, made on the spurs of moments by my devoted husband.' ... And now adieu. Assuring you always of my unbounded affection and love, your devoted Paul.

All that late summer and autumn John struggled on, half in heaven (the countryside), half in hell (the war factories), frequently unwell but perky and determined. Just before joining Carrington at Mr Hooper's farm in Dorset he and his sister, and Rupert Lee, had been caught in an air-raid on the West End. '[We] were in a cinema and the sound of the aerial guns was most thrilling and uncanny, especially as we were not allowed out to view the spectacle', he told Carrington. 'One bomb fell very near me at the back of the Russell Hotel but luckily did little damage except to shatter all the windows in Guildford St, another further on near Red Lion Square, where there was both fire and loss of life. A dreadful but wonderful scene was the spectacle of three fires raging in various parts of London, seen from the roof of Paul's flats. People were very calm about here and I was surprised to find my feeling was mostly that of indifference as to whether one fell on me or not. ... Tonight I go with Rupert to Queen's Hall and tomorrow home to do some fishing. We went shooting on the 1st. I think a picture might be made out of it, the line of guns and the opposite lines of corn and the stubble, very strong white yellow.' A few weeks later, when the threshing bands began to set up their machines in the stack-yards, he began work on one of his first confident and inimitable large oils of this annual scene. It was in many ways a time when all kinds of things began to 'come together', the drama of the farming year as a rich and inexhaustible subject for him as an artist, and his first tentative realisation that the tall, dancing 'German' girl must be his friend. Although still not very well, he revisited Wittenham Clumps and went to Garsington Manor for the first time. He told Carrington:

Estimable Dearie,

> Here is a good letter for you, but I have not been to Duncan Grant's party owing to a cold and headache. I had a most marvellous walk from Clifton Hampden. On the way I saw the potato digger at work and also a motor plough, but as I came up round the back of the Wittenham Clumps a fine sight burst on my gaze. A terrific purple Prussian blue storm cloud in layers covered the whole of the sky opposite the sun; against this the two clumps shot up, crowned by their woods of beech of a brilliant gold orange in the sun. In the foreground were green wild-rose bushes with bright red hips and an elder bush growing from a pollard stump whose leaves had turned a fine claret red. These colours against this sky produced an effect which at once arrested one's admiration and wonder. To add to this a rainbow appeared also, not to mention lesser items such as a hawk hovering bright against the storm clouds, and crab apples gleaming against the same background. I stood for some time wondering at these 'natural phenomena'. Certainly Berkshire has more fascination for me than any other county.

I had a long talk with the engine driver engaged in steam ploughing and drew the engines. It is a splendid sight and gives a great idea of power.

... Today I formally offered myself for his Majesty's army and was rejected as unfit. I have a certificate. I felt like a sheep going to slaughter and reprieved by the butcher's whim.

I heard from Christine. She asked me over there [Forestholme, Gerrards Cross]. I shall go and get her here [Wood Lane House, Iver Heath]. Babs [Barbara] suggests Quinton in stead of K— 'An uncommon name, certainly', said Father. 'I don't remember having heard it before.' ...

I so much enjoyed my weekend [at Garsington]. It was good seeing what I did see of you.... Lady O was very kind and wrapped me in an immense fur coat for my drive, waving to me till the last moment.... Shall I ever settle down? I wish I had not to go to Gloucestershire but Father thinks it madness to refuse 30/- a week and I have no money at all. He seems to have grown more warlike and thinks art must go to the wall, and truly I think it will do so for all Lady O's entreaties.... I *like* you better than any one else I know (of womankind) and would gladly go to Timbuctoo with you, but as that can't be I must be patient and wait for some one else to like me. It seems foolish but these times make one need someone closer to one in affection and acquaintance and yet I should almost fear to have another 'affair' so-called in case I bungled again. By this you see I have been looking back, which is bad, but easier than looking forward. However I must be thankful I ain't in the army.

Weekends at Garsington could be fraught. Once it rained the whole time and Lady Ottoline's 'lions' became so restless that – said John – she drove the whole pack of them out of the house to play football in the barn. She herself played goalie, wearing striped socks. D. H. Lawrence was there 'looking sulky'. The difficulty with so many of the young guests was, to put it plainly, that they were promising but broke. The uproar of the war made their aspirations appear frivolous in the eyes of their families. But at Garsington there was wealth and understanding. Also a sense of haven. It was this autumn that Carrington first met Lytton Strachey at another country house, that of Clive Bell and his wife. Carrington was nursing her convalescent brother Noel in Hove and the Bells were just a few miles away. She described the meeting to Christine. Neither of them had the faintest inkling of its consequences.

87 Carlisle Road,
Hove, Sussex.

My dear Christine,

Thank you so much for your letter. But I hope to see you again soon, so I will not write a very long letter. It's been a mixed time down here. Some bad Balkan crises, and some good times on the downs, and some fine talk with Noel, who is so beautiful, and so unlike all the Slade people. I believe we are leaving next week. I have been able to do very little work and I have had the hump badly over it. But Brett, as you say, is a grand mainstay and prop to one. Are you going to be a 'Lady companion' to her sister? I am sure you do not like her! But if the children are real it won't matter so much, will it? I am now writing to try and get a job in London. Really making a move on at last. But I know I shall hate it and long for my garden and the little barn at home, directly I do come to London!

Well last week the Clive Bells asked me to stay with them near Lewes; just about eight miles from Brighton were we are. So I went. It was indeed a romantic house buried deep down in the highest and most wild downs I have ever seen. Duncan Grant was there, who is much the nicest of them, and Strachey with his yellow face and beard. Ugh! I used to walk along the ridge of the downs every morning early when the sun was just rising, and the wind at the top was more fierce and powerful than anything you could imagine. It roared in my ears, and I had to lie flat down on the wet grass in order to look at the land below, and the sea beyond Newhaven which shone all silver. We lived in the kitchen and cooked and ate there. All the time I felt one of them would suddenly turn into mother and say, 'What, breakfast at 10.30! Do use the proper butter-knife!' But no. Everything was behind time. Everyone devoid of table manners. And the vaguest cooking ensued – Duncan earnestly putting remnants of milk pudding into the stock-pot! They were astounded because I knew what part of the leek to cook! What poseurs they are really!

. . . Brett told me a wonderful story of the woman who read your hand! What

---

Opposite: *Portrait of Teddy*, Dora Carrington, *c*.1912. Pencil, 254 × 1980 mm. Private collection. Photograph courtesy of Tate Gallery Archive. Over, left: *Dora Carrington Cooking*, Christine Kühlenthal, *c*.1915. Ink, 204 × 164 mm. Ronald Blythe. Right: *Head of Gordon Bottomley*, Paul Nash, 1922. Crayon and pencil, Carlisle Museum and Art Gallery.

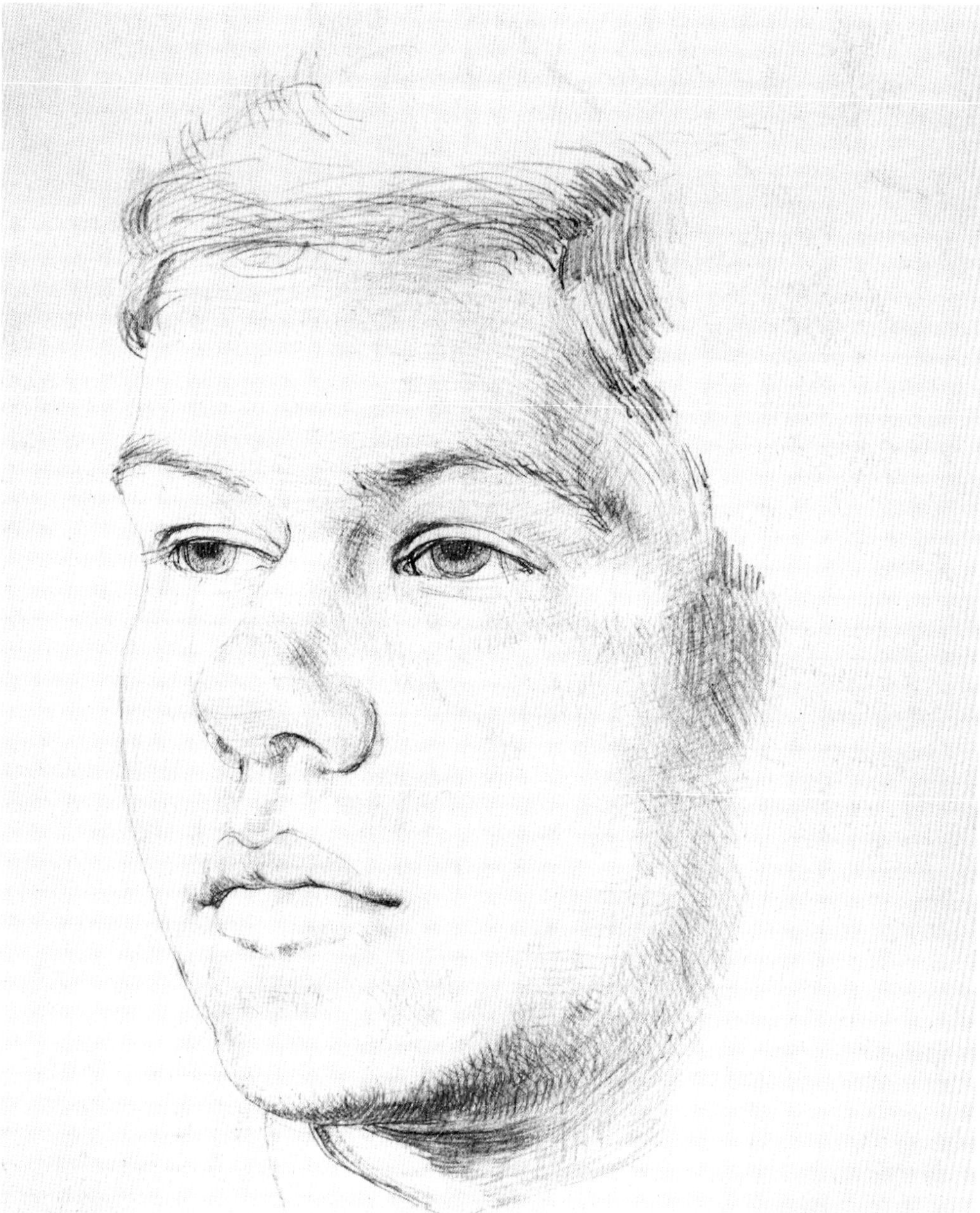

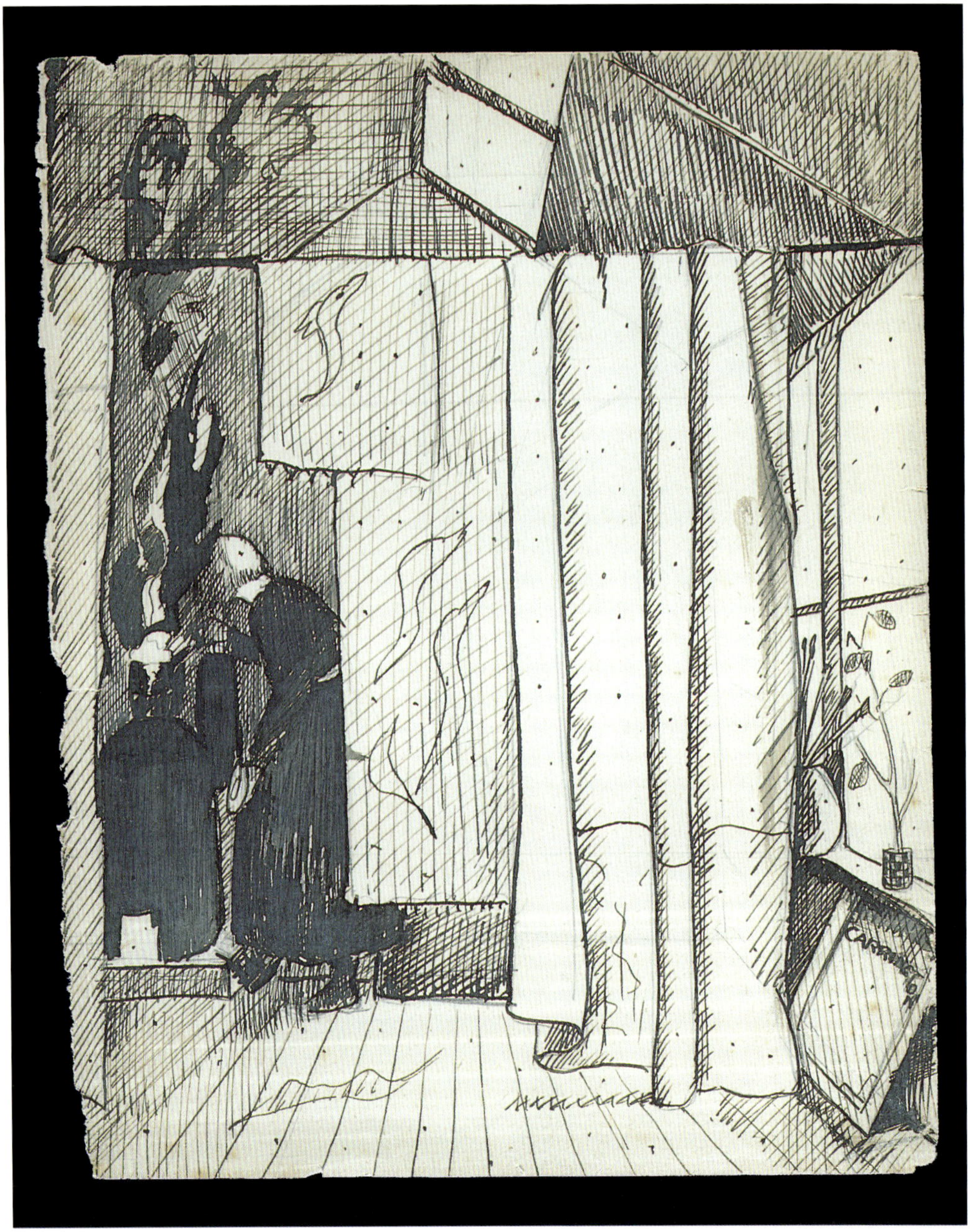

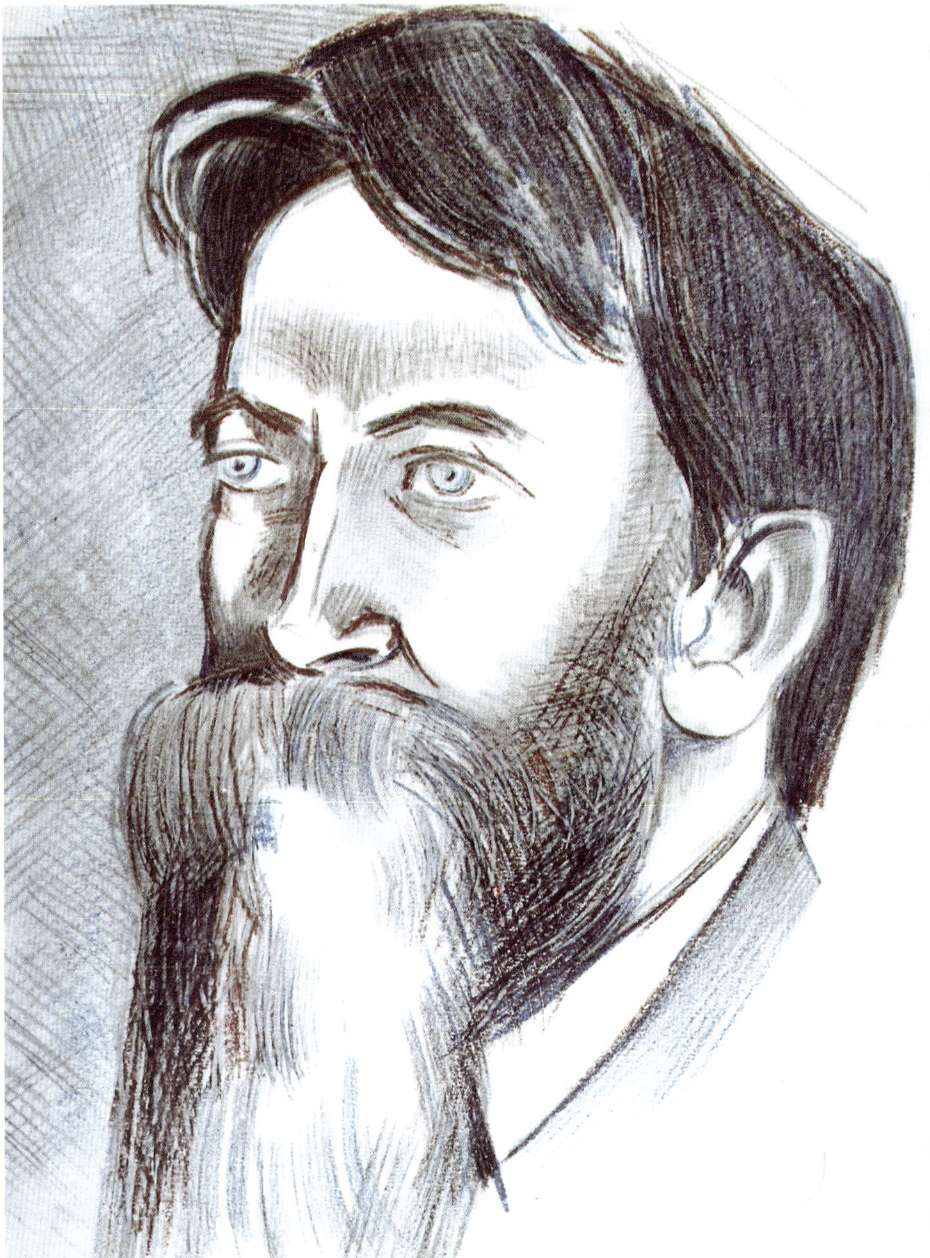

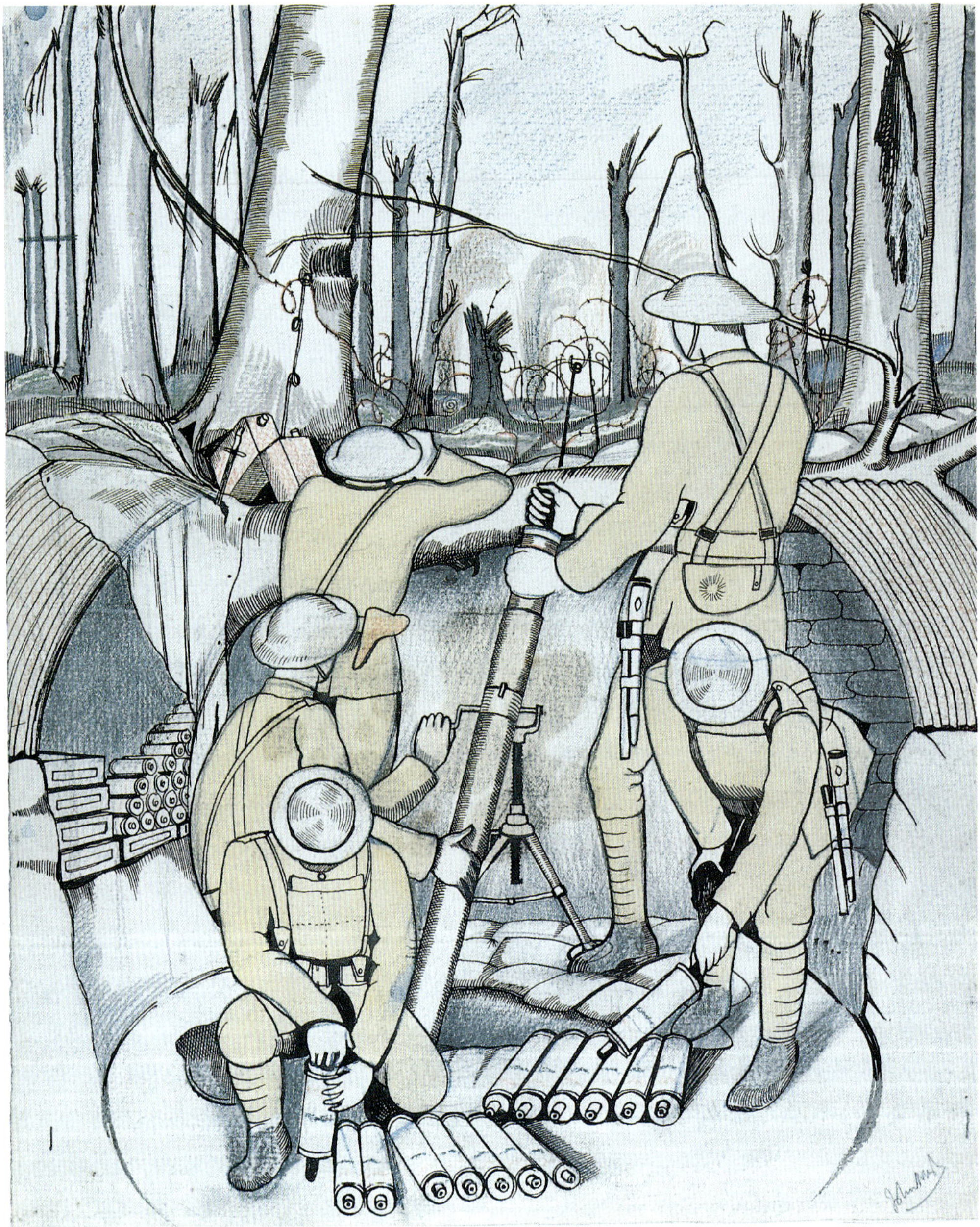

a life for you. Poor Christine! But I do not believe it! Noel goes to London today to have his arm examined. I shall miss him. You would love the country here. I found a good cottage on the downs where they take two people for 18/- a week. Shall we go one day next summer? This I mean in all earnestness.

A complete escape to her own remote dwelling-place would remain Carrington's ideal for the remainder of her life. Her first Christmas at Hurstbourne Tarrant had proved to her that she would always perch like some awkward bird in the rafters of a conventional house. Unlike most young people, she would not grow out of her unorthodoxy; it was there to stay. Which meant that she could not remain for much longer in her blue-ceilinged den above the drawing-room taking comfort from the sight of a thatcher mending a barn, and relishing 'being really dirty and untidy' after rabbiting jaunts with the country lads. She used up an enormous amount of energy and imagination transforming attics and nooks. 'Yes, yes, you shall have my room when you come,' she told Christine. 'I've really done every bit of it for my friends. I am not going to paint the walls after all. Only the blue cupboard with flowers.' Earlier in this letter she had confided 'the trees make me so happy that the Balkans don't matter.'

But it was less the view from her window that Christmas Eve than the arrival of 'My sailor brother' which delighted her. 'I love him. He's not Balkan. I was so pleased to see him. My eldest brother and sister are so particular and gentlemanly, and beautiful snobs. One has great fun annoying them. Teddy looked so lovely and dirty in his sailor's clothes, and his luggage in a big sack on his back!' David Garnett wrote that this brother 'played a large part in her dream life' and that her 'sexual love was unconsciously directed to him'. Teddy was an A.B. on a minesweeper but would soon die as a soldier on the Somme. His was to her the most terrible of all the deaths of the war and when the war was nearly over she told Lytton how she hated returning to Hurstbourne Tarrant 'because everywhere in the house I see his things and in my rooms all his school books, the queer boxes, and carved things he made, old chemistry jars, boats, and in the drawers his note books, drawings of engines, and frigates. You remember in that poem the room with the quick silver? It was all so like him. He wasn't a bit intellectual, only so charming. Really like one of those south country

---

Opposite: *Trench Mortar Firing at Evening*, John Nash, 1918. Watercolour, 352 × 286 mm.

people, or a sailor. But mostly I think I loved him for his exquisite beauty and strength. I cannot forget one of the last days he was at Hurstbourne. In the afternoon I found him fast asleep on the sofa, curled up. His dark brown face, and broad neck, the thick black shiny hair and the modelling on his face, like some chiselled bronze head. You don't mind me talking now. But it's been so heavy inside lately.' That Christmas another brother, Edmund, had told them about his sailor friend 'Taichioskfy', nephew of the great musician and who himself played 'the violin awfully well', and Carrington told Christine, 'I was so excited for no reason at all.' Now 'I sit above them all in my little room and write to you.... Today I distributed mistletoe in the village to all the passers-by.... Goodnight dear Christine.'

Measureless Commitments

If the world was one step from the edge in 1915, by the new year it was rushing towards tragedy – and madness – unprecedented. Although huge armies were now massing in France for some ultimate conflict between the righteous and the accursed, compulsory military service for single men was made law in Britain for the first time ever. It sent a frisson of fear and unease through the population. The nation's much-vaunted freedom seemed to have been put on hold by its frowsty politicians, and its far from admired militarists appeared to be too much in charge. But to criticise the war even faintly brought every kind of accusation down on one's head and to say that it should be put a stop to here and now, as Bertrand Russell and a few intrepid others did, brought screams of rage. Press coverage of what was happening was slanted and lying, and few really knew what was going on. The shell factories were booming and while the new civilian soldiers were paid a pittance, those exempted from serving because they could not be spared from 'war work' were collecting wages they could not have dreamed of only a few months previously. Conscientious objectors were abused and mocked. Nothing was too bad for them. Those who refused to have anything to do with fighting even when their application for exemption was turned down needed the courage of the old martyrs.

John himself was still wandering from war work to war work when he heard that Claughton's petition had been refused by the tribunal. He told Carrington: 'Poor Claughton will go to prison I fear on Nov. 30, rather than use any force. Surely all things are wrong if one is put in prison for following, as it were, Christ's life for a pattern, when the world is supposed by now to know what Christianity means? I don't know. Things are more puzzling every day. There is a feeling here (mostly paternal) that I must, if I have an opportunity sacrifice my art to war-work. Thus do most people think that artists work for their own amusement and edification. I wish you were an heiress with a marrying propensity. I know what I'd do, and double quick too! And now, dearie, I will close having no more to say to you, and being puzzled and bothered by chilblains and the war and other minor worries.'

Both John and Carrington were now drawing and painting steadily, and showing at the Cumberland Market Group and New English Art Club exhibitions. She had in April 1915 discovered a studio in Yeoman's Row, a quiet spot tucked away off the Brompton Road 'opposite the underground nearly', where Christine was often a guest. 'Will you come and sleep with me sometimes? I will have a sofa and a bed. It will be so kind if you will. So cheery, as I shall get lonely all by myself there often. It's a nice big room and Duncan Grant has lent me all his furniture!' She was also visiting Christine – 'When it gets fine Noel and me will come down to Jordans and meet you there on a Sabbath.... Dour faced creature, my love to you.' Neither John nor Carrington could any longer pretend that their activities were regarded with tolerance or admiration by their families. After the withdrawal from the Dardanelles, after the blood-bath of Verdun, after the Somme, after the daily casualty lists, and with the deafening clamour for more sacrifice, more patriotism, their dedicated pursuit of art was seen as trivial. Time enough for that kind of thing when we've beaten the Boche.

Paul was stationed at Romford that spring, where he taught map-reading. It meant that he could see Bunty fairly easily, as well as London friends. Although it was impossible to do much in the way of painting, both the calamitous nature of the war and its numbing mindlessness were beginning to sow protest and dissent in him. He and the poet Edward Thomas, a fellow soldier in the Artists' Rifles, would tramp to country pubs and put the world to rights. Thomas was ten years older than Paul and far more decided in his views.

This is no case of petty right or wrong
That politicians or philosophers
Can judge. I hate not Germans, nor grow hot
With love of Englishmen, to please newspapers.
Beside my hate for one fat patriot
My hatred of the Kaiser is love true:–
A kind of god he is, banging a gong.
(from 'This is no case of petty right or wrong', 1915)

Although far from fit, or at least far from robust, and subject to unspecified infirmities which often laid him low, John felt honour-bound to get into the army at all cost and at least escape the looks and questionings which any male under forty still not in uniform had to endure. A summer letter to Carrington told her, 'I may be going to have another medical board when I may be put back to Home Service. If not, I shall go to the Artists which I hear is again open for recruiting.' More dramatic for Carrington was what came next.

> I have been seeing a lot of Christine and we have had very jolly expeditions, to Jordans among other places whither she told me she went with you.... You do not know Christine so well. I do. I have taken more trouble and patience to 'unravel' her, as you say. I don't wish to brag about it over you because she really unravelled herself to me, indeed probing is little more than questions and answers. If the former is evaded the probe can't do its work.... I have done a little work, not very much. I have been idling rather, I fear. Dallying. Christine and I went to Queen's Hall on Friday.... We had a fine concert. Eroica Symphony and a Mozart concerto.... Strachey. I have always been repelled by his outward appearance....
>
> Yes Christine is a rare creature, you use an apt expression....
>
> P.S. Christine and I love each other. Please write to me.
>
> The P.S. was designed especially as a climax. C. and I arranged it but in using the words I was not thinking of being dramatic, only it seemed the best way of expressing it. Engagements and publicity of *any* kind, like champagne, are not for war-time. You will be secret I know dearie. Please write and tell me if I can see you and if you are sad and happy as I am. Yours Jacko.

Carrington's life too was speeding towards commitment. Her first task when she got to 16 Yeoman's Row was to distance herself from Mark Gertler without hurting him too much. 'Please do not be unhappy: mentally at any rate there are happy times before us.... I think it best if I do not see you for a bit. As it nearly sends me mad with grief, at seeing you so miserable.... When we are both calmer we will talk it over. Please let me alone for a little while, as I cannot bear it – and my Mother is here now which fills me with despair. But dear if only *you* will be happy, it will make me happier also.' She didn't tell him that four days later she would be meeting Lytton at Euston with 'Incredible internal excitement'. But then neither did she bring Paul and John and Bunty and Christine into her letters to him, which was reasonable enough. It was not that her friends were being compartmentalised, as she would be accused of doing, but that she had a strong sense of her friends being in their own special spheres. 'Mon chère grand-père Lytton' – she was learning French (and to ride a motor-bike) – had mysteriously brought her to enthusiasms and pleasures she had never before known. She found herself, to his delight, reciprocating his camp wit and his seriousness. She had just returned from a holiday with him in North Wales and the die had been cast. They would live together. That Christine and John were settled too came as a relief. It was partly the result of her match-making. She wrote:

My dearest Christine,

Jack has written and told me! I am so glad. Indeed gladder than you will believe. As I love you both so much I can write without reserve. Did you know when you wrote that last letter to me? I just read it again and wondered! Rainbows bring strange things about. What of Rainbows? I saw two complete double rainbows in Wales twice, and the landscape behind the rainbows through it. Like this [drawing] and they shone through a cow! Think of it. What a sight. It came as Lytton Strachey was reading *Tristram Shandy* to us over the fire. What a life.... Lytton was indeed a splendid companion to have with one, as he read poetry whenever we asked him, and made us laugh heartily at his lewd old-fashioned jokes.

But more of my adventures when you meet me. What times. What heydays and holidays. I am sad they are all gone and I am here drearily! drearily! alone with my Mother. Jack wants to come down for a day. Will you come also? I may get Mother to let you stay the night. If I say your name is Christine Penn or Penzance, or any extravagance you choose! Then we could go and picnic all day on the downs. Could you I wonder bring a bicycle? As then we could get about so much easier – and Jack bring his. . . . Christine, are you very happy? I almost envy you. For I think Jack is such good company. How he made me larf with his comick jokes.

I am all of a tremble learning French diligently every evening! Reading poetry and so many books. [Lytton had introduced her to Rimbaud's *Le Bateau ivre*, and to Donne and Shakespeare.] I rush frantic from one to the other without taking in anything! I went to Coombe on Saturday and my misery was so great. I nearly wept to see the house neat and *newly* painted, and smoke from the chimneys. To think that I might have lived there if I hadn't been so stupid as to never let anyone see it who might have taken it. But the country was [so] lovely that I then felt it would never really be taken from me, as I could always lie on those downs. . . . I am so distracted to think of how I shall live this winter. . . . I have done so much since I last saw you, and you also have felt so much. What things there will be to talk of when we meet. My love dear fawn. Write to me soon x x Carrington.

Immediately before John joined up, Carrington was bustling him and Christine off on the great quest for a house for Lytton. She told Lytton that she had maps of every square inch of the country and was in correspondence with every auctioneer in Newbury, Marlborough and Reading. She packed Christine and John off to the house agents at High Wycombe – 'search diligently and write me news of your successes in the evening as there is no time to be lost. . . . Can you take photographs of any possible houses for me with your Brownie? I'll pay for the film and will develop it.' She herself was travelling all over the place to find a home for Lytton while he remained inert: '40 miles in one morning did I bicycle for your sake revered uncle! Searching the highways and hedges for your blasted house! 40 miles!!' She found John's and Christine's happiness pleasing, yet disturbing. Just before it was announced she wrote, 'I wonder many things about you and Jack. What you know about him that I know. What you do not. What he is like to you? What you are like to him? But of course I shall never know. Nobody gives minute enough descriptions, and all the things that I always long to know I should not dare to ask.' It would be a whole year before the house agents sent her news of the Mill House, Tidmarsh – 'Electric Light, Bath H & C, Rent £52, 3 years lease, Nr. Church and P.O., London 65 mins.' John had by then been long on the Western Front. His letters to Christine, and hers to him, were typical of the correspondence between men in the trenches and women back home. His experience was beyond her comprehension. As for Carrington, the war was the boring sound of noises off. Not even the wounding of one brother and the death of another awoke in her any remote interest in what was actually happening in France and Belgium, neither was she able to understand John's hunger for letters. Christine wrote wistfully, 'At the Slade ... sitting in the window, waiting to ask Tonks to sign my NEAC paper, the trees in the quad are just in leaf, pale green, you remember how they looked, but alas blue-clad soldiers are strewn about all over the grass, and there's no sign of Carrington and Brett walking around the paths, or of you and Paul in large black hats and mutton cutlet whiskers looking like a couple of Guy Fawkes.... What about this old war, are events working up to a climax?... Never has the future seemed so impenetrable. One thing is certain, that I even love you more with the increasing difficulties that surround us.'

It was shortly after this evocation of student days that Edward Carrington was killed. Carrington was on her way to see Leonard and Virginia Woolf when she heard that he was missing. Her world gave a sickening tilt. Months later she would write in her diary, 'Awoke after a horrible dream. Mrs G. Jones was lying on the grass and showed me some photographs of three boys in vests and sailors' breeches, one was Teddy. Then she said they had been lost. Presently Teddy came in himself and I remember rushing at him, telling him how I had thought he was dead and how I closed my fingers into his hard fat cheeks. Very brown and kissed him and hugged till I nearly crushed him to atoms.' This was the day, April 13th, 1917, when she had to say goodbye to Mark Gertler and go with Lytton. Mark sobbed and wanted to die but she felt that she must leave him. She contrasted Mark's love for her with 'The unreality, and coldness of Lytton'. That night she kissed Lytton on the mouth, 'all enmeshed in the brittle beard and my inside was as heavy as lead'.

John and Christine had made love in the Chilterns beechwoods during the summer of 1916 and had also made a bargain, the gist of which was that they should be as one, yet 'free'. This bargain would hold but its 'freedom' would become the worst kind of, for her, imprisonment, though this not until after the Armistice. From the fighting itself there came a series of superb letters which were the prologue to the official war paintings, and outpourings of the desire which Carrington had managed to stifle.

My sweetest love,

It is particularly your letter of Nov 28 [1916] I am answering.... It is the one where you wonder that there is anyone who loves you enough to write you twelve pages. My sweetheart, I do assure you it would not be practical to write to you as I love you, else no envelope could hold it. My dear one, shall I confess I gave way myself to tears when I got this letter.... I did not know you nearly cried in the wood then. I wish you had that I could have kissed your tears away.

[*Several letters later*] I wish Carrington would write to me again, please ask her to. Now my sweet love, a little endearing for you before I send this off. First one full kiss (in the major) on your lips, followed by a squeeze then a pause, and an attempt to stroke your knee (for which I get a clout, doubtless); this is reconciled by a 'nosing' kiss behind the back of your hair just where it ends.... We must always be kind to each other.... Never let the sun go down on your wrath.

[*18th December 1916*] What do I think of it? Well I don't think too much, this life is not conducive to it, but I find myself dreaming as usual at landscapes on the march, but not on parade.... Yesterday I went on the range to fire off a rifle for the first time. Extraordinary feeling. I thought I had shot myself.

[*25th December 1916*] Now I am going to break off a little to read that excellent and wonderful book *Lavengro*. Today is Christmas Day ... we went for a long walk in the course of which we alighted on a roadside inn. We went in and had coffee. I have never seen such a neat, bright and burnished interior. The good dame of the house kindly gave me a lovely Christmas rose, the first flower I have seen since I left England. Pure white. This morning we had a few carols at church and the Beecham Opera-man sang *Nazareth:* he made a good thing of it. [John Nash would give one of the soldiers in his painting *Over the Top* the face of a singer he had heard at Queen's Hall 'because so many lovely voices had been lost'.]

How I should like to see you in your black dress when it is made, for I don't ever remember seeing you in black before, and it usually becomes many women. If anyone asks whether you are in mourning for your love, tell them I was drowned in black mud. Make clear however that I was in the Artists' Rifles and not in a Navvies' Battalion.... I never felt the future so obscure and impenetrable.... Though you are 22, in April I shall be 24, and then where are you? If anything happens to me I am satisfied if I have made you happy at all for a short time, and that is nothing to what I hope to do if I come back alive.

The war is a terrible muddle now. Everything seems so hopeless, and men grumble and are tiresome, and you have to restrain them altho' you may agree with them in everything they say. This is the curse of authority. There seems no heart left in anyone. I am more cheery than a good many.... But do not think I am mentally 'going under' for I am strong beyond what I ever thought I was.

Carrington told Christine that she wished she had seen John before he sailed. He had called twice but she was out. 'I will certainly write to him. Do you know where he is in France? If he is at Rouen, Noel is there, you might tell him so. I am all distracted and half-mad again. I cannot remember anything, and the accumulation of "undone" things mount daily in my head.' On Boxing Day 1916, on the day after his love-letter to Christine, John wrote a brave and painterly letter to Carrington. She had just finished painting Lytton's portrait and it was in her room. 'To bed now, and have you sitting in your green armchair staring at the impossible book, all night and I shall find you there in the morning. So goodnight. What dreams in store? Who can tell' – she wrote in her diary. It was incredibly cold and snowing. There was a piercing wind. As well as brave, John's letter to Carrington was that of a young man who knew that the world to which he belonged was going on merrily enough without him.

December 26th 1916

My dear Duckie,

(Ought I now to so address you!) I am much to be cudgelled for not answering your long and good letter let alone to thank you, or was it Brett, for the chocolate, which I do now most gratefully, though I have long since nourished myself with it. Well you see I am out here and of course you realise that I can't do much in the way of describing where I am to you owing to the censor's vigilant eye. The country is reminiscent of the Aston Downs in Berkshire though the trees differ somewhat and the valleys are full of rows this way and that of rigid poplars, making as it were hedge-like planes set perpendicularly at different angles, and then of course the houses are different. The people and customs I suppose are of the most interest as being so different.... I don't think I care for France as I should for Italy. Noel may know exactly where I am but I cannot get to him without special leave – which is almost impossible to obtain.... My life is now spent in performing fatigues, weight lifting, dish washing, room cleaning, gutter sweeping, utensil swabbing etc., dirty work and such as makes one wonder if you are really a soldier. However I don't dislike it. We have just spent

Christmas here. May it be the first and last. A great accumulation of food – marvels in the tinned line, cakes, puddings even, and then we all went out and had champagne.

Alas duckie I feel sorely tried to write to you in my old way, not because of my change of situation (cardiac) but because there is so little to speak of. On the whole monotony is prevalent and the chief pangs (if one might say so) of pleasure are to be found in letters from my love and all kind friends, and other little details, stray sights – sunsettings – men with unexpected knowledge akin to you, good fellowship and eating! What a strange life is this same army life, though we are lucky to be safe out here, mind you. How I have longed for some of those days in Dorset, and days latterly with my dove in North Bucks, and then the uncertainty of the future for her and me. Well it is no use thinking over-much about it. She, thank God, is tranquil and brave and that helps me, which with that resignation which the army does teach you, helps to keep us going at all. I expect Paul will be sent out now soon, which is no pleasant news unless I could see him. What affects me and others too are these tempting chances of peace which are being put aside. It is not unpatriotic to desire it surely? Now come John Nash, let us be brighter. Now what about this bending position! I suppose you are at your inscrutable joking again, but what of it all the same? Roger Fry is indeed a good and kindly man I opine and you do well to help him at Regal Hampton [Paul, John, Carrington and other young artists had assisted in restoring the Mantegna cartoons at Hampton Court under Fry's jurisdiction]. My love told me you liked my *Viaduct*, and I know you always say when you really like my efforts, so that I was glad I wrote to Paul to get it photographed.

Alack and alas I had no letter from Christine or homester Christmas parcels owing to the old mailboat running amuck. I should like to hear from you re NEAC show and other town news ... how are many of our boon companions, Mark and others? Do you remember how unsettled and searching I was when in Dorset with you? Now I feel like a man who has gone away and left his riches (heart) in a safe bank. Oh how true you were, dearie, when you said that Christine was a rare and to be probed creature. Well I am running away with myself yet I thank you for recommending me to her. What a civility you did me. Why should you not of all people know how I am entangled and engulfed in her sweetness. Is this irksome to you? But remember I asked you more than once! ...

Well now I must stop and return to barracks (I was writing to you in the Church hut). It is getting on for dinner time. Please may I, though not deserving same, receive another letter from you? My love to you, dearie, and to all the homesters around you, from your Jacko.

Paul had been undergoing officer training all that autumn, and just before Christmas he joined the third battalion of the Hampshire Regiment as a second-lieutenant, arriving in France on 22nd February 1917. His first letters to Bunty from the trenches possess a literary sparkle and excitement. He soon met Noel and began to make sketches, the first drawing being one 'of trenches under a bloody sort of sunset with a crescent moon sailing above', to be called *Winter Trenches*, and the second was 'a rugged looking landscape with a scarred hill in the background and stick-like trees'. He posted six such drawings to Bunty asking her to get them mounted and framed and sent to Goupil. John too was directing his career from afar, sending careful instructions to Christine about where to exhibit the work he had left at home. Paul's active service was brief. On Friday 25th May, just three months after his arrival at the Western Front, he fell in the dark and 'limped back into the dug-out feeling rather as if I had been broken in the middle like a doll'. He had been drawing no man's land from the trench parapet, had accidentally stepped backwards into a void and fallen heavily. A broken, floating rib caused acute pain and soon he was a patient in the Swedish Hospital, London. He and John had not seen each other. Paul sent Bunty a brilliant account of these weeks, complementing and in many ways matching his brother's letters to Carrington:

[*March 7th, 1917*] Flowers bloom everywhere and we have just come up to the trenches for a time and where I sit now in the reserve line the place is just joyous, the dandelions are bright gold over the parapet and nearby a lilac bush is breaking into bloom; in a wood passed through on our way up, a place with an evil name, pitted and pocked with shells, the trees torn to shreds, often reeking with poison gas – a most desolate ruinous place two months back, today it was a vivid green; the most broken trees even had sprouted somewhere and in the midst, from the depths of the wood's bruised heart poured out the throbbing song of a nightingale. Ridiculous mad incongruity! One can't think which is the more absurd, the War or Nature; the former has become a habit so confirmed, [so] inevitable, it has its grip on the world just as surely as spring or summer.

Thus we poor beings are doubly enthralled. At the mercy of the old elements which we take pains to study, avoid, build and dress for, we are now in the power of something far more pitiless, cruel and malignant, and so we must study further, build ten times as strong, dress cunningly and creep about like rats always overshadowed by this new terror. Of course we shall get used to it just as we are almost accustomed to the damnable climate of England. . . .

Last night there was a heavy shelling, in fact the line is not the place it was; the Boche is very restive and jumpy, and I am not surprised. The clouds roll up in these parts and their shadows already fall over us. I have no fear. I know there are numerous things I want to say to you, but my mind is wandering today – it's raining and the earth and trees and all green things exude a moist perfume and make the soul dream wearily. . . . In the *New Statesman* you sent me, there is a short notice upon Edward Thomas saying the best thing he did was the verse written while he was in the Artists. He wrote under the name of Edward Eastaway.

[*End of March, 1917. In the Train to the Front Line*] Not quite there yet – we left the base on Monday – a wet, unwholesome day. . . . It was a most strange journey, lumbering along about two miles an hour. . . . About nine we stopped with a terrific shock. . . . The train emptied like magic, and I soon found myself in a cosy shanty, half-peaceful cottage, half war-like in construction. An open grate with a log fire glowing, bowls of flowers, attendant nymphs – English ladies in tweedy skirts, country hats, aprons and smiles . . . it yawned with kindness and hospitality and, best of all, the tea was made without sugar. God bless all sporting British ladies in short tweed skirts and tightly veiled country hats who live at odd places on dreary railways in homely huts, half-cottage, half military canteen . . . dispensing hot tea . . . and stout buns.

. . . By the way, before I forget it, do you remember Nevinson's small etching of the 2nd bombardment (or was it the 1st) of Ypres? I should still like to have it if possible. . . . It is a part of the world I'm interested in.

[*Good Friday, 1917*] Oh, these wonderful trenches at night, at dawn, at sundown! Shall I ever lose the picture they have made in my mind. Imagine a wide landscape flat and scantily wooded and what trees remain blasted and torn, naked and scarred and riddled. The ground for miles around furrowed into trenches, pitted with yawning holes in which the water lies still and cold or heaped with mounds of earth, tangles of rusty wire, tin plates, stakes, sandbags and all the refuse of war. In the distance runs a stream where the stringy poplars and alders lean about dejectedly, while farther a slope rises to a scarred bluff the foot of which is scattered with headless trees standing white and withered, without any leaves, done, dead. As shells fall in the bluff, huge spouts of black, brown and orange mould burst into the air amid a volume of white smoke.... In the midst of this strange country, where such things happen, men are living in their narrow ditches, hidden from view by every cunning device, waiting and always on the watch, yet at the same time easy, careless, well fed, wrapped up in warm clothes, talking, perpetually smoking, and indifferent to anything that occurs. Unless a shell falls into the trench there is no excitement, and even this provokes the minimum of disturbance. All day long, with only a few intervals, the shells pass overhead, always the same sound as of a body leaving [tearing] the sky like canvas.... Of course the heavy trench mortars throw over shells that can be plainly seen heaving through the air, tumbling over and over till they fall, and then a second's pause and then a bang. The earth rises in a complicated eruption of smoke and bits begin to fall for yards wide, splashing into the pools, flinging up the water, rattling on the iron sheets, spattering us and the ground nearby.... I go round the slimy duck-boards down the trench with the sergeant, seeing that all is well, sometimes inciting a listless sniper to fire, or the Lewis gunners to play a burst just to show the Huns we are really awake. At intervals we send up Very lights and the ghastly face of No Man's Land leaps up in the garish light, then, as the rocket falls, the great shadows flow back shutting it into darkness again. One could write for ever of these strange lights.

[*April 18th, 1917*] I have been a good deal worried over the papers lately, for ... we can see things are in a bad way.... Something must be shamefully crooked in the works of England. We read about profiteers, we see cartoons depicting them as monsters eating the people's food – but why are they allowed to live? No one in our country ever seems to have the simplest notion of grappling with things – we are a shilly-shallying people unable to deal with decision.... As I read, it just seems as if I heard all the pap being made and dripping, dripping into the foolish blubber mouth of the people which greedily laps it up, loving it so – the great brain fodder, the food of the little gods. I seem to see the label on the bottle, 'specially prepared for His Majesty and all His people by Northcliffe and Co. and the damned almighty Press.' It is intolerable – I cannot read the papers

– it's just humbug, from end to end. We need a spirit to stamp out cant and lies from England. . . . You speak of a revolution that will come at home if war grinds us to famine; it would be a pity to nurse your sorrows and your wrongs until the men return, that is when revolution will come. Out here men have been thinking, living so near to silence and death, their thoughts have been furious, keen, and living has been alive. Hammering in their minds are a hundred questions, festering in their hearts a thousand wrongs. The most insistent question is 'Why am I here?'

[*May 2nd, 1917*] There is a quiet confident strength, an easy carriage and rough beauty about these men which would make your heart jump and give you a lumpy throat with pride. The other day as I watched them I felt near tears somehow . . . [Edward] Thomas is dead . . . I brood on it dully. . . . It will not be so very long before we are in the fight. I shall not fear then. I only pray I don't think of you when the moment comes – only of my men. But if I am hit, then it does not matter, and I can think of you at the last and forever after till we meet again. Do not fear, I am not morbid, and you will never hear me speak of death again.

[*May 12th, 1917*] The whole country, the quiet of it, the sweet springtime, the hours of leisure when everyone can roam about, have all combined to make us sad and sick with longing for the end of this awful unending madness. I cannot get things straight at all. What is God about? . . . The cause of the war was probably quite futile and mean, but the effect of it is huge. No terrors will ever frighten me into regret. What are the closing lines of Tennyson's *Maud*? – '*I have felt I am one with my native land.*' This is the emotion and it is a satisfying one to rest with when every other has turned bitter and dead. The men, you know, make me think I have been very lucky in joining the Company. . . . I believe when the time comes, they will follow me over the top to a man.

Grist to the Mill

The historian A. J. P. Taylor believed that Europe's history in the old sense ended in 1917, and World history began. The death and birth pangs of that terrible year support his theory. On 6th April America declared war on Germany and that same spring the Tsar abdicated and Lenin arrived in St Petersburg. There was mutiny in the French army and industrial strikes ran like wildfire across many nations. The xenophobia which had until now helped to fuel the war had burnt itself out. Once-confident governments saw that they could be overthrown. Socialism spread over frontiers and offered radical alternatives to the myths of ages. In the field, and on both sides, chiefs of staff began to plan a gigantic military solution to the impending disaster.

The little circle of Slade friends was breaking up and being scattered in all directions. Claughton's, John thought, was the worst of all, for he was en route to Dartmoor after spells in Dyce and Wakefield prisons, having refused to don the King's uniform. He had been sentenced to labour in what were known as Home Office Work Centres, ending up on a Buckinghamshire farm during the harvest of 1918 – that same harvest which John had painted in *The Cornfield*, his 'thank-you' picture for having survived the trenches. Emma-Marie (Kechie) Tennent married Claughton in 1919 and they withdrew into a simple Franciscan quietness on the Norfolk coast for the rest of their lives. John was shocked by the tribunal's refusal to accept Claughton as a conscientious objector, and so force him into those actions which landed him in gaol. He wrote to him frequently but rarely received an answer. He felt he owed him everything for making the future so plain to him on their Norfolk walks.

Carrington ceased to drift in 1917 and took her own deliberate direction. On 18th October she found the newspaper opened at the casualties page and there was Teddy's death. 'It was a year ago and now they announce it officially,' she wailed to Lytton. 'It's rather worse being here [at Hurstbourne Tarrant] with all his books and things about, and where I saw him last, and the remoteness of my parents. Forgive me for writing but I wanted you so badly. One is not even left alone to cry. Dearest Lytton I love you so much.' Lying beside the newspaper was a letter from the house agent describing a property called the Mill House, Tidmarsh. Two days later she was scribbling happily from a Newbury teashop, 'Tidmarsh Mill it is to be.' She and Lytton Strachey had discovered what to all their friends and their families was a frankly unbelievable joy. John was more perplexed than hurt when he heard of it. He thought that they would continue to be close and that he would have to make the same kind of concessions for Lytton as he had for Mark, but that he and Carrington would continue their intelligently revised relationship. Carrington however seemed to think – and hope, maybe – that her bringing John and Christine together was sufficient amends for some defection on her part, though this was not so. She remained of enormous importance to him and although he was engaged to Christine he could not imagine life without her. From now on and until she died all his dealings with her were dominated by his insistence that the threads which once held them together must not be severed. It was a testy, wounding business on his part and he knew her well enough to know that it was everything she disliked, but he could not let her go. His wonderful letters to her from the front, and soon his superb paintings of the war, were all part of what she was blotting out from her life. From being so vulnerable, she had become a woman who had no compunction at turning away from what she no longer needed to see, to hear. Her chief loyalties from now on were towards Lytton and her dead brother. And, of course, towards herself as an artist, although she was to remain touchingly unsure of who she was, and where she stood, in this respect. John would not have been able to help her there.

Paul during the summer of 1917 was indeed 'lucky Paul' for the accident which returned him from Ypres to London for five months gave him time to prepare himself to become an official war artist. His exhibition of eighteen drawings of the

---

Opposite: *Spring in the Trenches, Ridge Wood,* John Nash, 1918. Watercolour, 352 x 286 mm. Over, top left: Bombing Section, Artists' Rifles, August 1917. John Nash is seated on the ground on the left; he became a Trench Mortar Instructor and wrote a handbook on its use. Ronald Blythe. Below, right: Sergeant John Nash, Artists' Rifles, Second Lieutenant Paul Nash, official war artist, and Christine Kühlenthal, Iver, 1918. Right: *Ruined Country: Vimy,* Paul Nash, 1918. From *British Artists at the Front: Paul Nash,* Country Life, 1918. 'Not far from La Folie Wood. The battlefield of April, 1917, is seen overgrown with rank verdure and many coloured weeds.'

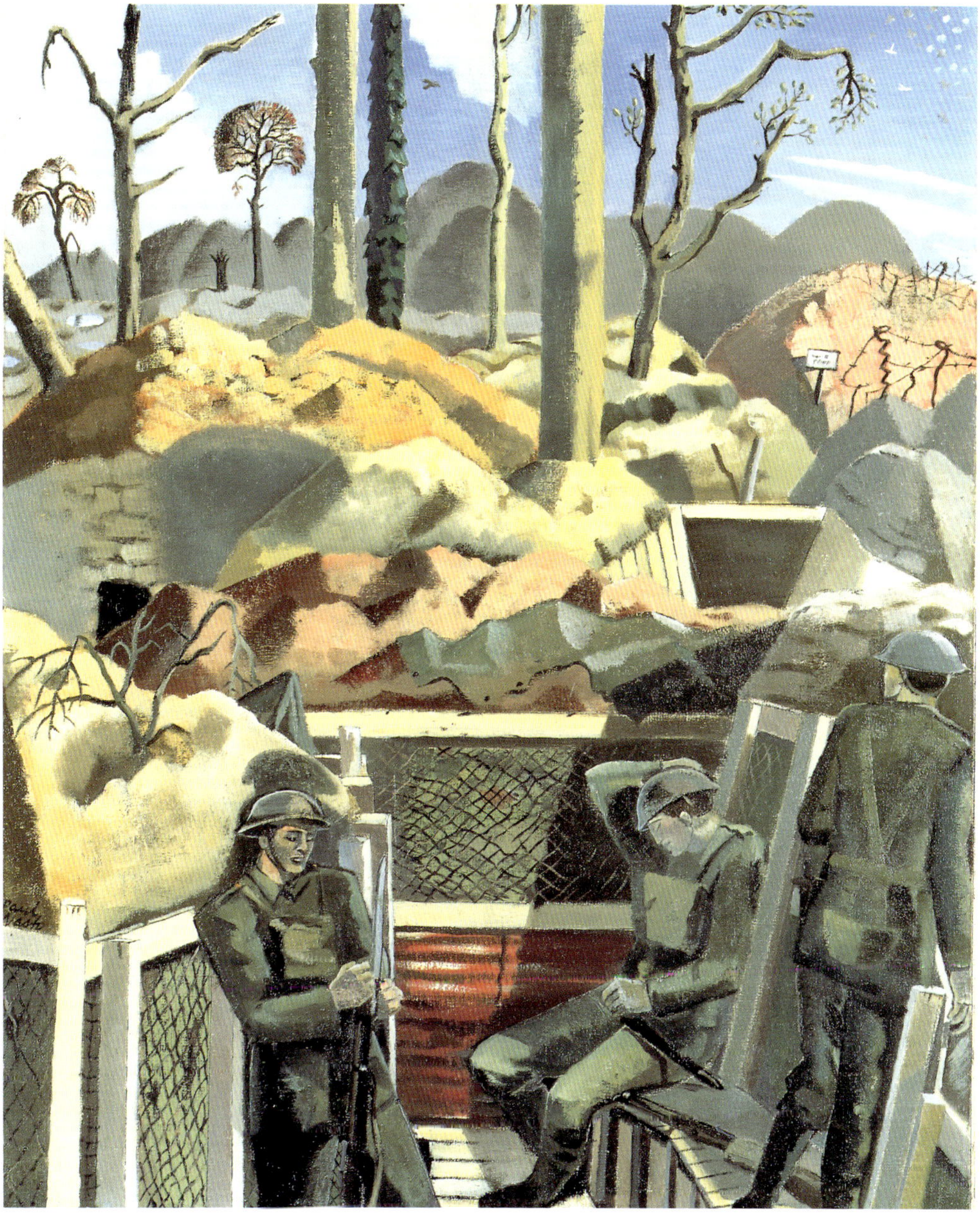

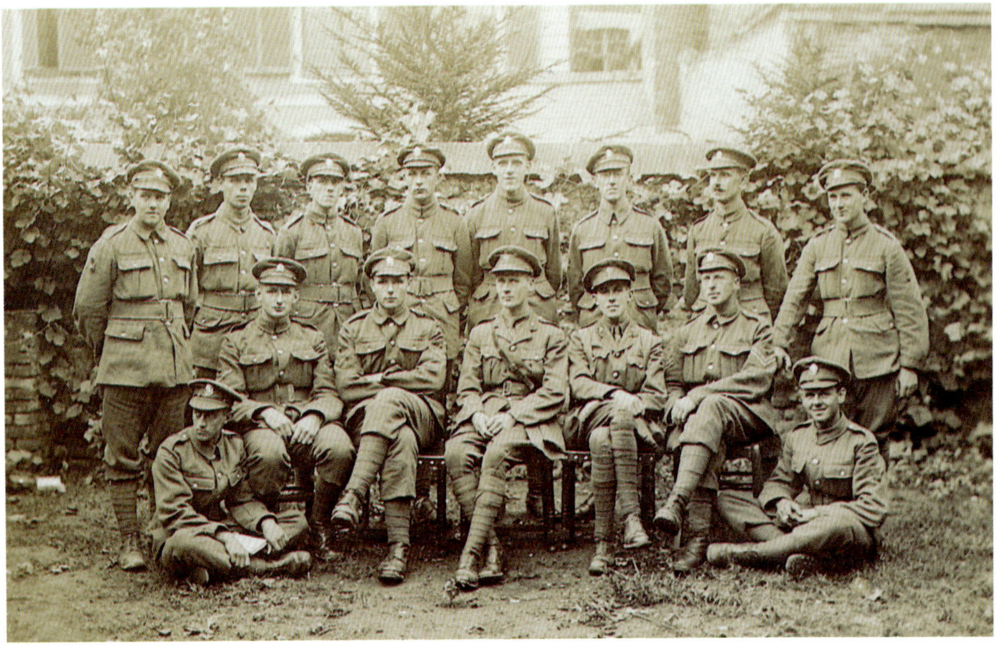

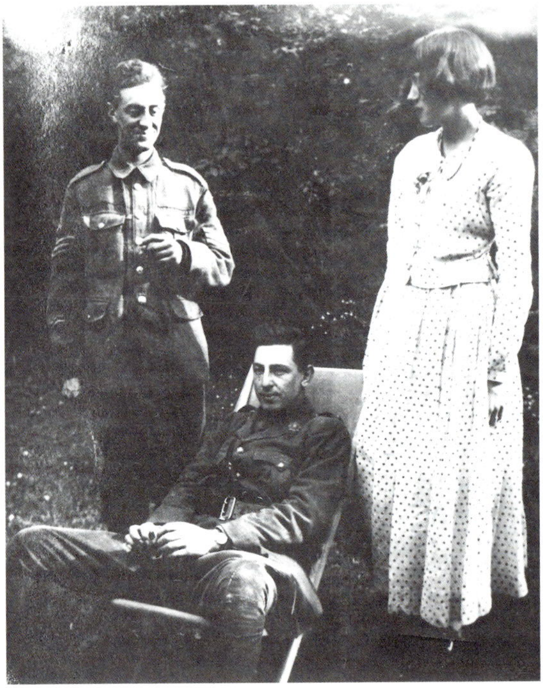

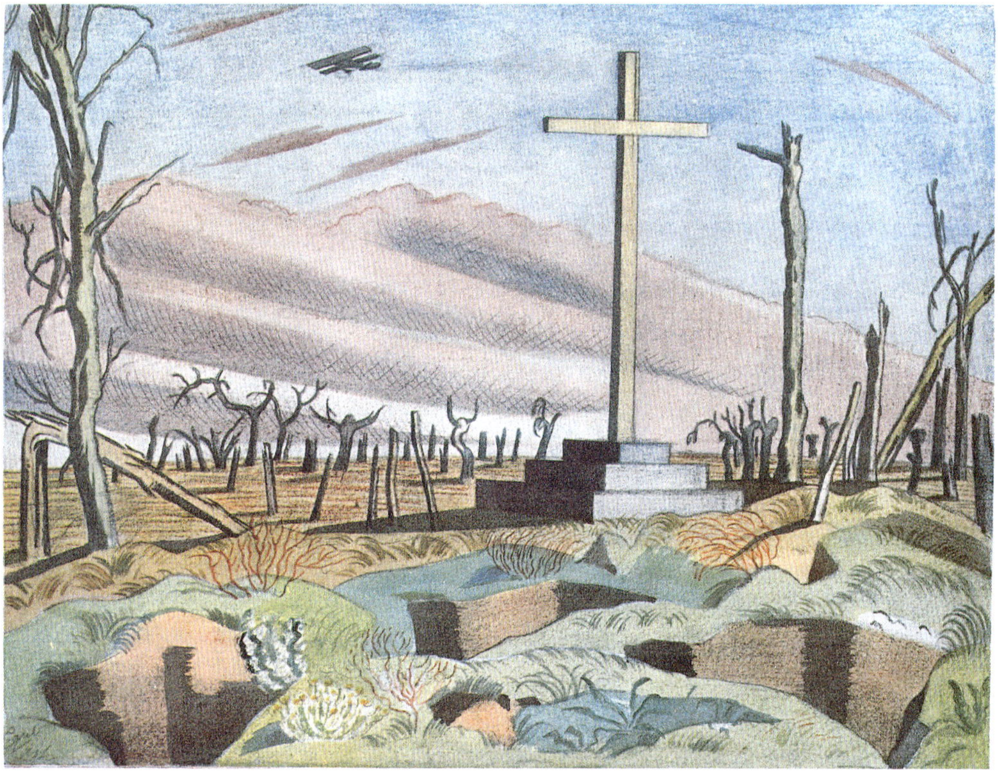

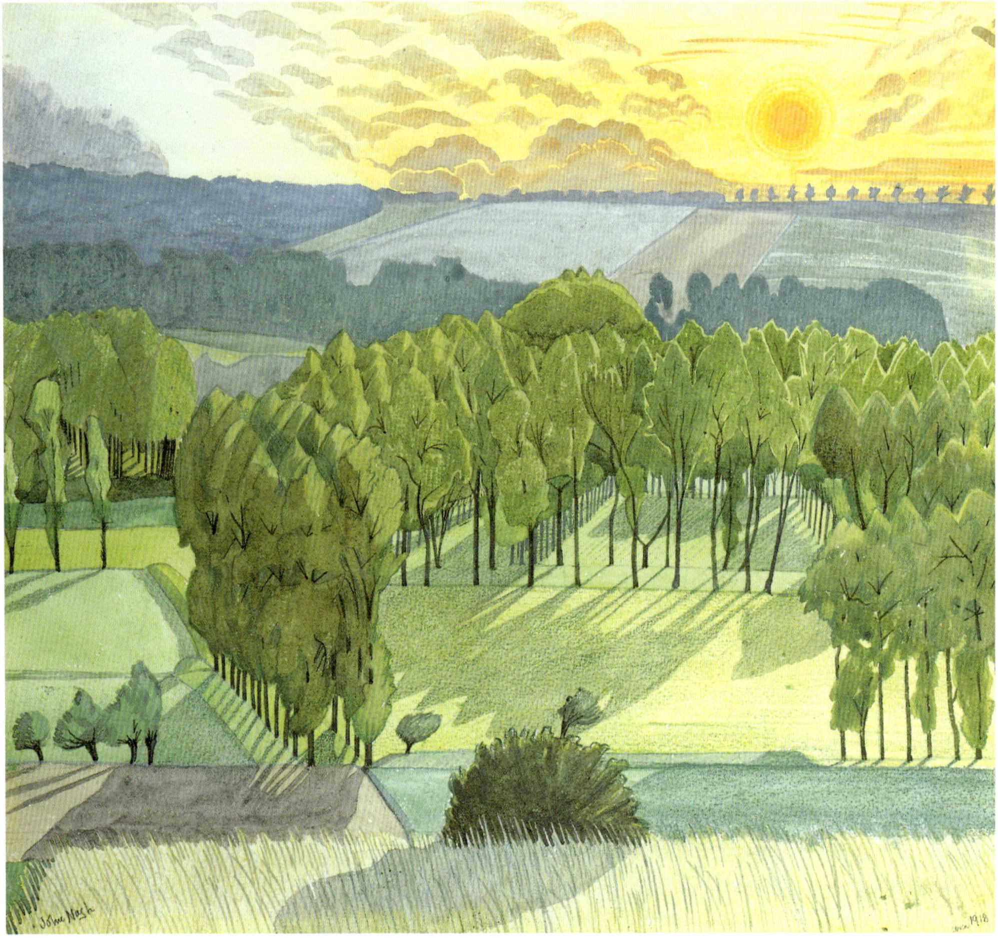
John Nash
1918

front at the Goupil Gallery in July revealed his potential and he set about gathering sponsors, Eddie Marsh, of course, and others. The novelist and historian John Buchan had been appointed a director of the newly invented Ministry of Information, and he was bombarded with Paul's applications. Paul was within five hours of sailing to Egypt on a troopship when the call came. He was elated. 'I have had a miracle of an escape', he told Bunty. 'Would you like to ring Buchan up and worship him over the phone?'

If the salient he had left in May was terrible, that to which he returned in November was beyond comprehension. Paul had witnessed the before and after of Passchendaele. The first thing he did was to find his brother.

> [*19th November 1917*] I motored [he had been given a chauffeured car] down to take the old man out.... The prevailing idea that he is depressed and hopeless is entirely wrong.... He is a real soldier and very proud of it. Of course, he is dying to get home for a bit ... but I assure you he has borne all the rough times magnificently, and he has really had it very rough. He is simply splendid and never stops talking of the good friends he has made.... I have just returned, last night, from a visit to Brigade Headquarters up the line, and I shall not forget it as long as I live. I have seen the most frightful nightmare of a country more conceived by Dante or Poe than by nature, unspeakable, utterly indescribable. In the fifteen drawings I have made I may give you some idea of its horror, but only being in it and of it can ever make you sensible of its dreadful nature and of what our men in France have to face. We all have a vague idea of the terrors of a battle ... but no pen or drawing can convey this country – the normal setting of battles taking place day and night, month after month. Evil and the incarnate fiend alone can be master of this war, and no glimmer of God's hand can be seen anywhere. Sunrise and sunset are blasphemous, they are mockeries to man, only the black rain out of the bruised and swollen clouds all through the bitter black of night is fit atmosphere in such a land. The rain drives on, the stinking mud becomes more evilly yellow, the shell-holes fill up with green-white water, the roads and tracks are covered in inches of slime, the black dying trees ooze and

---

Opposite: *French Landscape*, John Nash, 1918. Pencil, watercolour and bodycolour, 350 x 382 mm. Formerly with Spink and Son. John Nash frequently referred to the lines of poplars in his letters home from the trenches.

sweat and the shells never cease. They alone plunge overhead, tearing away the rotting tree stumps, breaking the plank roads, striking down horses and mules, annihilating, maiming, maddening, they plunge into the grave which is this land; one huge grave, and cast up on it the poor dead. It is unspeakable, godless, hopeless. I am no longer an artist interested and curious, I am a messenger who will bring back word from men who are fighting to those who want the war to go on for ever.

All through 1917 John's commitment to Christine rushed ahead. The only thing which could stop their marriage would be his death. His commitment to Carrington, though different or 'other', was hardly less determined and the year was half-way through before he scented that she was cutting herself adrift. From the Flanders mud John threw the kind of strings which used to hold them together but now nine times out of ten she failed to catch hold. He sensed that she was no more sorry for him than for those who had made the war, and that he was now in it, of it. Just after Paul's accident he wrote:

My dear Carrington,

(I employ this more formal term for censored letters to people who haven't written to me recently.) I want to write to you but my brain is rather awhirrrrrrrl owing to there being in this café a mirror in front and behind me so I see quite fourteen mirrors in the one opposite me and fourteen of my faces which is both bewildering and tiresome. However, here goes, though I ain't got much to say. Well, I have been jogging on the same old round till, wading through depths of snows and squelch we have at length reached sun and balminess and opening flowers and burgeoning trees. Here we have anemones white, pink and even pale mauve, oxlips, cowslips, opaque French blue periwinkles, kingcups and violets all a-blowing to soothe our jaded nerves and tired senses after work! But as yet I can only see one tree out all over the landscape from our window and that is a chestnut. Very tardy burgeoning. I often think and wonder what you are doing, and compare our lives now with when we were together in Dorset. How will it all end? Am I fated to disappear in fragments in a front line trench, or return with one leg (very lucky!), or more curious still 'intact' to my Christine? I have no presentiments or ideas, only I heartedly wish it was all over.

How do you do, Miss Doron Carrington, and what? I hear vaguely about you from my dove.... I would like a good long letter from you all about the little world in London, our old associates, latest gossips and re London Group etc. Paul I am thankful to say is at present out of the line for a bit.... How I wish I could get leave to come and see you all and tell you all the curious and interesting things that have happened to me.... Even if the war was to stop I dare swear we should be the last to leave this blessed land and would probably be employed to fill up all the trenches.... Let this be a reminder of my existence.... I still think and know I know nobody except Christine better than I know you. But I am maundering on and had better stop. Please write to me soon, your loving Jacko.

Paul too was puzzled and reproachful: 'Carrington dear, you have sedulously escaped me during my brief spell of liberty in this country and, faith, I am not pleased at it. You never came to my Private View and I have not seen you since you came so boisterously in to tea with us.' This was at his and Bunty's flat in Judd Street. Exactly where Carrington's latest move was he couldn't discover. As with a previous girl, he remembered the street but not the number and wandered frustratingly up and down Frith Street in search of her. He wanted her to send out cards to say that his *Ypres Salient* exhibition at the Goupil Gallery was to continue through July. She was to distribute them 'discretely'. In spite of enthusiastic reviews and having sold seven drawings, 'I shall be in pocket just five pounds!' He told her that John was at Arras, that he and Bunty had been staying with the Drinkwaters in the Cotswolds, and that he had a poisoned nose. Carrington had been so busy finding witnesses to speak up for Lytton at his 'conscience court' and at his medical, making her peace with Gertler, going to Fitzrovian parties, working hard and house-searching that the silent weeks and months where the Nashes were concerned hurried by without her noticing. Both brothers had become terribly eloquent on matters she did not want to see or hear. Just before Passchendaele John made a masterly attempt to catch her unwilling eye.

My very dear ΔΩPON

Though I have written to you and you have not answered me, and though my present existence has been worthy of your compassion in that respect, yet will I as I have often done before forgive, and not only write you a letter, but e'en start a new block with that epistle. The block is called The Patriot and has 8 flags painted on it. I have no material to work on, no remarks of yours to comment upon, but I will not press you. I must try and entertain you with what news exists and is allowed by the censor to be recorded. You must know that I have been in the line off and on since I last heard from you, gaining many curious, grim and amazing experiences. You will imagine that I have got all I can out of it, as is our wont. I would not have missed this experience for anything, now that I have been through it, but there, I will say no more. I am always thinking these things over. How I wish I could tell you my thoughts and impressions by word of mouth. Mostly I come to the same conclusion as many other artists or writers. Nothing changes.

The whole surface of the earth for miles is disrupted and pitted by shells so closely as to render easy walking impossible. Decay in war material, human composition and natural objects (trees) is everywhere, yet Nature is uninterrupted. Cornflowers and many kinds of others bloom over the trench-tops and all is covered with a thick growth of merciful herbiage. Birds sing and swallows fly about among the shells and machine-gun bullets. You expect almost to see eternal night or winter, yet the sunsets are as wonderful and the nights full of stars. 'Of course' you will say – yet it seems unreal somewhat. I daresay Noel has often described to you the cacophony of sounds marshalled in a night bombardment. Machine-guns tatting and cackling like a lot of silly women or recently disemburdened hens – a maddening noise – then a sniper's bullet with a sound of a carter's whip cuts the silent intervals. A soft 'phut' and up curves a Very light, falls, flares, casting two diagonal shafts of light from the ground, then darkness again. Now let the batteries start with numerous reports and the crump crump of the shells exploding. You hear our shrapnel shells screaming overhead and bursting in the air in golden flashes. I have seen what I was told were burning oil shells bursting into cascades of yellow-red stars amongst a blasted wood, and red lights rising and falling like slow fishes in the firmament of the night. Amongst all this din – as I mentioned to Christine – I noticed on the parapet in front of me where I stood shivering with cold and wet and not a little fear – a very small fly seated stupidly tranquil on a clod of earth. It seemed such a tiny atom and yet . . . it appeared to out do all this spectacular din by the intensity of its stillness. . . . There are less aesthetic scenes which do not bear describing. This is an 'indecent' war and modern 'improvements' have not tended to minimise their horror.

I remember one thing – very fine – it was late evening afterglow and the trench's dull decayed earth colour was silhouetted against the sky. An aeroplane flew over firing on the Boche trenches with its machine-gun, a straight line of flashes from the machine slanting across to the trenches like a taut golden chain.

I must not prolong this letter further, the censor must be considered, and you must take it as a sparkling reminder of my existence, rather than a decent epistle. Please write soon a good longer letter recounting your travels, experiences, present mode of life, condition of heart, mind and health, etc. and oblige your good friend.

Carrington had no intention of not obliging someone whom she was beginning to think of as an old friend, rather than a good friend. She recoiled from John's stunning pictures of the Front. Now that Teddy was 'Missing' whatever small allegiance she may have at first felt towards her country in wartime she now abandoned. The war was stupid, vulgar, boring and she found John's brilliant accounts of it unanswerable. So in a sense did Christine and Bunty, but for different reasons. The fact was, as so many soldiers discovered when writing to women back home, the Front was uncommunicable. The more powerfully it was described, the less its unique awfulness and strange beauty were conveyed. John did not tell Carrington or Christine about the most important thing which happened to him on the Western Front in 1917. He fell in love with a comrade, 'But not as a comrade'. He loved this young man more or 'other' than he loved girls and when he was killed he never in all the long years ahead tried to re-experience this love. To understanding remarks about it being natural for men in such conditions to share emotions they might not feel in the normal way, he would simply reply, 'It was not like that.' Like David's 'passing the love of women'? 'Something like that, I expect.'

If John never mentioned this turmoil and grief to Carrington, neither was she able to tell him that for sheer unspeakable loneliness the years between leaving the Slade and finding Lytton were the worst years of her life. But by the summer of 1917 a single-mindedness of purpose gripped her and although she looked as though she had joined Fitzrovia, she was well on her way to that country-house of art which had been beckoning ever since she became a student. The domestically helpless and inert Lytton allowed her as a matter of course to find their perfect house and the search was stimulated by her parents deciding that Hurstbourne Tarrant was too large for them and were themselves on the move. And this after only three years in Hampshire. It suited Carrington for it meant that in the confusion she could undertake a 'looting expedition' and bring a cartload of furniture from Ibthorpe House to Tidmarsh Mill without her 'frightfully stingy' mother being any the wiser. While painting hard in Frith Street and working at the Omega, and learning wood engraving at the Arts and Crafts, and with her affair with Mark Gertler still dragging on with misery on his part and fibs on hers, she was exhilarated by the strength and reliability of the currents which were bearing her away.

Little of this great surge to freedom was seen in Christine's letters to John. She and Carrington went to classes at the Arts and Crafts and earned their thirty shillings at the Omega. Roger Fry had opened the Omega Workshops at 33 Fitzroy Square in 1913. It was a design centre where the designers remained anonymous although they included many famous artists, and where penurious young artists could decorate furniture and ceramics for three mornings a week, earning thirty shillings. Customers could also purchase copies of the Italian masters and learn how to use colour in their rooms. None of the furniture, pottery and so on was made on the premises, only richly transformed there.

While John in his letters contemplated death, Christine wrote:

> I went to tea with Carrington after the Arts and Crafts and in the evening had to help Norah with the cutting-out of a blouse. Carrington sends her love to you. She is very well and rather depressed, and seems to be going to numerous parties in a wonderful Russian fancy-dress with red top-boots. Brett was also there, and did not seem quite so deaf, I thought. Carrington is perhaps coming to the Arts and Crafts with me on Tuesday to learn Woodcuts. She will work in my room, but I'm afraid it sounds too good to be true.... I am again working here [at the Omega Workshops]. What a lot of funny jobs I've done and who ever thought I would turn into a dressmaker? All the morning I've been making a green and yellow, and black and white and khaki check dress for Nina Hamnett, and now I'm having my lunch hour as stipulated in the Workshops Act.... When I came home yesterday, there was your letter waiting for me. I'm so excited to get a letter from you that I simply choke over it. I mean I read on and on and never grasp a word of what you are talking about. With a green envelope I always make a violent effort to read very slowly, stopping every page or so for five minutes to take breath.... Dearest love, do you know what bird it is that makes a noise like a machine-gun? Every morning I am awakened by this strange throaty chuckle.... My dear, dear love, when I think of the noise that you have to stand I feel I cannot bear it.

I have gone to the length of putting your photo on the mantlepiece! It's a pity it is not of you in khaki.... Mother said, 'I'm glad to see Jack's photo standing over the fireplace, perhaps it will help you to be more tidy'.

Dearest, I quite understand how bored you must feel with your present life. ... I'm glad you told me what to expect, it is always best to do that. When the worst comes to the worst, or whatever you choose to call it, I'm sure, darling, you will manage very well, and as to being heroic, one does the jobs as they come along, I suppose. Looked at as a whole it seems impossible, but one lives only a minute at a time.... Once you thought you could not leave me, and yet you did, and how well I remember that evening, and how I walked back into the sitting-room and warmed my hands by the fire, and presently Paul came up saying, 'The old man seems very cheerful....' It is very selfish to wish to be dead, unless one is alone in the world and you say he [a fellow soldier who wished he was] has a dove at home. Well I repeat it is unkind, unless she is the kind of dove I once learnt about in a little song at school, who 'Before a year had passed. Had bought another poodle-dog Exactly like the last'. I have come to the conclusion that it needs a good deal of best quality love to make life worth living these days.

John had written sombrely:

I left this over last night because I felt depressed and unable to write a good letter. I have no reason to be cheerful particularly now except that the day's work is over and I am free from this eternal mud, and walking through it, and also treading with every muscle braced in your left leg on these everlasting duck-boards, a dreary and most tiring job. I am always physically tired but with just enough 'go' in me to do another day's work. So we dither on. My best friend is on leave and has been for some time on a sad occasion, his Mother being either dead or dying, and I miss him.

By the time this letter reaches you it will be John Nash without the N [use of his middle initial, N, was a coded indication for duty at the Front]. I am sorry Esmond is wounded, I hope not seriously: he is lucky to be in England.... I feel in such a clotted state – no mind at work.... I wrote to dear Carrington yesterday. I do hope to hear from her.... I have never once heard from Claughton tho' I have written twice at length.

... The only thing I can feel sure in – I question so many accepted dogmas – is that I am right so long as I love you and am kind.... I am really over-passionate, yet if every other venture, even if my work failed, I would not have existed in vain if I can love you.... You will not laugh, remembering how troubled I was for the moment before I first kissed you in that old fir wood on the hill.

Christine had, almost from the beginning of their relationship, noted that the amusing talk for which John was famous appeared to surface from a kind of inborn darkness, and as his letters from France grew more and more apprehensive, so she began in the only way she knew to counter his melancholy. While he was posting back to her his books and drawings in case he himself should not return, she began an efficient and practical campaign to direct his attention to Work, a word which to her overcame every fear and horror which life could offer.

I was going to tell you about your pictures. I went to Bulstrode Mews to fetch the New Englishers yesterday and there learnt, as I told you in the letter-card, that *The Orchard* is sold to Sir Charles or Henry or Percy Younger of South Audley Street. I took the other two up to the Goupil, where I met Paul who had been to *Colour* [magazine]. I think they will reproduce *The Viaduct* and one other. We chose an oil of a farm roof and fir-tree, haystacks and elm-trees. Can it be your *Stable?* And for America *Steam Plough,* two Dorset landscapes [painted when John was on holiday with Carrington], N. Bucks and one also of Bucks, I think, very green of a wood, with Brussels Sprouts down one side of a hill, and a field with grass tracks down another hill to meet them, and Apple-trees to the right.

Marchant [William Marchant, a London art-dealer] is now quite amiable with [Harold] Gilman and his group.... I met Gilman on Thursday and he told me he had seen someone home on leave who had seen you lately. You'll be so stout and strong when you get back I shan't be able to recognise you. I have been so thin and lanky living on war rations (which by the way are more than we eat in the ordinary way, but from the papers you'd think it was only enough to keep body and soul together).

Every now and then the cryptic Field Service postcard would arrive at Gerrards Cross. There were too the usual terrifying hold-ups. The postman was longed for, the telegraph-boy was dreaded. 'Still no news from you. I try not to be anxious and put it down to hostile submarines, but you know the listening for the postman feeling, don't you? What is most trying are the kind enquiries from the family. No letter from Jack yet? It makes me freeze up.' And then there was the commiserating stranger. 'I met a

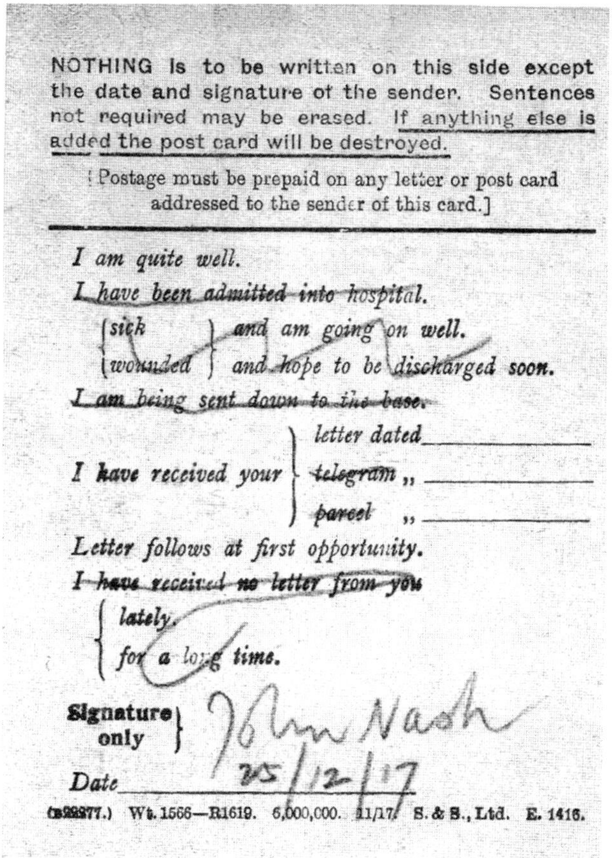

NOTHING is to be written on this side except the date and signature of the sender. Sentences not required may be erased. If anything else is added the post card will be destroyed.

[Postage must be prepaid on any letter or post card addressed to the sender of this card.]

I am quite well.

~~*I have been admitted into hospital.*~~

sick / *wounded* } *and am going on well.* / *and hope to be discharged soon.*

~~*I am being sent down to the base.*~~

I have received your { *letter dated* ______ / ~~*telegram*~~ ,, ______ / ~~*parcel*~~ ,, ______

Letter follows at first opportunity.

~~*I have received no letter from you*~~ { *lately.* / *for a long time.*

Signature only } John Nash

Date 25/12/17

(B29277.) Wt. 1566—R1619. 6,000,000. 11/17. S. & S., Ltd. E. 1416.

The 'Green Card' Field Service Post Card, by which relatives could quickly be told how the sender was faring, a simple method of reassurance.

woman-lady who shook me by the hand and then put her left hand on top of the whole, and gazing in my face, said, "And where's the Sweetheart?" The letters became a mass. 'Your Green Letter [official envelope] came last night. I keep all your letters as my most treasured possession. They all live in a drawer with Carrington's and some early ones of Norah's. It is nearly full up now, and as Carrington's and Norah's were first there I have a sentimental dislike to throwing out the old love to make room for the new, but something will have to be done.' Norah and Christine had been living together at Gerrards Cross until April 1917, when Norah left to become a landgirl. 'We had a miserable time trying to separate our possessions and get hers packed up into trunks, and we got into a thoroughly reminiscent state over old clothes and fancy dresses, and drawings. I little thought that the end would come like this. There would be quite a cheery feeling in leaving to be married, but this is so unsatisfactory. Poor

Charlie, I shall have to take him for walks as of old, and the Gerrards Cross folk will have a new-old subject for conversation over their bandage and shirt-making and tea-cups. It is nearly six months since I have seen you.' Christine herself was now attending London County Council classes twice a week to train as a press and advertisement artist. 'There is not one word to be said in favour of it, and at first I thought I could not bear to do it ... but it is necessary to earn money, and only proper and right, I suppose, to be independent of one's parents – or husband, may I say?'

Whereas Carrington turned her face from the carnage, particularly now that Teddy's features stared from it, Christine began to regard it critically and recklessly, considering where she stood. Her letters to John shift from the conventional to the alarmingly astute.

> There was a kind of adverse peace feeling in the air a few weeks ago. I mean nobody wanted it. You know what has been happening at home, I suppose? How Mr Asquith was kicked out, and Lloyd George walked into Downing Street saying, 'We will not lay down our arms until our object has been achieved'. If that is the case, I doubt if we shall see the end of this in our lifetimes. Mrs Pankhurst got up and said a few words the other day, but she was instantly squashed, worse luck. For once I felt in sympathy with her. At any rate she had the courage to say that we have all been making fools of ourselves long enough. I've been wondering about sending you that good little book [perhaps Bertrand Russell's protest against the continuation of the war]. Are your things likely to be pounced upon, and would you get into trouble for having in your possession a book which is not calling this a glorious war? Or don't they care what you think?
>
> Everyone seems to have that craving for something to cling to, and one must find out what comforts one best. With us it is surely music and landscapes.... I think our love for each other is something in the nature of a religion.... Do you remember, love, climbing up that steep lane to the village I thought was Stokenchurch [Buckinghamshire]? We passed a bull browsing in the hedge and beheld the whole countryside spread out below us. The Juniper Hill, and beyond that the other hills, and you turned and kissed me with the joy of it all. I doubt if one could get a better or more religious feeling than that. It has suddenly occurred to me that we are hunting for something we have already got.

I don't know what to think about the war. Most people seem to think that the end will come about August after another Big Push, but today an Inspector came round to see Mother with reference to her staying in London for a few days, and he was very gloomy and depressed about it, and thinks that it will be a long time before we come to terms.

John was at Arras now and throughout the early summer of 1917 he was in training for the Third Battle of Ypres, or Passchendaele. 'I have been up the line with a party of men last weekend (sounds rather like a pleasure trip). We were in the front line trenches for over 48 hours just for experience and by Jove we got it! On Saturday night at ten o'clock, I wonder what you were doing? I was standing on the step with my gun and fixed bayonet by my side peering over 800 yards of tangled wire and grass trying to see if Fritz was coming across to pay us a visit while round about fell, flew, and whistled respectively 5.9 shells, whizzbangs, pineapples so-called and machine-gun bullets. I never knew when I was not going to be blown to bits, but I do assure you I thought it curious myself that my feelings were not of fear. What was unpleasant was the wet, sleepiness and continual looking into darkness.... Surely there will be some recompense for us? I have thought it over so often wondering why people allow themselves to continue in misery for the sake of justifying the idle boasts of a few misguided statesmen. And why God or the gods can allow it to continue to the extinction of everything that is likely to raise up people's minds.... Did I tell you that I found a fly-orchis and others of that genus? I had a long letter from Carrington the other day: she seems to have been enjoying herself at the sea.'

While John was being initiated into trench warfare, Carrington and Christine, and a host of other young people, were taking part in a 'Monster Matinée' at the Lyric Theatre. It was one of Lena Ashwell's shows in aid of her Concerts for the Front and it had originally been staged at the Chelsea Palace Theatre on 20th March, when Christine described it to John. 'There has been so much to do for the [Augustus] John Chorus ladies.... The scene will represent Morris, Swinburne, Carlyle and Rossetti a-talking, and walking in Rossetti's garden in Cheyne Walk.... Then there will be the Gertler Girls and a Conder Ballet, and many other attractions to weedle sums varying from £3.3s. to 2/8 (including Entertainment Tax) out of the pockets of foolish people.... However, it's great fun making the dresses. Carrington, Brett, Barbara Hiles, Sylvia Meyer, Faith and I are all in it, most of them as boys, but I'm going to be a girl because I thought you'd like it better.' They made the dresses at the Omega

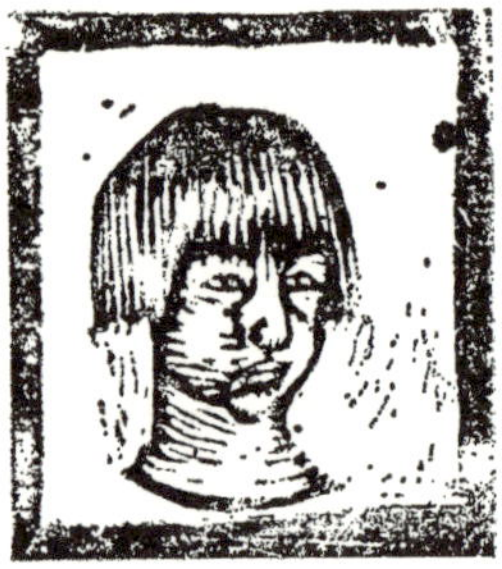

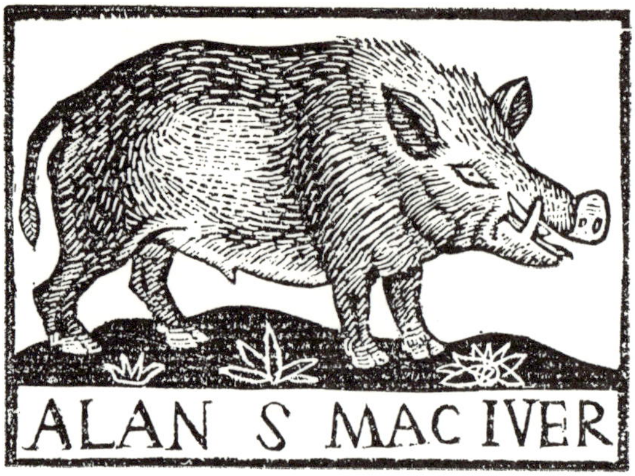

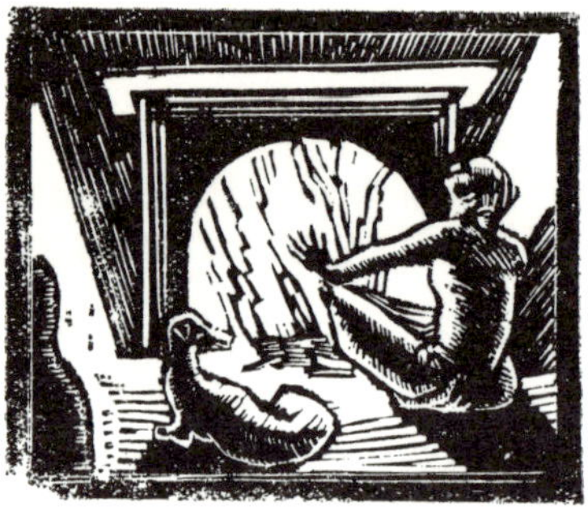

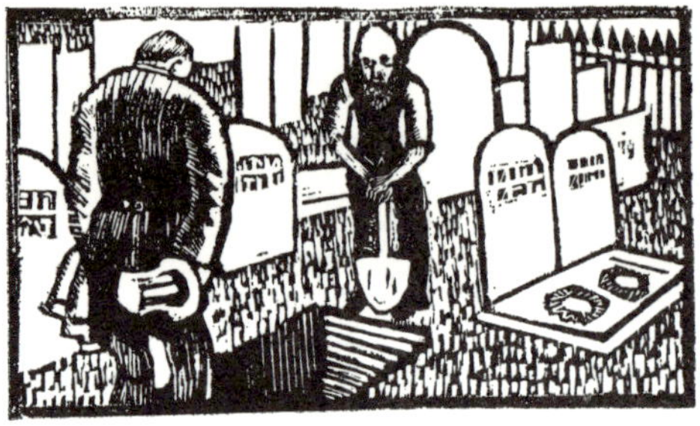

Carrington, woodcuts printed from line blocks.
Self-portrait, *c.*1916. Bookplate design for Alan S. MacIver, *c.*1920.
'The Fireside', and 'The Grave Diggers', for *Two Stories*, Hogarth Press, 1917.
(Courtesy of Harry Ransom Humanities Research Center, Texas.)

– 'the amusing part of it is that Carrington and I dress in everyday life like a John lady, so that we shall have to appear in our own clothes.'

Christine loved dressing-up, dancing and theatricals, and in the Lena Ashwell revue she and Carrington and the other girls fell into Dorelia attitudes and sang:

John: John:
How he's got on:
He owes it, he knows it, to me:
Brass earrings I wear,

And I don't do my hair,
When I walk down the street,
All the people I meet
They stare at the things I have on:
When Battersea-Parking
You'll hear folk remarking:
'There goes an Augustus John.'

Now that she was engaged to John Nash, Christine was less susceptible to the little non-deliberate woundings of Carrington's behaviour and she would occasionally tell John about some typical let-down with her because he complained so much about the sparsity of her letters to him. But never again would there be the conscientious landscape pages, the careful drawings and the mutual badinage. Or rarely again. John had gone to that tedious war. Christine and he now took to sharing what they hoped was a light-hearted acknowledgement of her notorious failings. John had only been in a snowy France for a few weeks when Christine wrote:

> I took my lunch round to Carrington's house and ate it with her. She says Noel met Paul about five days ago ... Noel so much wants to go for walks with you because he is so lonely with no friends to talk to. I wish you could manage to find him. She is coming to the Arts and Crafts with me to learn Wood Cuts. Isn't that good news. She's coming with me tomorrow for the first time. I'm so pleased to think of seeing her twice a week.

In her next letter Christine reported:

> Need I tell you that Carrington did *not* come with me to the A and C yesterday? I called for her punctually at ¼ to 10 and she came running downstairs looking so beautiful in a black jersey coat and very good green skirt, and golden head as usual, saying, – 'I'm so sorry – I'm afraid I've got to go and paint a man today – I'll come on Thursday!' You know her ways. Always so charming that one would forgive her anything. She has done a woodcut of Jasper [her dog] and is sending you a print. Noel Rooke who teaches Wood Cuts is an old admirer of hers. Who isn't, I'd like to know!

Christine faced the last Big Push with apprehension. At home the 'war whoop', as Coleridge described the fanaticism of his day, had subsided and people, especially the young, were openly sceptical about what was being planned. Field-censors blocked out place-names and troop movements but could do little about the freely spoken criticism of the war which filled the letters to and from the trenches. Christine now realised that the odds were against John returning to her.

My dearest pocket Hercules,

... I don't know what to think about the war. If the powers that be think it will really end this summer, I'm so afraid that they'll push all the people training for officers into the finale.... When one realises how silly people are, and to what lengths of suffering and misery they will cheerfully go, all for the sake of what they are told is patriotism, it seems as if it will never end. And then to think that it was started, as I am sure it must have been, by a lot of beastly financiers, all wanting to make money for themselves, and the way in which people have been stuffed with lies to make them go and fight ... But I'm sure that some folk find a lot of consolation in the thought that they have given their best – their life for their country and a great cause. But I could never feel that.... Sometimes on a fine summer's morning one has to answer one's own prayers.

Earlier that year she had admitted that having to hide her dread of what could happen to them 'has closed up a large part of me'. She said, 'I know I'm constantly putting things aside as not safe to write ... writing is difficult work and needs careful handling.... Good Mr Stubbs is to come and play at our wedding. I want him to burst forth into that Toccata thus! [*A line of music.*]'

She sent him parcels of biscuits and dates, Mexican chocolate and *Wuthering Heights*, also a score of *The Magic Flute*. She took his work to the London galleries and 'spoke good of his name'. No one had ever before cared for him like this. He was overwhelmed. 'My darling,' she told him, 'I will do all I can to look after you and make you happy if you do get back, you may be sure of that.' There was one thing she must know. She prefaced it with a topical analogy. 'A little armoured-car insect is lying on its back struggling to get up. I shall have to help it to its feet in a moment, poor little tank. Now I'm going to ask you a question. Did you "want to make love to me" before our business-like compact? But I believe you have already told me that you did, but were frightened that I would laugh. So it's not a question after all.' But it was – a huge question – and not about sex at that moment but sex in the future. The 'business-like compact' was to do with having one's cake and eating it too as long as one was honest about it. No monogamous Balkan business. Theirs would be a glorious open marriage.

Charlie married Norah in the summer of 1917 and Christine often stayed with them in their minute cottage. Norah was her earliest friend and lover. With the 'business-like compact' in mind, Christine wrote wide-openly to John, 'Charlie and I take it in turns to sleep with Norah, which again I think is very kind of him. The charwoman thinks it the most extraordinary thing she has ever heard of. I forget how she found us out. Well, Charlie comes home about 7.30 and we have an awful rush to get dinner ready at the critical moment. We cook on a gas-stove in the back kitchen. It is a tiny little room, about as big as a railway-carriage, and I suddenly thought that we looked like two chefs in a train restaurant, both busying ourselves over basins and stirring saucepans. There is only one candle to light it with and we seem to run round each other in a stooping posture. Can you picture us? In front of the sink is a board to stand on, which tips up if one stands on the edge of it. This train idea is so grown on us that we can almost see the telegraph wires flash past. The little cat of course travels with us. Charlie comes in cold and tired but ever gentle and loving, and by the time we get to Birmingham he is partaking of a plate of hot soup. Yes, I think their married life is most successful.'

No sooner had John sent his Borrows and other treasured possessions back home in preparation for the Big Push than he found himself in the company of a gipsy soldier. John was elated. England's highways rose and dipped before him. 'Did I ever tell you about a man in my Company who knows all the Wells and the Dodds, and the people about Wallingford, and that country most intimately? It was a curious coincidence of a man knowing two separate parts of the country as intimately as I did. The other part of the country referred to is around Cromer, which I have so often visited with Claughton. I was talking of Borrow also and it happened that he knew a lot about gipsies. In fact he had undoubtedly gipsy blood in his veins, since he was well met by them and entertained and addressed as "brother", which does not happen towards anyone. He mentioned several families living which appeared in *Lavengro* and said that they still used portions of their undoubtedly unique and ancient language. This man lives close to Horncastle in Lincolnshire where the great horse-fair takes place mentioned in *Romany Rye*. We have since had many talks on the subject. Some of his experiences are very curious and he is full of fine perceptions for things natural and curious. He is by profession a farmer and has been more or less independent since he was fifteen years old. He is very dark skinned and has a Romany nose. I hope he will be spared – I don't like that word – for us to meet some time in wild parts of England.'

Painting the War

John's account of Paul's flying visit contrasted greatly with his brother's 'real soldier and very proud of it' description of him. It left him discontented and frustrated. 'First I will tell you that Paul arrived yesterday [19th November 1917] quite unexpectedly and took Game and me out. We had not much time – just had a meal and a chat, and saw his new drawings and whizzed back again, but the change was very pleasant. P. is very well and has done some more interesting drawings – he is leaving this unhealthy area. I think he found drawing a little hazardous and is going to another part of the line. I fear I may not see him again while he is on the job.... Paul thinks he might work a job for me – like the camouflage dept of the R.E. ... I can't tell what will happen to me.... Goodbye, dear love ... if only Paul could work me a specialist Bombay job! [slang for an easy-chair job]. I'm sick of the damned subject – let's leave it. Perhaps I shall get leave. Why do I not get any luck? I have got Carrington's letters.' A week or two later Paul wrote to say that the critics were mixing them up. It was the first intimation of something which would prove to be an irritant for the rest of their lives. There was also some reaction to the young artists' view of the war, causing John to explode. 'May the very worst kind of boils and blisters break out on the faces of all those sniffy slug drivelling journalists for reflecting in such a dirty manner on our patriotism. I'd like to have 'em all out here for a bit. Grub orderly every day, I'd give 'em and then they'd be as filthy as their writings. God curse all journalists.' He asked Christine to send him Thoreau's *Walden*. 'Books are fearfully scarce here. Now I do beg.'

Opposite: *Oppy Wood, 1917, Evening*, John Nash, 1918. Oil, 1828 × 2122 mm. Trustees of the Imperial War Museum. Over, left: *Over The Top: 1st Artists' Rifles at Marcoing, 30th December 1917*, John Nash, 1918. Oil, 795 × 1075 mm. Trustees of the Imperial War Museum. 'There was not a shot for a while, suddenly the Germans opened up and that seemed to be every machine gun in Europe.... We never got to grips with the enemy but were stopped in sight of them. We had to "hole up" in craters and shell holes till nightfall.' Right: *The Mule Track*, Paul Nash, 1918. Oil, 610 × 914 mm. Trustees of the Imperial War Museum.

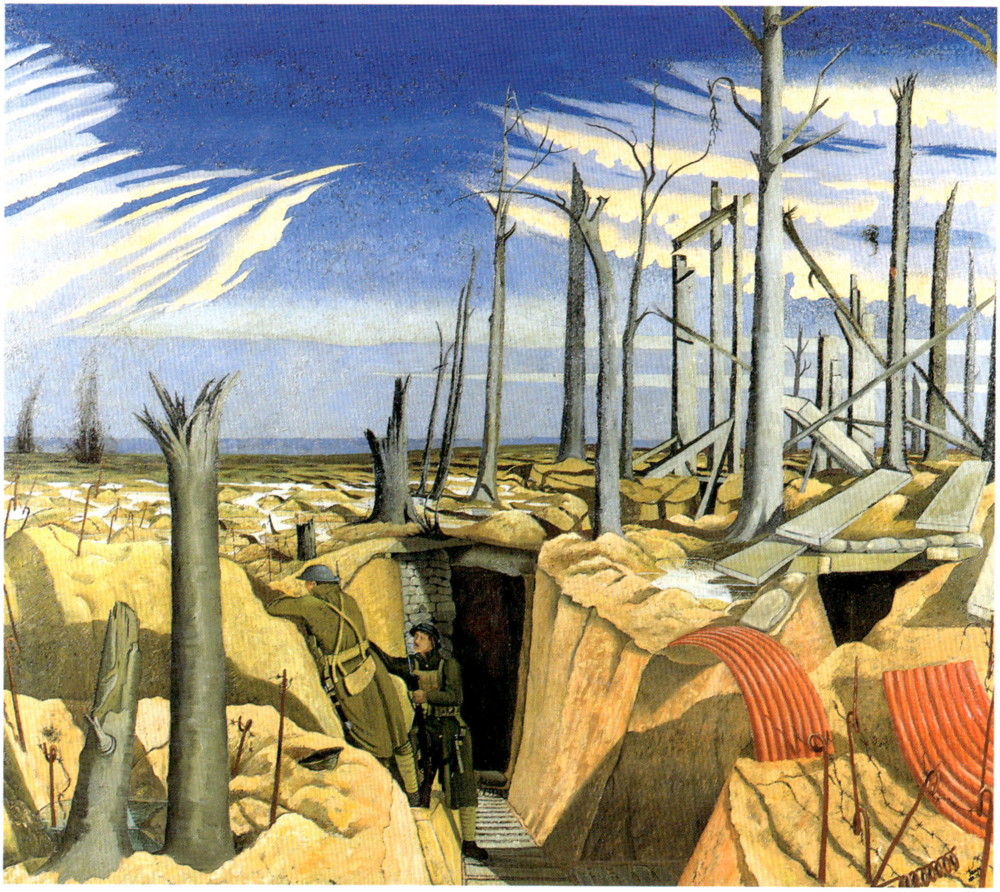

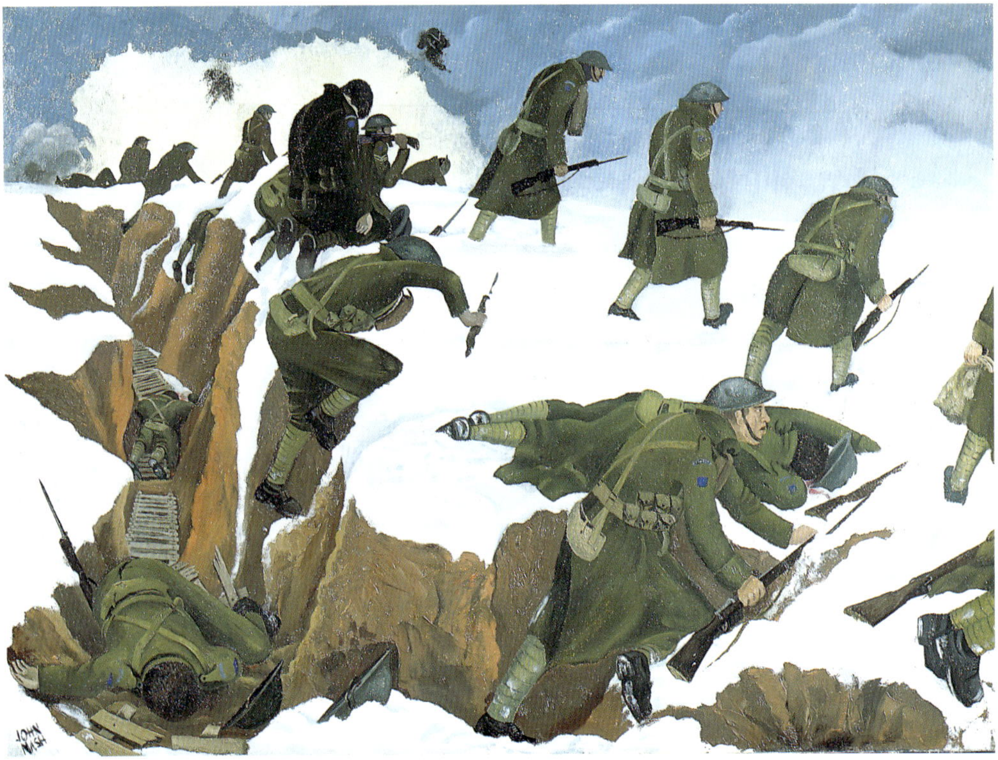
JOHN
NASH

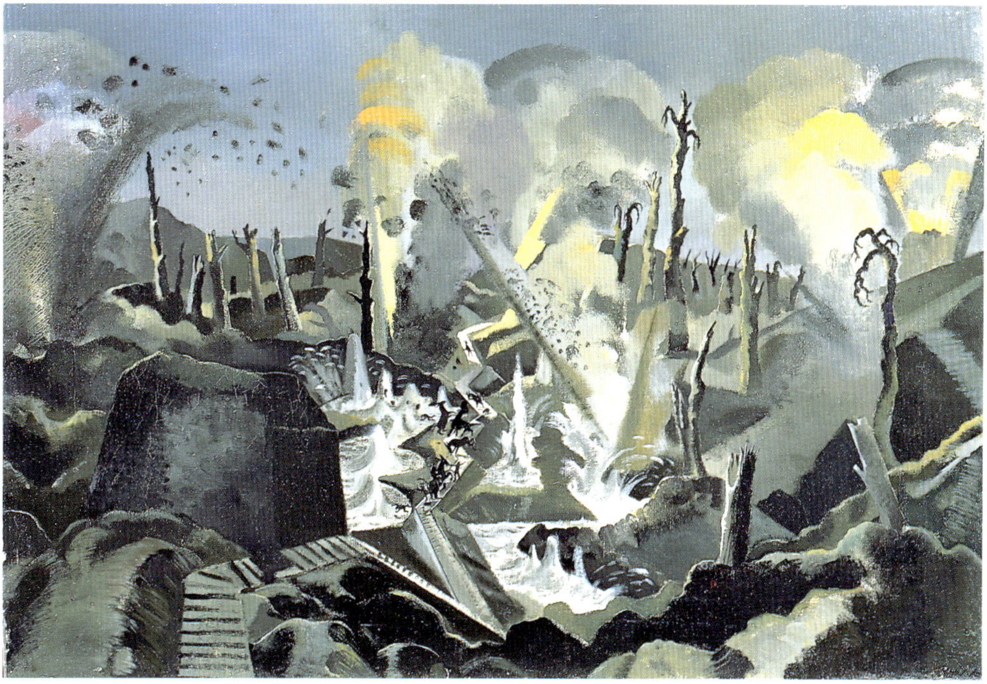

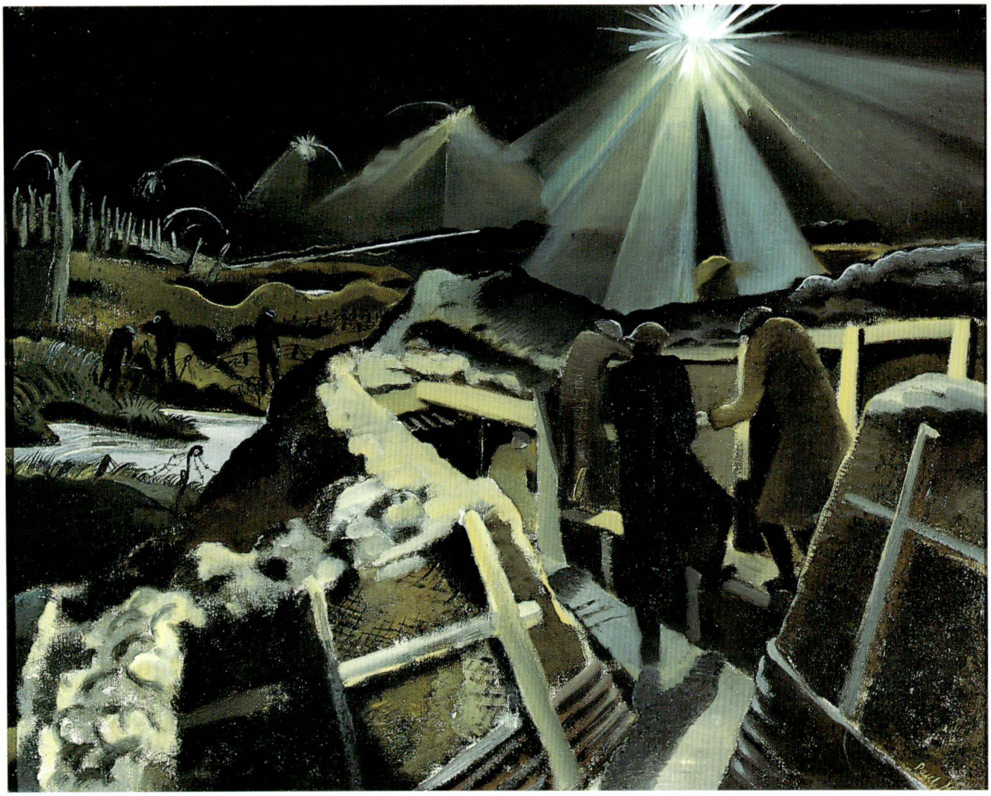

His Christmas letter to her was all blotched with snow. Tucked inside it was a letter to Paul, who had now returned to London, begging him to do all he could to get him an official war artist's commission. He believed that he could not escape being killed for much longer, especially with his being 'unlucky'. His natural fatalism now had to make way for, what was for him, the wild certainty of a glowing future – if only the war would let him have it.

... This is Xmas Eve. I spent last night with 3 of my men in an advance post – a perfectly uncovered shell-hole. It was strange to watch one's rifle freeze all over and one's coat get covered with rime, and my wasn't it cold! There is a chance of being in the front line tonight and for Xmas Day. I don't mind telling you I shall be glad to get out of this. We are 700 yards in advance of our company on an iron-bound (by frost) road. I am curled up in a little 'funk' hole covered with a 'welter' sheet and the shells which are bounding and bouncing somewhere none too far shake the earth ... a bit of shrapnel cut my coat this morning – aye, and one of our own guns it was. Nothing but bully beef and rum until your mouth feels like nothing on earth.... It is like an unnecessary dream.... I heard the partridges chirping early this morning between crackling bursts of machine-gun fire.... We could hear Fritz working and talking, and we seemed far more part of his operations than of our own.... And now quite a lot of mud has trickled down my ear and I am so cold and cramped that I must stop a moment and warm my feet.

Xmas Day. We got back safely and got a good sleep in a dug out. I had my ration of pudding, not unlike cold clay, and also Audrey's [his stepmother's] excellent tinned turkey, but I have such a headache owing to rum and fatigue. We slept most of the day. A man gave me a cracker and we gravely pulled it while great shells bounced overhead to its tiny report. We then sang carols and I have to go out again to the beastly position tonight. Now goodbye, my darling.... Enclosed is a letter for Paul. Will you give it to him. It is about the War Artist job. Your own love, Jacko.

Opposite: *The Ypres Salient at Night*, Paul Nash, 1918. Oil, 712 × 914 mm. Trustees of the Imperial War Museum. 'At intervals we send up Very lights and the ghastly face of No Man's Land leaps up in the garish light, then, as the rocket falls, the great shadows flow back, shutting it into darkness again.'

Whilst John was writing this letter, Lytton and Carrington were settling into the Mill House at Tidmarsh and enduring its terrible cold. Each had discovered a perfect companion, impossible to believe though it was to everyone who knew them. Carrington had fobbed off her parents' suspicions with the unlikely tale that she was joining a household entirely composed of ex-Slade women. Lytton had sent *Eminent Victorians* to Chatto and Windus and was resigned to its refusal when instead he received a delirious acceptance. He was amazed and, what was more important, he discovered himself about to be solvent. Also properly cared for and waited upon, as John soon would be by Christine, both of them to the end of their days. Messy, wintry, beautiful Tidmarsh Mill House was rapidly transformed into a comparatively warm sanctuary. Carrington's genius for home-making flourished. She cooked, scrubbed, decorated, hammered, gardened (having learned much from John), shopped, entertained, lit fires, hired 'hags' (charwomen) and brought the ramshackle building to colourful, if not exactly cosy, life. She had fled, from her parents, from the war, from Mark Gertler, and with all the necessary ruthlessness which flight entails. Out went everything and everyone which she no longer required. She was able to convince herself of the honesty of this. The Tidmarsh furnishings came from all over the place, articles quietly stolen from Hurstbourne Tarrant during her parents' move, chairs and crockery from Omega, beds from friends, a big wheel-back chair, sacks of plants. 'Are you getting a little cheerful now old Yahoo at the prospect of Tidmarsh?' she asked Lytton. She rigged up a studio for herself in the tank room. It was done.

While all this was happening, Paul's pleadings on his brother's behalf, along with Eddie Marsh's and others', bore fruit. The Ministry of Information added John's name to its little list of official war artists and he was returned from the Front, only to be arrested as a deserter before his commission and uniform arrived. It was the spring of 1918 and on the Somme the German and Allied armies surged to and fro in bloody seas, advancing and retreating, winning and losing. That February the Ministry of Food rationed butter, sugar and meat, and it was less the privation of such measures than the reaching out by the state, as it had done two years before with conscription, into the nation's much-vaunted freedom that was bringing an added alarm to the subjects of King George V. John Buchan's men kindly suggested that John Nash might care to return to the trenches at the country's expense to 'refresh' his memory before starting on the war pictures. He asked them how anyone who had seen the Western Front could forget it. But there was something they could do for him and Paul –

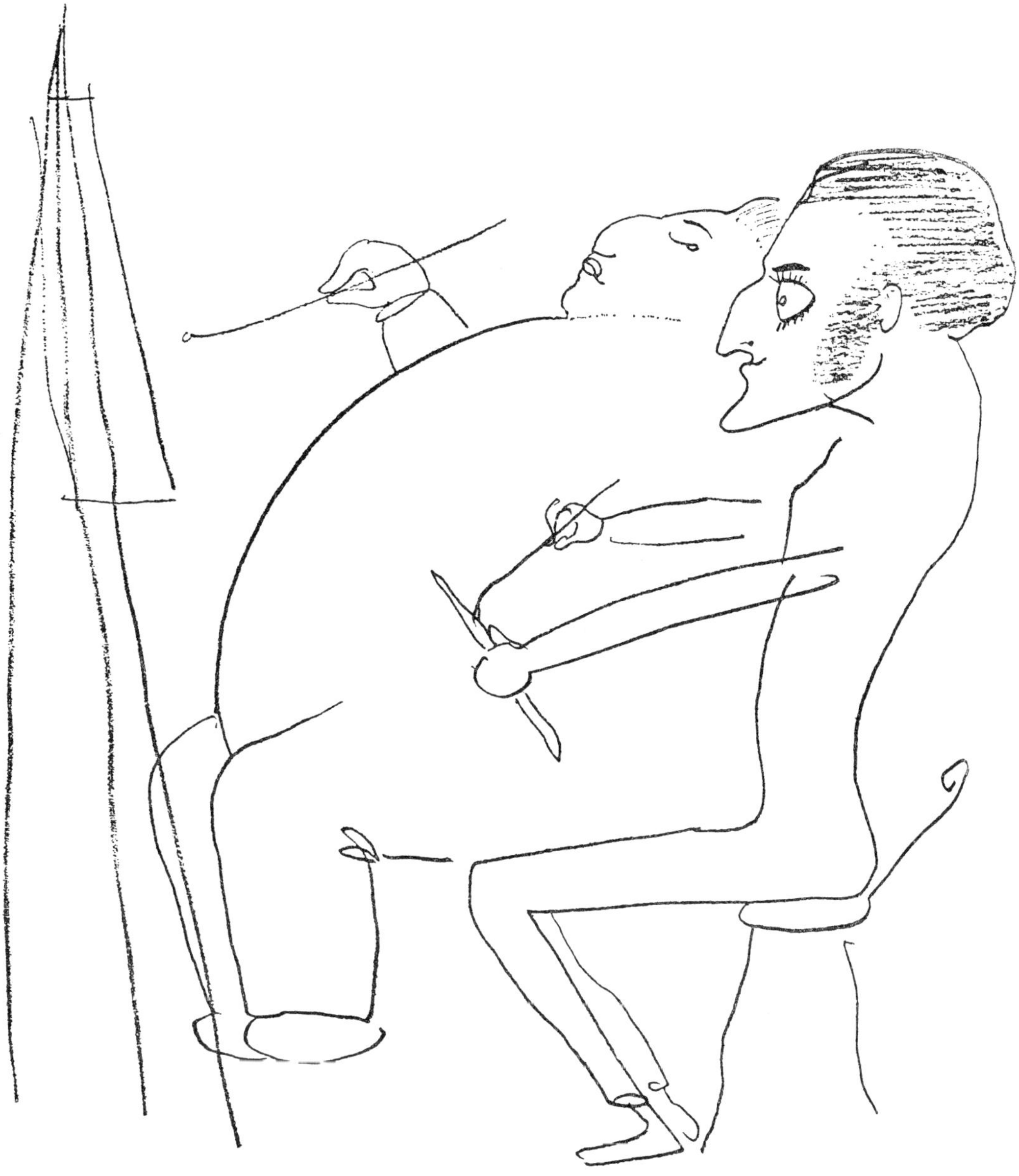

Pencil sketch by John Nash of himself (foreground) and Paul Nash
at work on their war paintings in the seedshed at Chalfont St Peter, 1918.
Ronald Blythe.

bring a load of War Office barbed wire, duckboards, gun chains, corrugated iron and other objects to Chalfont St Peter so that they could be accurate about the measurements. And this was done. A huge lorry full of W.O. equipment arrived and its contents duly signed for. The brothers were to receive thirty shillings a day as official war artists and were jubilant. It was a fortune. Paul insisted that they must be scrupulous and never stop work until six o'clock. Only then might they do their own 'art-work'. Which is why an evening light falls across *The Cornfield,* John's thank-you for not having been slaughtered. He and Christine were married at Gerrards Cross parish church that April, with Gilbert Spencer as best man. After a bicycling honeymoon John and Paul rented a shed on the common at Chalfont St Peter where they could paint the war pictures side by side. This shed had last been used by Belgian refugees for drying crops of belladonna and henbane, and it was, as a friend John Lewis said, 'in this drug-laden atmosphere that John Nash painted one of the greatest of the first war paintings, a scene based on the Battle of Cambrai called *Over the Top: 1st Artists' Rifles at Marcoing.*' In 1919 John had to make a copy of it for his old regiment, working this time in the cellars of the Tate Gallery. While the brothers toiled in the seedshed, their wives played Scarlatti, Schubert and Bach to them on the piano, bursting into little flights of cracked song. Now and then government inspectors came down from London to make sure that they were hard at work, among them John's old teacher-in-oils Harold Gilman.

Once settled into the discipline of the seedshed and the pleasures of marriage, John nevertheless became tantalised by the nearness of Carrington. Pangbourne to Chalfont, what was that to so seasoned a cyclist? He routed her as he had so often done before, but she did not come. Like everybody else, he offended her about her relationship with Lytton and had to retreat as best he could:

> I think we will not continue the argument. It is neither seemly nor proper that friends of such long and excellent standing as ourselves should toss such a heavy and prickly ball about from hand to hand. I am sure you will at least credit me with sincerity of feeling in writing what I did, even if you will not believe me when I said I liked Lytton. I am now going to bury the bone of contention. Let no roaring jackal disinter it from its resting place.
>
> Now you shall know that I am wedded and bedded, and on this head I expect a storm to break on me for not having written before. Christine and I have settled down [at a house next to the seedshed] and Paul is just down the road at

a good farm, and we both use a large room for our bloody war pictures.... I wish you would come and see us. We could put you up. I like being married and Christine is very lovely, and I only hope that she is as well pleased with me. I will not write a long letter now but will wait to see if you are *fâché* with me before committing myself further. Please write.
Ever yours with love, Jacko.

P.S. I am a little Lieutenant now, dearie.

When Paul was working beside his brother in the poisonous seedshed a second exhibition of his Western Front drawings, this time at the Leicester Galleries during May 1918, was beginning to establish him as one of the chief artist-critics of the war. Arnold Bennett, no less, had written the introduction for the catalogue, describing the impact which these stunning pictures had made on him: 'The interpretative value is, to my mind, immense. Lieutenant Nash has seen the Front simply and largely. He has found the essentials of it – that is to say, disfigurement, danger, desolation, ruin, chaos – and little figures of men creeping devotedly and tragically over the waste. The convention he uses is ruthlessly selective. The wave-like formations of shell-holes, the curves of shell-bursts, the straight lines and sharply-defined angles of wooden causeways, decapitated trees, the fangs of obdurate masonry, the weight of heavy skies, the human pawns of battle – these things are repeated again and again, monotonously, endlessly.... They seem to me to have been done in a kind of rational and dignified rage.... Their supreme achievement is that in their sombre and dreadful savagery they are beautiful.' Later, John Rothenstein would declare that the drawings which Paul made while at the Front, and the paintings of the Front in retrospect, were his greatest achievement. Paul would not have this and would play down this work in the future. John, who had fought as a sergeant in the gore and mud of those human swamps, had, he said, barely lifted a pencil. Art had to wait until Chalfont St Peter, the government's and his own. Neither he nor his brother felt that the war pictures were theirs in the complete sense. In September 1918 John told Carrington, 'There have been lovely cornfield scapes about here, binders in battalions working in the fields – the whole vale of Amersham a mass of corn. I plod on with my work, which will not interest you. In the evenings, when we think we have worked honestly enough for the old Ministry, we draw landscapes but cannot carry any out or show them.... Do write to your old picture-producer and send a good letter and news.'

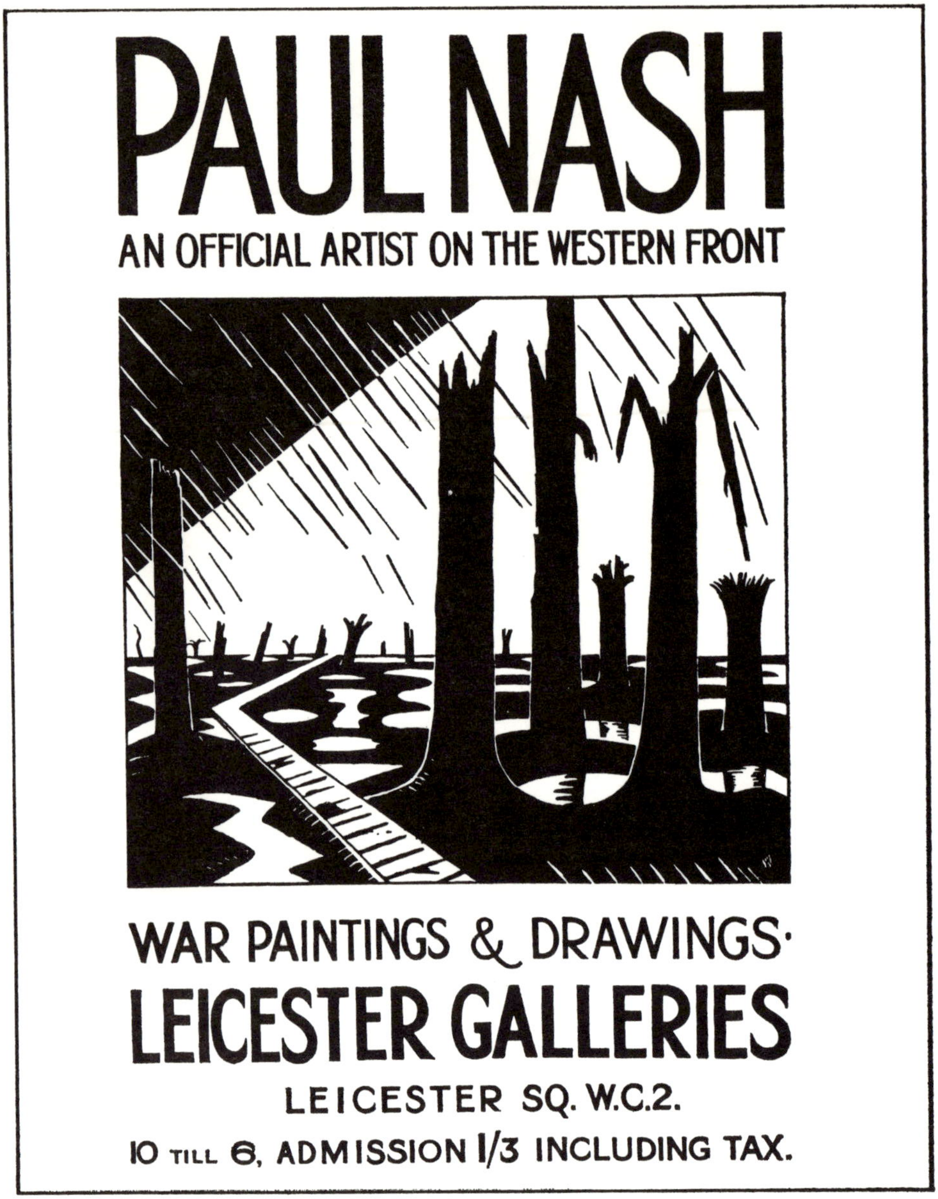

Paul Nash: poster design for his second exhibition of war work, May 1918.

It was during this late summer that two books revealed all too clearly and bitterly the gap which was growing between him and Carrington – indeed between him and many of the young people whose world had been a part of his before the trenches – and how, from now on, there could only be some kind of reaching-out and reminding. The first of these books was *Mendel*, the novelist Gilbert Cannan's fictionalised account of Mark Gertler's and Carrington's love affair. It horrified the pair of them. 'It's ugly and so damned vulgar,' said Carrington. John Nash agreed. Yet *Mendel* also was proof that the girl he had known as a struggling art student and hardy companion on long walks and bicycle rides, and as a faithful correspondent, had become in some curious and indefinable way a celebrity. Lytton Strachey's own sudden fame touched her to an extent, but she herself had begun to exist in an unwanted prominence which, for John, made her more unreachable than ever. 'I also read *Mendel*,' he told her. 'I suppose it is true that the book represents certain people known to all of us, yourself included, but tell me, will you, did Gilbert Cannan make use of this "copy" without consulting you? Or did he intend a compliment by its publication? I was so depressed by the book; it seemed so tangled and rather sordid (if you will forgive my saying so). The characters, if they are intended for *certain* people, greatly distorted either for good or evil, and to my mind a considerable amount of personal feeling and rancour is expressed in pseudonyms; but chiefly I was sad after I had read it.'

His reaction to *Eminent Victorians* was awkwardly polite. The many-houred days of toil on the official war paintings, and his thrilling rediscovery of the Buckinghamshire countryside, had left him unfit for its witty iconoclasm. Having begged Carrington to 'filch' him a copy, he admitted to her that 'Lytton has a fine satire at his command. I am not clever at expressing my feelings for the craftsmanship itself, and I fear to appear like a cheap reviewer. You will understand when I say that it *is* a good book. I was really excited by the life of Manning, the contrast of that successful and somewhat vulgar prelate with Newman, the really spiritual and cultured man in his quiet background, is wonderful; besides, the narrative reads like a piece of prose fiction. That and the life of Gordon kept me in great suspense.... It would be a little impertinent to congratulate Lytton on his book but the wish lies in my clotted pen yet runs not onto the paper – with love, yours ever, Jacko.'

Carrington now wrote 'Dear Jacko and Christine', which he found 'over cautious' and disliked. But he too was more than cautious when he told her that 'Poor Bunty had a nervous break-up and she and Paul have returned to their flat, where I can't help thinking they are more in their element.' Paul was more concise in his autobiography – 'We fly from Chalfont.' It was *opera bouffe*. The good-looking young artist had seduced a married woman and her husband was threatening to kill him. Both Bunty and Christine were obliged to view the terms of their own marriage contracts with the Nash brothers, Paul with his 'wife and wives', and John with the painful freedoms laid down in the woodland pact. It disturbed him that Carrington should see him and Christine so exclusively wed.

As for the Armistice, it left him financially insecure and in an emotional limbo. 'I fear my picture-income, commission, position, etc. may all end at the end of February [1919]. The reason lies chiefly with H. M. Treasury. I am working to get my discharge by then if possible. [Paul was demobbed on 13th February.] Therefore come and see us before we become totally poverty-stricken. I hope your lord is well. My old woman is troubled by bad circulation but otherwise very brisk. I have Gilman and [Bernard] Adeney and Ginner coming down today to inspect my large masterpiece [*Over the Top*]. ... We lead a quiet life here, sitting of an evening as now by our fireside, playing and reading. I have not been out much owing to the Painting, a hole in my shoes, and also I don't feel free for landscape – how I long for "my ticket".... The day I get free from the army I shall take a clean sheet of paper and go out and try and surprise myself. I fear we shall have an awkward "interim" time – financially, I mean.... Do you know anyone who wants to buy a drawing? How should you. Well, what more have I to say to you, miss? I wish we did not live so far apart. I remember a time when such a state of affairs would not have lasted long.... I suppose you have periods of wishing to see certain people. It is not discontent but a consciousness of something lacking – temporarily just as one suddenly desires marmalade and now one can only get lemon ditto, which is a very poor substitute. However, people who desire things off the table are always troublesome, so we'll dismiss it.'

The Spanish 'flu began to rage across Europe before and after the Armistice, carrying off more victims than the war itself, including kind, helpful Harold Gilman, to whom John owed so much for tutoring him in oil-painting. John came down with it in September 1918 and he wrote groggily to Carrington, 'I've got bloody Spanish 'flu and though I am now down [from being in bed] and on fine days totter out in the sun, I am not yet strong enough to ride out to see you, a thing I have been meaning to do, even at the risk of your displeasure.... I am sadly pulled down from a blooming young man ... to a wretched wight, all skin and bones.... Before I was ill I went to see

Sickert who gave me much praise, which is gratifying, and more advice, which is useful. There is an indescribable glamour around Sickert, whether you care for him or not; one feels he has been in such good company. He told me about his friendship with Degas since he was 21, and Whistler. He is now 58, and no signs of getting "groovy" [furrowed] or tired. I greatly admire him. He is a fine talker too. He has just returned from Bath and opened all his bundles of drawings which he had done there to show me.... Please write to your old cracked up Jacko. My sincere regards to your good gentleman. That you are happy in your work and as tranquil in mind as the present permits is the wish of your Jacko.'

He and Christine, whom he rarely mentions in these letters, had moved to a furnished house in Horn Hill Road, Chalfont St Peter and he told Carrington, who had run away from such an interior, 'The people from whom we rent this place have a wonderful collection of Indian *objet d'art.* They have left a wonderful cow sculpted out of a small log of wood ... the expression of his eyes are of indescribable benignity.' Mrs Wheeler, its owner, gave this sacred creature to her young tenants and it became a beloved house-god all their lives.

Not only did John tell Carrington little about his life with Christine, but he was sketchy too with regard to the intellectual world into which he was swiftly being drawn, now that the war paintings were finished and he had to find a way to make a living. Christine made a little money from her brilliant dressmaking but they were desperately poor and had to watch every penny. Her father Mr Kühlenthal was impatient with them and told John to be a commercial artist, at that time quite a profitable business. Neither was his own father uncritical of what appeared to him their self-chosen penury. John's fireside description of them to Carrington as 'playing and reading' gave no idea at all of the richness of their first year of marriage. They subscribed to Margaret Anderson's *Little Review,* which made 'no compromise with the public taste' and was thus serialising Joyce's *Ulysses* and introducing the work of T. S. Eliot, Ezra Pound, William Carlos Williams and John Rodker, and were playing Scarlatti. John and the Australian poet W. J. Turner became the theatrical critic and illustrator for *Land and Water.* These ink drawings of *La Boutique Fantasque, Kissing Time* and *The Belle of New York,* and many other shows, were funny and sophisticated. Claughton Pellew had taught him how to engrave on box-wood, and throughout the 1920s to sell a single engraving for three guineas or to illustrate a novel or a poem gave him and Christine a sense of security. She would cycle to Gerrards Cross to save the 5s/6d fare and make meals from 'nothing'. He found her loving, even adoring, but now and then sharply astute, wifely, yet holding back from giving him her complete self. Her intellect contained a rigorous element from her German background, also something cosmopolitan, and this in spite of the fact that she was now teaching English country-dancing. He was proud of her but was glad that they had made the pact. He was not equable and was easily sunk in gloom. Once she wrote in her journal, 'John: It's no good once you're married you're done for, you can't be free!' To which she replied on the page, 'In my relations with Jack I have always aimed at not attracting him in any way, or playing upon the physical side by dress or movement, or touching his emotional nature by crying in front of him, or wheedling or pleading with him against his reason. And I have been successful in as much that he tells me that he does not feel connected to me. That seems to me freedom obtained.' Presuming that all men shared John and Paul's tastes, she dubbed them 'polygamous tadpoles' and found constancy in women. The journal became a haven for the girl who should have been an artist, a musician or a dancer; who should have been able to stare out openly from the picture but whose gaze let her down. 'What exquisite pleasure in the fact that someone comes to see *you* alone, and not because you know the beloved ...' says the journal. She envied Rupert Lee's wife Rosalind and Bunty because 'they are always willing to forgive anything.'

In February 1920 Christine admitted, 'Jack did not marry the person [Carrington] he fell in love with, but I have fallen in love with him since I married him.' This early recognition of what had happened deepened their relationship, although it was too sweeping, or too conventional, to say that John had fallen in love with Carrington. It was nearer the truth to recognise that their friendship reached a level at Mr Hooper's Tonerspuddle farm during the summer holiday of 1915 which convinced John that he had a friend for life, and this after what he believed was a long period of the standard playfulness which must precede any serious relationship, let alone an affair, between a man and a woman. Something in Carrington's letters to him at the Front told him that he was more likely to be a special friend of a certain part of her life, and that was all. Christine saw the situation clearly where she herself was concerned and never for one moment either wanted or imagined any future in Carrington's direction. Had her

---

Opposite: Pen drawing by Nash found among his letters to Carrington, possibly an illustration to the theatre articles by W. J. Turner in *Land and Water*.

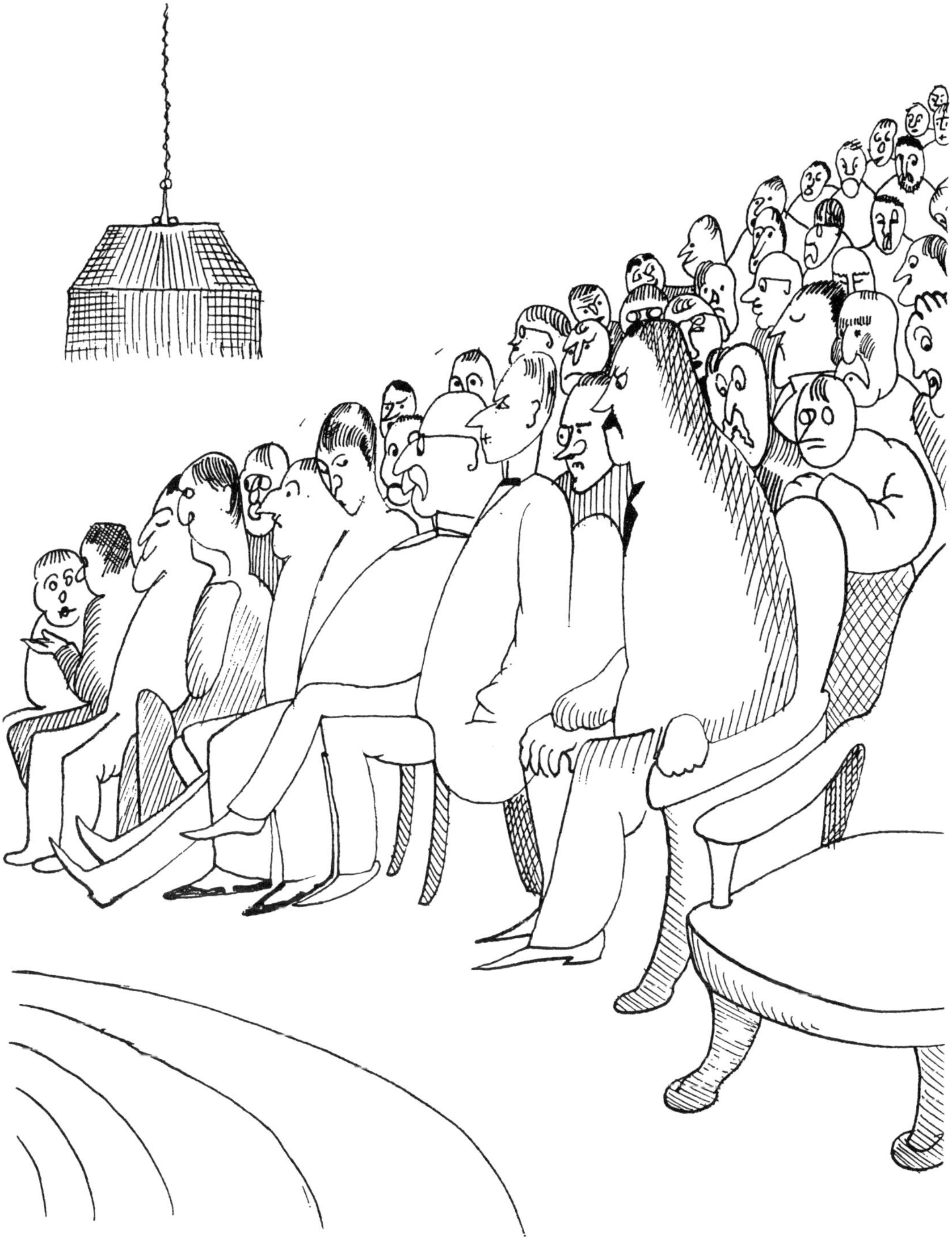

poor eyes not given out, she would have become a good artist, and it would have been this which would have utterly changed her marriage, not John's hopeless pursuit of the 1915 Carrington. Something Carrington wrote to Gertler in January 1919 could well have applied to John and Christine, and to other 'first' friends: how she had 'suddenly realized a few moments ago what a beastly ungenerous nature I had created inside my frame ... my letters to you are like woodcuts, limited in their technique, and that certain elements, as colour, will never be able to be shown.' For some two years she and John Nash were funny, witty, landscape-adoring companions, he so learned, she so enchantingly fresh, naive, magnetic – and lost. When he naturally sought to prolong their situation she with ruthless commonsense pointed to Christine Kühlenthal and told him, 'She's the girl for you.' He agreed (there was no mistake), but surely not to the exclusion of herself? 'Yes', was Carrington's eventual answer. It made its painful way to him via letters which were not like the old letters, and visits which were not like the old visits, until her suicide in 1932.

A fortnight after Carrington's death John received in the post the final volume of Marcel Proust's *Remembrance of Things Past, Time Regained,* in which the translator had written on the fly-page, 'My dear John, I want you to have this book. Begin by reading from p.210 to p.274.... For me this is one of the greatest books ever written.... Ever yours affectionately, Stephen Hudson.' In 1925 Hudson, under his real name Sidney Schiff, had introduced John's paintings in a series called *British Artists of Today*. John and Christine were now living at Meadle, Buckinghamshire, and had a baby son, William. In the section of *Time Regained* recommended by Hudson there is the following passage:

> When we are able to take up our work again, the woman who posed to us for our sentimental reaction can no longer make us feel it. We must continue to paint her from another model and if that is a treachery to the first, in a literary sense, thanks to the similarity of our sentiments which make a work at one and the same time a memory of our past loves and the starting point of new ones, there is no great disadvantage in the exchange.... For we are not as faithful to the being we have most loved as we are to ourselves.

Last Pages

Meanwhile there were the establishing post-Armistice years, for art of every kind a fabulous decade of invention, energy and change. In April 1919 Carrington sent John into the wildest hopes when she wrote asking for a spare canvas.

My darling duck,

Of course you can have one of my canvases. The one that Newman has delivered to you is not mine but was ordered for Paul by mistake. You do not owe Paul the kisses and I fear he would not appreciate them as I could.... Surely you have mellowed like a lovely golden Rayon D'or(a) peach to offer me these favours. T'wert not so some time back! Well lovey I have written to Newman to release the canvas and you may, if you like, let the cost stand to my account, for on this my birthday, (which formerly you were not wont to forget) I must have the pleasure of doing a good deed.... I am ill with a filthy cold and depressed beyond measure by 'the situation', thinking I shall have to join the army again if things go badly or be put in gaol for disloyalty to George V and sympathy to the miners.... Who cares what an artist cares, a rush for miners or Government – but is our work to be interrupted again and further set back? [Strikes and widespread social unrest, and thoughts of what was happening in Russia, were leading to talk of civil war.] ... Half the bloody fools anywhere don't think how dangerous it is. I am here D.V. all the summer. When will you come and stay with us and pay me for the canvas, else I shall be obliged to dun you! Love and a kiss from me, ever your Jacko.

However, a few months later, it was 'Again I place my pride in my pocket, swallow my choler and choke down those feelings of emotion that *will* arise with the thought of your neglect of me. And what is the result – some dear little cuts for Dora! Three [wood]cuts are enough and I will stifle any temptation I have to cut at you in any other way.... Please commend me to Lytton.... Titles of cuts. 1. *Cats on Table*. 2. ditto on chair 3. *Amorous Approach*.'

A year later he was urging her to forsake her 'castle in Spain' for 'a hovel in Bucks'.

'We are in a small cottage in this charming village halfway up a hill on which is carved a Cross. Wonderful country. Could you ride? I fancy there must be a way through Nettlebed onto the range which terminates in *Bledlow Ridge*, which is just opposite us. ... Christine sends love and I send more.' The village was Whiteleaf on the Icknield Way. The Saxons had cut a protective cross on the escarpment which sheltered it. It was a far cry from Gerald Brenan's 'castle in Spain' or small house in Yegen. Carrington, her future husband Ralph Partridge and Lytton were squashed into it, having arrived on mules, not bicycles. Brenan, the young writer-artist, was not in love with her then, but he would be.

Paul came briefly to Whiteleaf with Bunty during the summer of 1919 and saw not only the chalk cross but a glimpse of his own sacred Clumps beyond it. This higgledy-piggledy place, however, was not for him and he was soon back at work in a studio in Fitzroy Street, though with frequent returns to Buckinghamshire. He and John were ridding themselves of 'the Nash brothers'. Paul was in search of those signs and symbols in a landscape which could provide him with an original language, and John knew that he himself needed to look no further for his great subject – the lie of the land as farming had left it. He was also worshipping plants. A floret of primroses in a ditch would halt him in his tracks. The beech-woods drew him into them. Fugitive ponds caught his eye. Agriculture was in the doldrums and many farms were bankrupt but he was too young to worry about such stagnation. He and Christine lived on pittances amid poverty. Other Whiteleaf neighbours included the biologist Eric Daglish and his wife Alice, and the superb etcher Francis Unwin, who had been at the Slade as long ago as 1902 but who looked young still due to the consumption which refined his pallid face. Unwin had climbed and sketched in the Bernese Oberland before arriving in Whiteleaf in a final attempt to kill his disease, but it survived the pure air. John felt that he had found a new friend in the Claughton Pellew mould, another Franciscan, although this time nearly ten years his senior. He saw Unwin's etchings with awe. They were not selling. Marvellous though they were, the heyday of etching was over. Both John and Christine loved Francis Unwin and would nurse him until his death at forty in Mundesley Sanatorium. He filled Whiteleaf with his inspiration and craftmanship, and showed John how to engrave and print. Like Claughton, he ended up on the Norfolk coast, though only for a few last months. Right up to the day of his leaving Whiteleaf John would find him, aproned and inky, at his meticulous task, and the walls of his cottage covered with prints of Sicily, Italy,

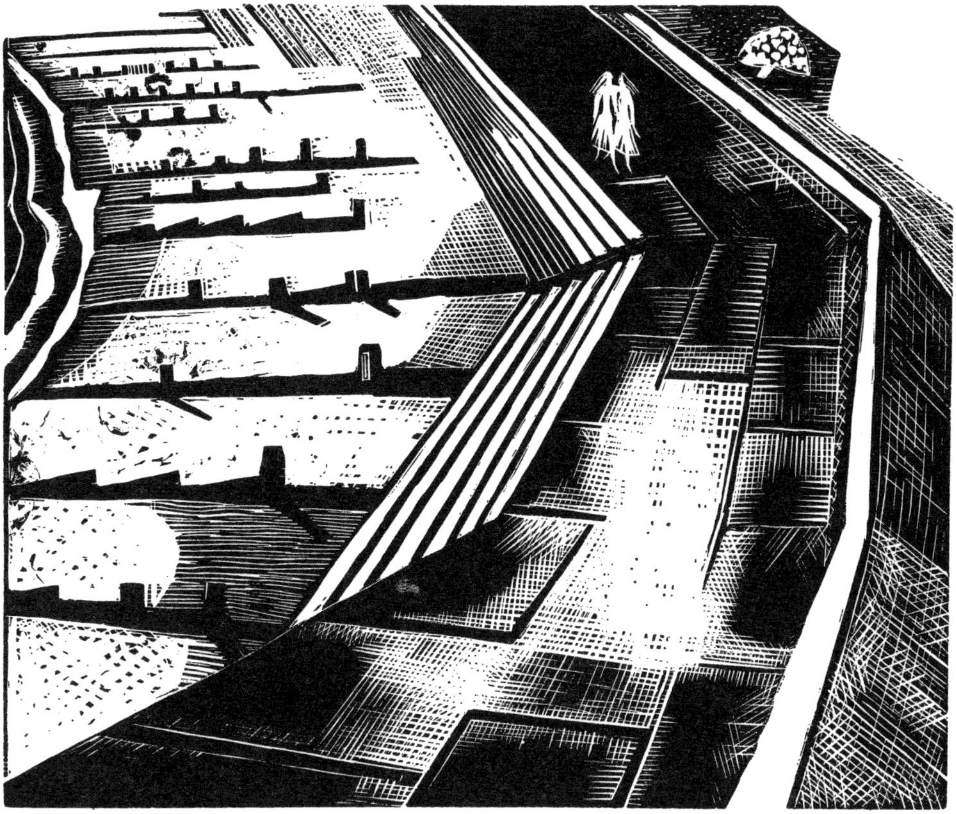

Paul Nash: *Promenade, 2*, wood engraving (printed from a line block) 1923.
Courtesy of the Tate Gallery.

the Alps, the huge industrial scenes in London in which he etched vast brewery interiors, and occasionally a reaper or a threshing machine from on his doorstep. Unwin taught John and John taught Daglish, who engraved enormous birds. They called their activity 'wood-chopping'. When one of John's Whiteleaf engravings fetched three guineas, Christine knew that she could buy enough food for a month. Francis Unwin had another function: Christine found that she could tell him about wives and wife, and freedom pacts. He was shocked. For him her low, bell-like voice had become too beloved to utter such things and he said that she must leave John. So even Francis had not understood. Leaving John did not come into it.

It was the French singer Raymonde Collignon who unwittingly separated 'the brothers Nash' by sending Paul off to look at Romney Marsh. There he discovered Dymchurch and the Futurist pattern of its immense sea-wall. This colossal structure ran two thirds of the way along the shoreline of the town, itself beginning to be gimcrack with holiday shacks and bungalows, and so not alluring. But the sea-wall! He saw a great grey staircase to the English Channel, a squared-up and precipitous concrete slide towards oceanic oblivion. It mesmerised him. He drew and painted it unceasingly, sometimes with haunting women. The formal repetition of its imagery drove him to study after study of its geometrical statement. Somewhere under all this Modern concrete 'lived' the Romans' sea-wall and John Rennie's sea-wall of 1803, as well as the pilings and patchings of all the centuries in between. And behind it lay Romney Marsh, sunken and full of sheep. It was here in this half built up, half empty spot that Paul Nash would 'find himself'.

Shortly after settling in Dymchurch he discovered a philosophical language in which to paint, as it were. It was that used by Sir Thomas Browne in his twin essays *Hydriotaphia, or Urne Buriall,* and *The Garden of Cyrus,* which Cassell the publishers had invited him to illustrate. He immediately posted a copy of this old book to John, but he at that moment was deep in another language, that of the Physic Garden in Oxford, where he was gathering material for his book *Poisonous Plants* (1927). He wished Paul well with his metaphysics. He could only speak Linnaean. Paul was enthralled by *Urne Buriall,* which, apart from being the most ravishing case ever made out for cremation, told him such mighty truths as 'Life is a pure flame, and we live by an invisible sun within us.' Sunflowers eventually burnt their way free of their roots. One of his drawings for the Sir Thomas Browne essays, *The Soul Visiting the Mansions of the Dead,* is of his mystical progression from his father's Bird Garden at Iver. Between Dymchurch and the discovery of this language Paul had come very near to death. A kind of delayed illness, maybe the aftermath of the trenches, plus the development of

---

Opposite: John Nash, Esmond Fitz Daglish and Paul Nash, in military uniform, *c.*1918. This photograph was kept by Barbara Nash, who wrote on the back 'I'm sure Jack wouldn't want this one of him to appear in print but it's good of Paul isn't it?' Tate Gallery Archive.
Over, top left: Dora Carrington riding her horse, Belle, near Ham Spray, Wiltshire, late 1920s. Hulton Getty. Below: Dora Carrington and Lytton Strachey under the weeping Ilex tree at Ham Spray, taken by Frances Partridge, May 1930. Hulton Getty.
Right: John Nash at Wormingford Mill, 1930. Ronald Blythe

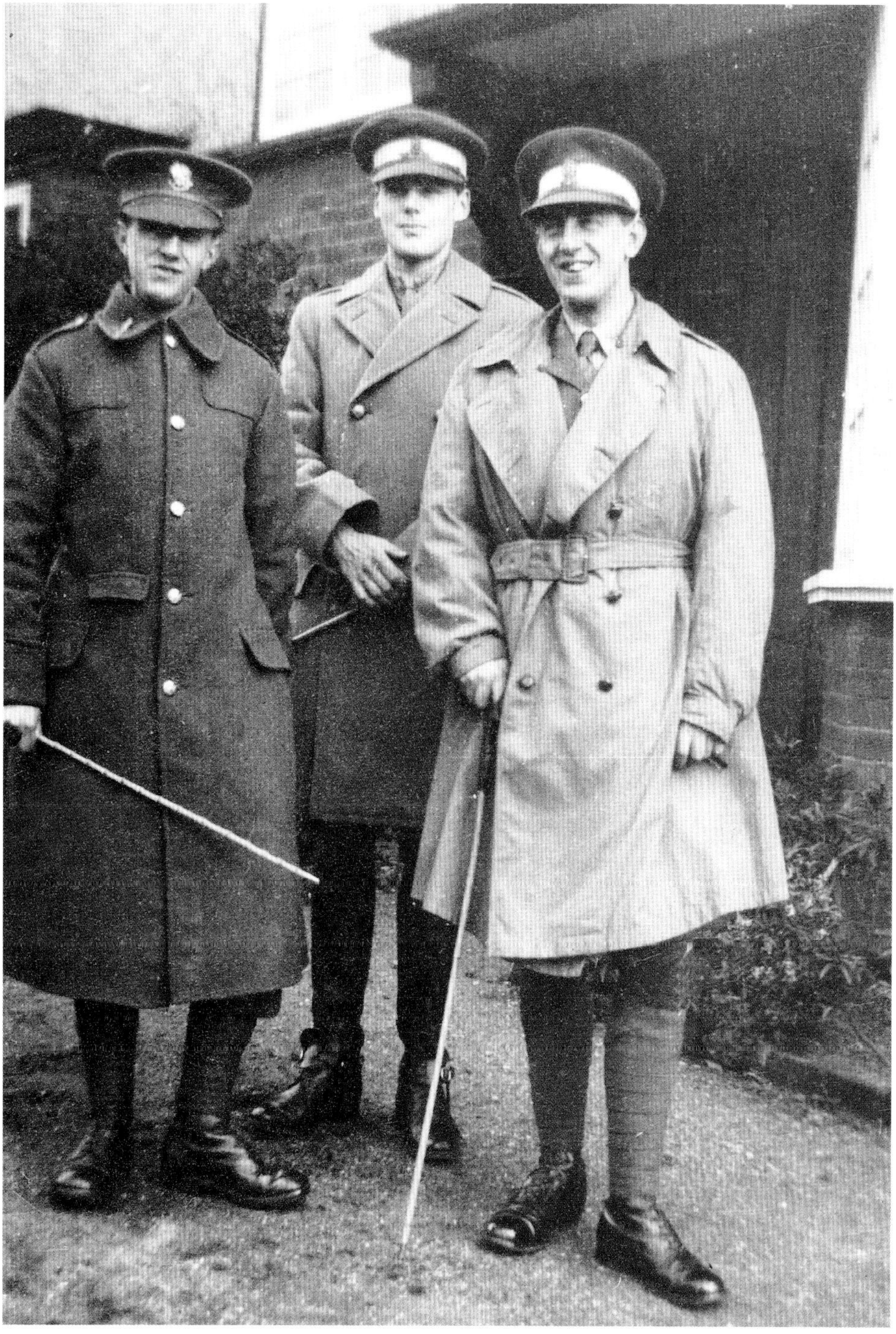

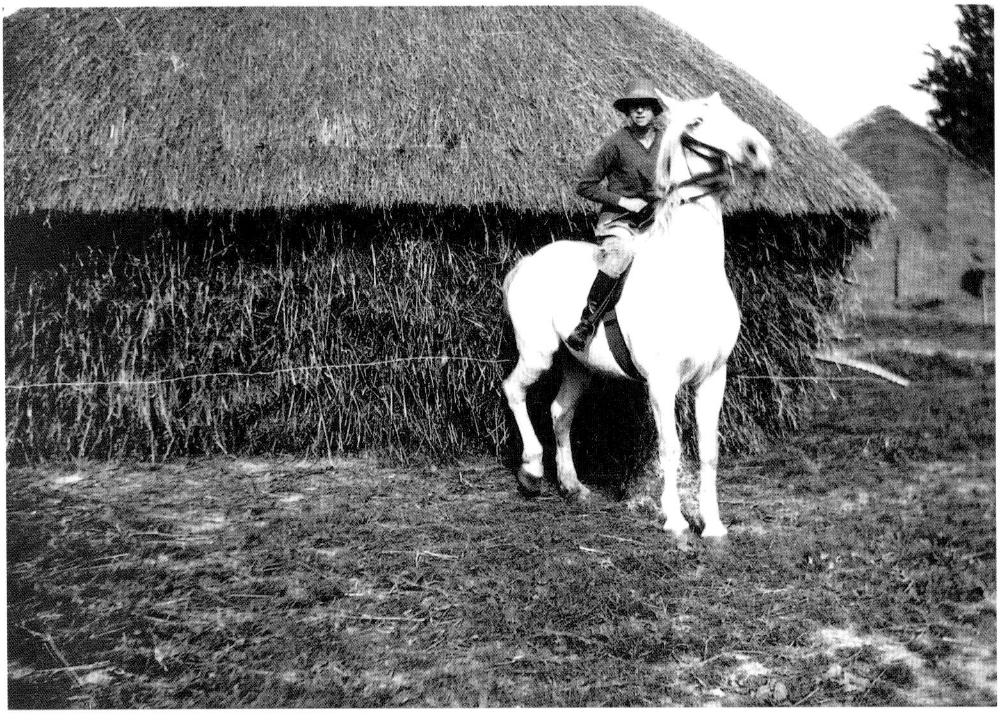

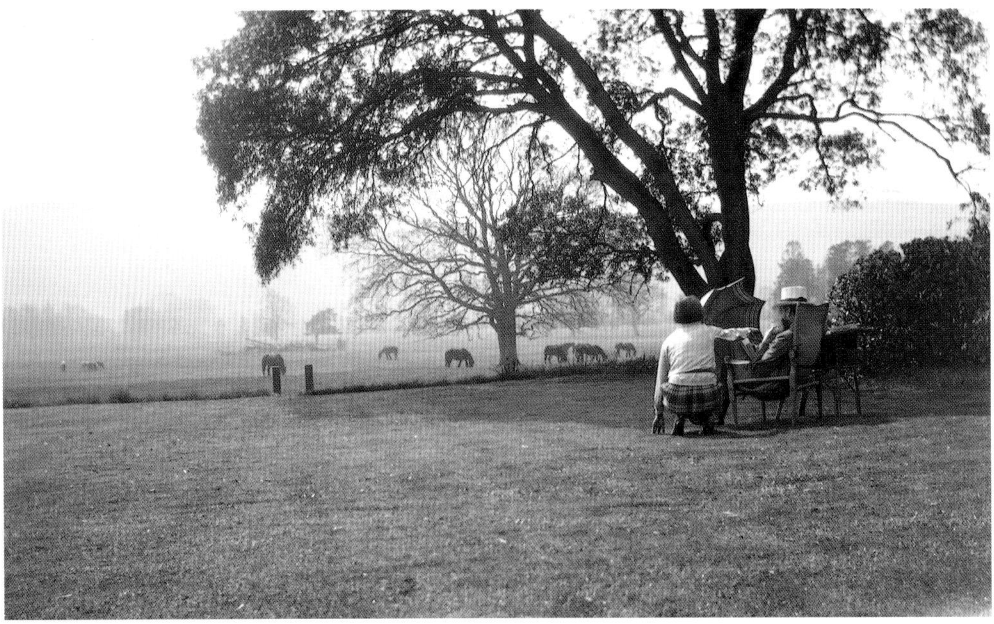

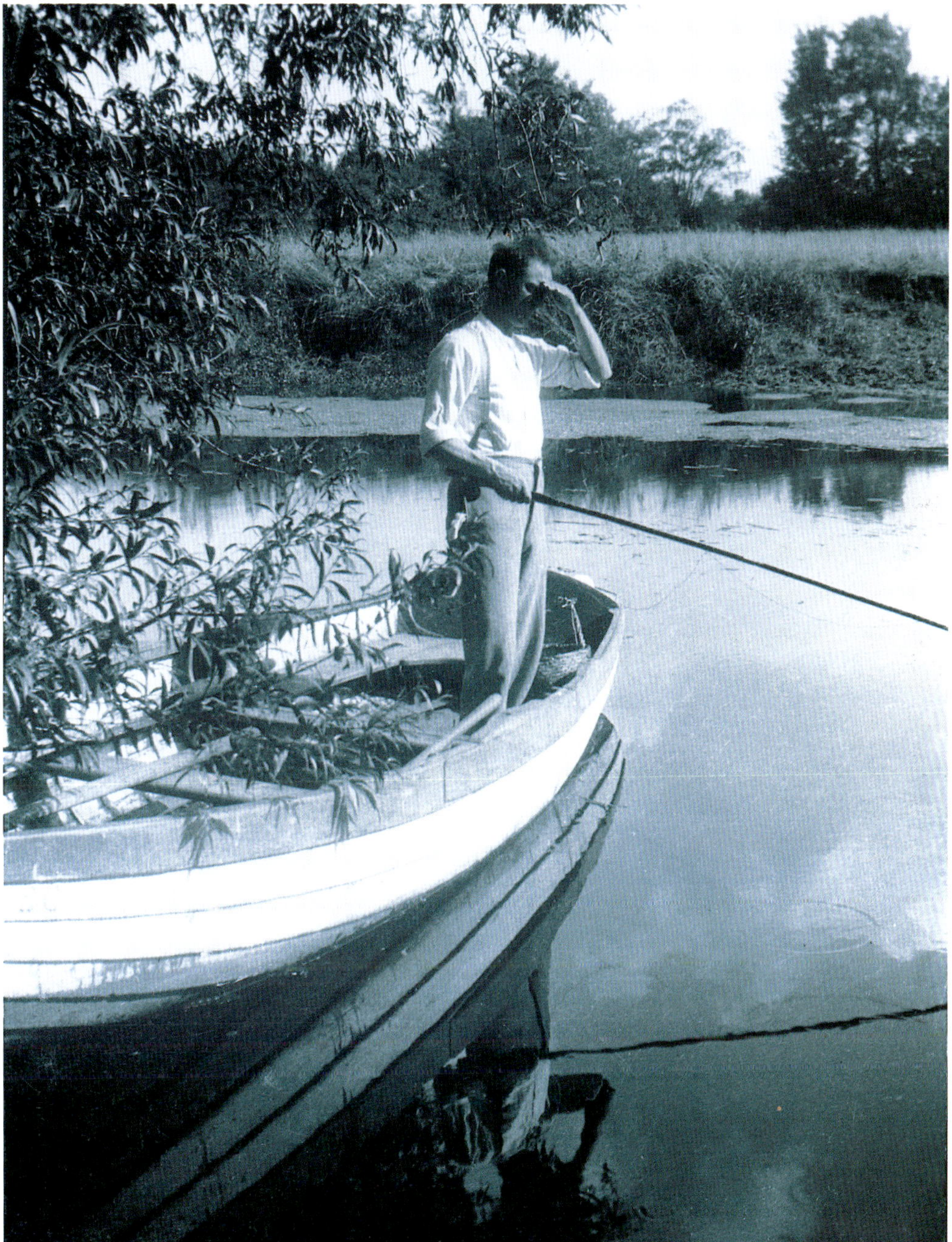

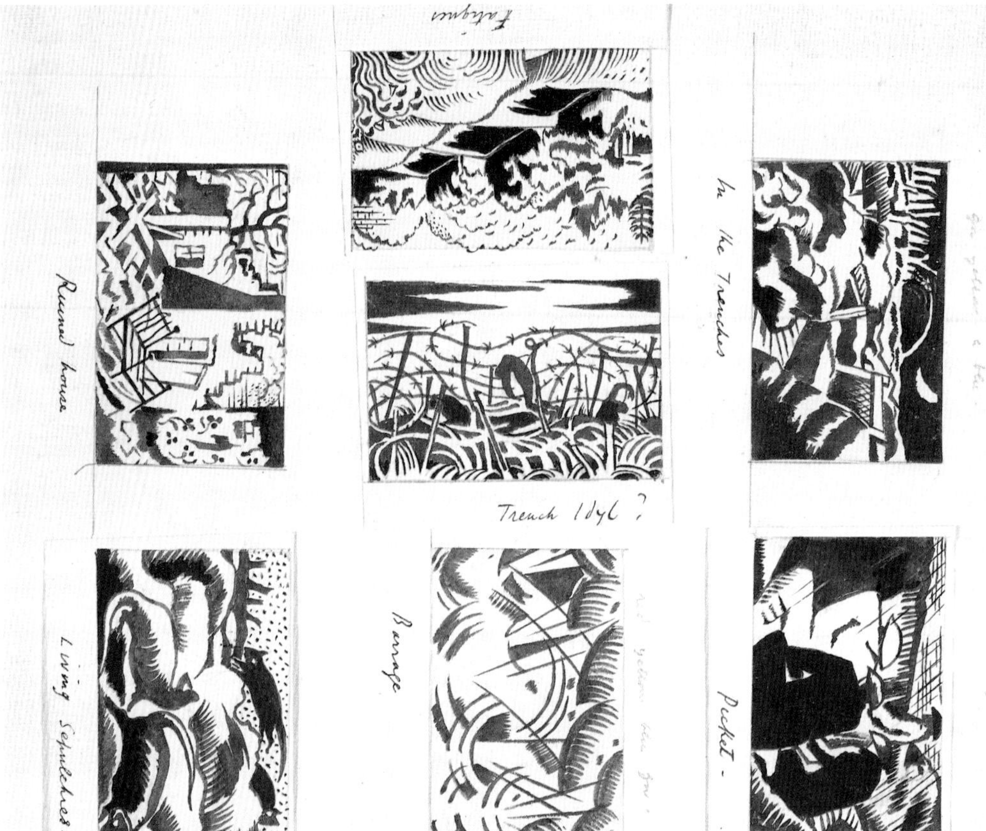
Fatigue
Ruined house
In the Trenches
Trench Idyl ?
Living Sepulchres.
Barrage
Picket.
Terror.
Bombardment

asthma, had struck him unconscious, after which it had become imperative that he should know where he was going, spiritually speaking. Clairvoyant Bunty was the perfect wife in this respect, being inventive and inexact.

Both John and Paul had settled to a hard-working regime of landscape painting, wood engraving and book illustration by the mid 1920s. Christine was settling to the conclusion that she could not be either the wronged wife or the frustrated artist. It would be too tedious – vulgar even. Unable to paint because of the glaucoma, and able though resentful to do just the housekeeping, she began a little deception of stealing a life for herself. John, though always courteous and kind, could only imagine one life – his own. He would not have liked to see her life flourishing separately beside it. So she found a way of letting it grow without him knowing. She possessed a gift for being amused by 'antics' and his drew her wry laughter and a few of what he described as her 'hard knocks'. She took what she needed to make this life for herself, but in a way which prevented him missing anything. It became her game and it intrigued them both, although John never learned the rules of play. Her music advanced by leaps and bounds, to his joy, and Mr Kühlenthal, now impressed by their marriage, gave her a new Steinway grand piano and a contract which said that he would pay to have it tuned for the rest of her life. She made friends with Susanna Sharp, Cecil's daughter, and they demonstrated his and George Butterworth's *Country Dance Book* teachings in the square at Princes Risborough. John could not be tempted to dance but he would practise for two and three hours a day on the new piano. Christine made new women friends, some of whom had begun as John's girlfriends, and, strangely to those who knew about her poor lightless eyes, she was seen every late evening at the finest sewing without spectacles under a lamp, the cats piled up on her lap and bits of a Dorelia-dress everywhere. She was untidy, he was neat. They both smoked like troopers. The atmosphere was one of a faintly mannered serenity which might now and then be punctured with a sharp remark. Both of them were enthralled by landscape, as he and Carrington had been before the war, and Christine would bicycle fifty miles, or make intricate train journeys, to find where he could paint. What he usually did was to make pencil and wash drawings on the spot and carry out the complete watercolour or oil in his studio. But it meant a lot of wandering and,

---

Opposite: *Original Pen Drawings for Images of War* by Richard Aldington, Paul Nash, 1919, each approximately 50 × 75 mm. Courtesy of the Trustees of the Victoria and Albert Museum.

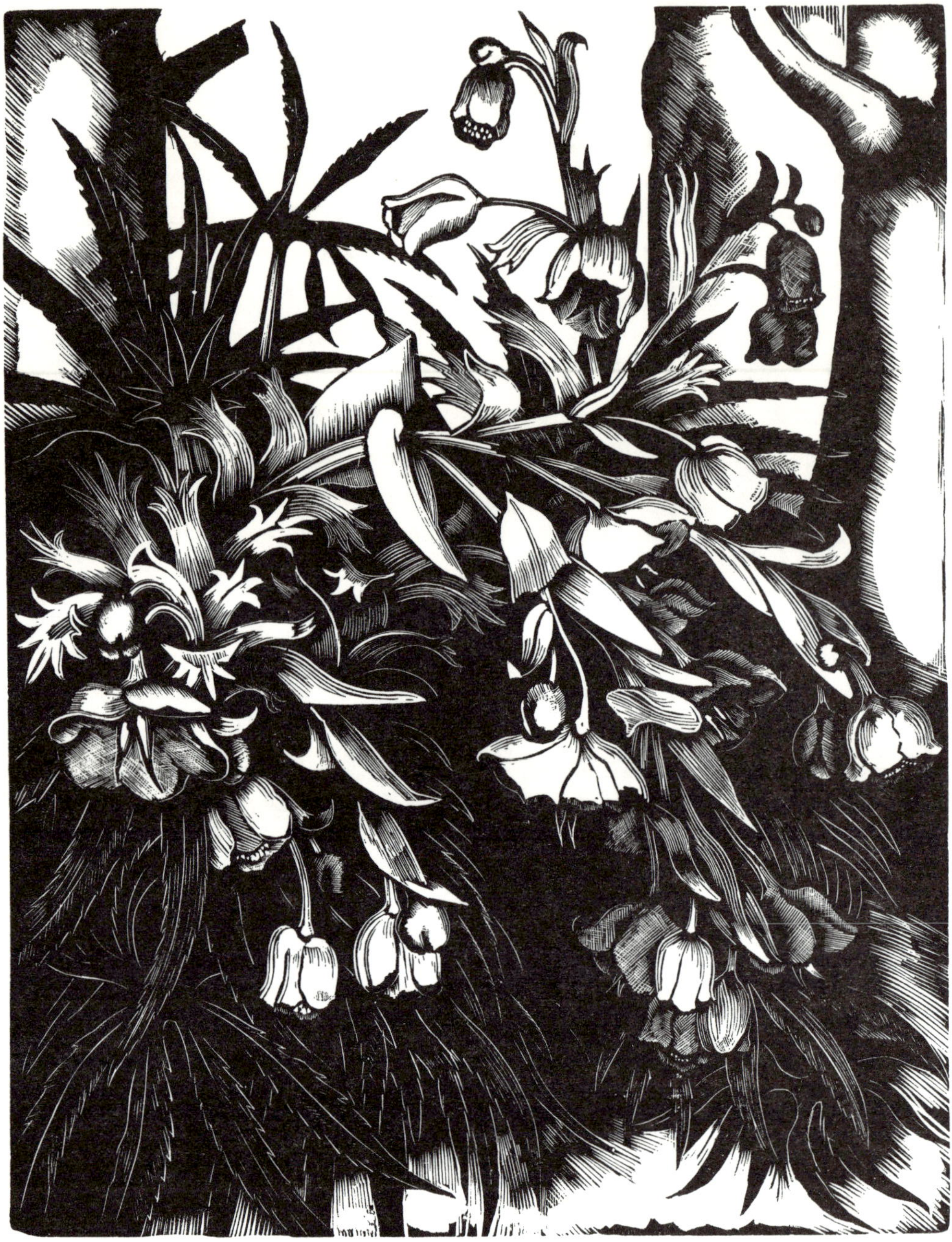

John Nash, *Helleborus Foetidus*, 1927

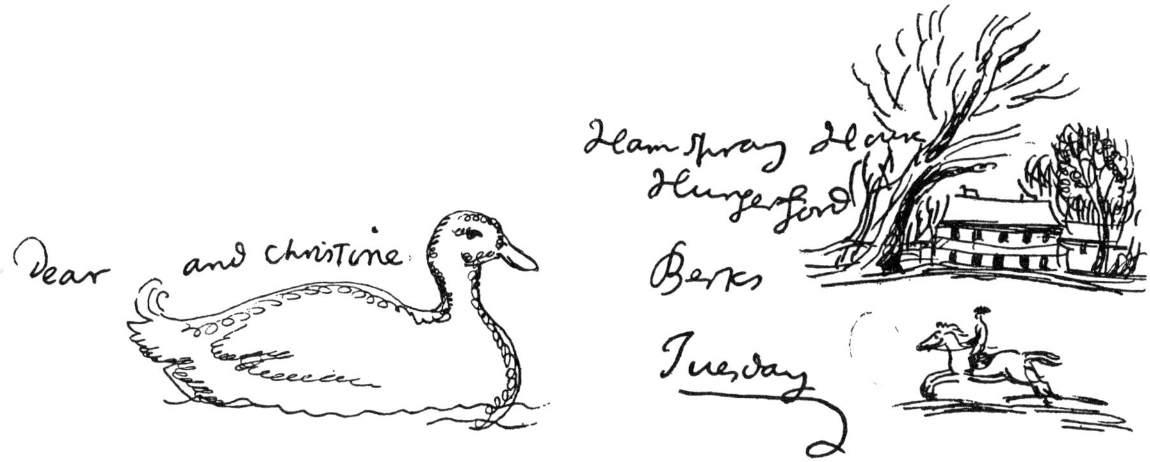

Letterheading, Carrington to John and Christine Nash, from Ham Spray House, 1929, one of her last letters to them.

inevitably, since he did nothing to discourage it, a lot of thinking about Carrington and their youthful landscape-mania.

Neither of them would see much more of her. Once when he was sketching in Bath during August 1926 John unexpectedly caught sight of her. 'Why do I write now, quite suddenly? Well, you see, I was climbing to the top of a tram t'other day in Batheaston, when, chancing to direct my glance, as they say, downwards, the rays of the sun struck on a car and on a beard in the car – no offence, I hope – it was undoubtedly Lytton. My attention was then "directed" to the driver – did I recognise a green corduroy jacket and golden hair or was I dreaming? Enough to start thinking of you again anyway.... Being in temporary possession of a car and passing [Ham Spray House] probably *next Saturday* ... I intend to call unless I hear you are away, for blood is thicker than petrol ... and I should like to see you again and see what you look like.'

Ralph Partridge would sum up John's hopeless pursuit of what even he in his heart of hearts knew he could never have when he told Rosamond Lehmann, 'She was an obsession to me – once she got into anybody's blood she was ineradicable.' It was Rosamond's husband Wogan Philipps who brought Carrington and John briefly together. Carrington wrote to John 'I have some friends near Oxford so I might make a sort of combined expedition to see you and them. The young man draws at your art school [Ruskin] – Wogan Philipps. Do you know him? He has a lovely wife whom I dote upon.' She had also heard of the death of John's father and this was the chief reason for her breaking the long silence. She had rather liked stern, puzzled-about-art Mr Nash when she came to stay at Iver. But she had not at all liked some of the things which John had said when he told her of the loss of his father. She had been less than enthusiastic about the proposed visit to Ham Spray after his glimpse of her in Batheaston and incurred his wrath:

Dear Madame perdix,

... Perhaps it is as well for I don't really know if you sound cordial, that is to say I am not *sure* of it and I should hate to find you changed. Perhaps I am sentimental and dwelling in this matter rather in the past prefer to keep my memories as they are. Besides you would be surrounded by people who would not wish to see me. Christine was not coming with me as she had already gone home. I said 'I' in my letter not 'we' but you, with your careful discretion, reminded me – what is the game, dearie? Do you think Christine would be jealous if you wrote to me alone without the 'dear J and C' or plural ducks [a drawing]?! Now I must say I wish I *was* seeing you if I could only pull your leg a little in private.... Well don't be angry with me because I feel a little sad at times that I should be so utterly cut off from you. Not a letter in so many years and then when I rise from the dead, so to speak, you can't ask me to lunch because you have friends. What am I, an enemy?... Despite this nasty letter I am ever yours Jacko.

And so the old friendship rattled on, hollow now at the heart, with John finding his way barred to what he still believed could be its renewal. Carrington protected herself from his accusations as best she could: 'I am (in spite of all your sly allusions to "intelligent friends" and "over-crowding") just as stupid and humble.... This [the countryside around Ham Spray] is really a most lovely place, to my mind equal to any of the "beauty spots" of England. Holds up its head to Grasmere and the Lakes. But I suppose I shouldn't be saying this – it's a long time since I saw any of your paintings, but then I very seldom go to London. I hope you succeed to your taste, and lead a happy life.... Give Christine my Fondest Love if it still means anything to her.... Your Carrington.'

All this because she had offered Ham Spray House to them for a painting holiday while she was elsewhere. It was kind but crass. 'My dear Duckie.... We were, it is true, rather "impeeved" when you wrote and offered your house to us. I suppose we thought you might imagine we should not want to go there if *you* were absent. It is not your house we wanted to see but *you* duckie, and every time I have been near you you have retired behind a hedge of friends and engagements, it seems – so I thought to myself, drat the girl, cannot she push through this rampart or throw it down to see an old friend?... So now, my dear, when you come back, if you are willing I will come over and see you, and belike I may hit on a day when you are alone or at least en-famille and not overcrowded with intelligentsia.... Please write and tell me I shall be welcome.'

The visit, John and Christine's first and last to Ham Spray, took place in June 1929. John had just retired from five years' teaching at Ruskin College. 'It was rather sad leaving all the lovely "gurrrrls".' But things were more muddled than sad when they drove away from Carrington, her gravel crackling beneath the wheels of Unwin's bull-nose Morris, which they had inherited. Their thank-you letters mixed duty with apologies and revelations. Christine wrote hers sitting in the car outside High Wycombe town hall while waiting for her dancing class to begin. It was 'good to find you as I remembered you, I won't say unchanged because one ought to develop a little in ten years and it would be insulting to both of us to imagine that we could stand still! However perhaps we have moved in the same directions. It struck me as being so strange too to remember how I always wanted to come to Hurstbourne Tarrant to see you, and now when I did come to just the other side of Inkpen Beacon, it was just as nice as I imagined it would be fifteen years ago.... I hope you really *will* come to see us, and so assure us that you were not disappointed either in our meeting....' John came away 'a little depressed feeling that I had blundered in making reference to your private affairs just before I went'. They had all three climbed up to the Beacon and stared around at the great view. He wanted to draw her *Arum Dracunculus* and she sent him a cutting carefully packed in her vacuum-cleaner box.

> I thought it was extremely kind of you to send it, cutting it all so ruthlessly; but I have kept your box. The plant was fine. I drew it half-opened and then waited till it came right out, when the stink was almost overpowering and I hardly liked to be left alone with the fellow – it is a rude Freudian plant no doubt....
>
> I was trying to remember for your benefit what exactly we *did* say as we left

you in the car. ['Of course it would have been fascinating to know what you and C. really said as you drove away. But I don't suppose I ever shall!'] I think I was a little sad and drove in grim silence for several miles. We agreed you had not changed – all the qualities which were so endearing, but I will not make you blush, if 'old women' like you can do so. ['Of course the rivers of time have, I suppose, rather worn our faces and furrowed our hearts, but otherwise I expect we will find each other not much altered']....

I have just finished a block for a book called *The Anatomy of Dessert* [E. A. Bunyard, 1929] – bi-sected apples, a melon gashed open, bananas protruding from their skins and half peeled apples also etc. Fun with the fruit shapes! Love from us both, ever your old Duck.

Carrington was both touched and disturbed by the visit and was sorry that John and Christine had not enjoyed it more. 'For with my penetrating eye (and ear) I saw you didn't – but I am an old woman, and rather battered by life and misfortune.... To tell you the truth I thought you seemed rather sad, but perhaps it was only my depressing effect, and the catarrh. I hope so. I mean that you are so gay and happy in general.... You are an owl to think I minded a hoot about your reference to my private affairs. It was nice of you to sympathise. Although to tell you the truth I am so happy in this Paradise with my cat that I hardly mind now.' Mind what? She could have minded that John rarely saw her as an artist like himself but only as a captivating woman. She was serious about her work.

Due to a series of domestic incidents 'the brothers Nash' were together when they heard that Carrington was dead. Paul and Bunty had moved from Iden to New House, Rye in 1930 in order to have room to care for her father, who was now widowed and ill. John and Christine had settled at Meadle, a hamlet near Princes Risborough which had once been a Quaker retreat, and which had retained much of that quietness. After twelve years of marriage, there was a few months old son, William – a miracle, a wonder, or 'the nicest chap you can imagine', as Paul put it when he arrived in March 1932. Then came the devastating news – something about an accident with her rabbiting gun. An inquest but no post-mortem. And no reason for them to think that, sad though it was for her, she had not been getting over Lytton's death in the way that people did get over death, by grieving and planning. Lytton had died five weeks earlier after an illness which filled the press, for he had become a celebrity, and they all knew about that. But now Carrington – *dead*? It was too soon for her to shoot rabbits. She would still have been worried and overwrought. The news ran around the old circle like a crazy flame. There had been an accident. It was what the coroner had said. But she had said in a poem called *Advice to Oneself* written after Lytton's death:

Turn down the wick!
Your night is done
There rises up another sun
Another day is now begun
Turn down your wick.
Turn down the lamp!
Time to expire
'Body and soul' end your tune
Retreat my pale moon,
And turn out your lamp.

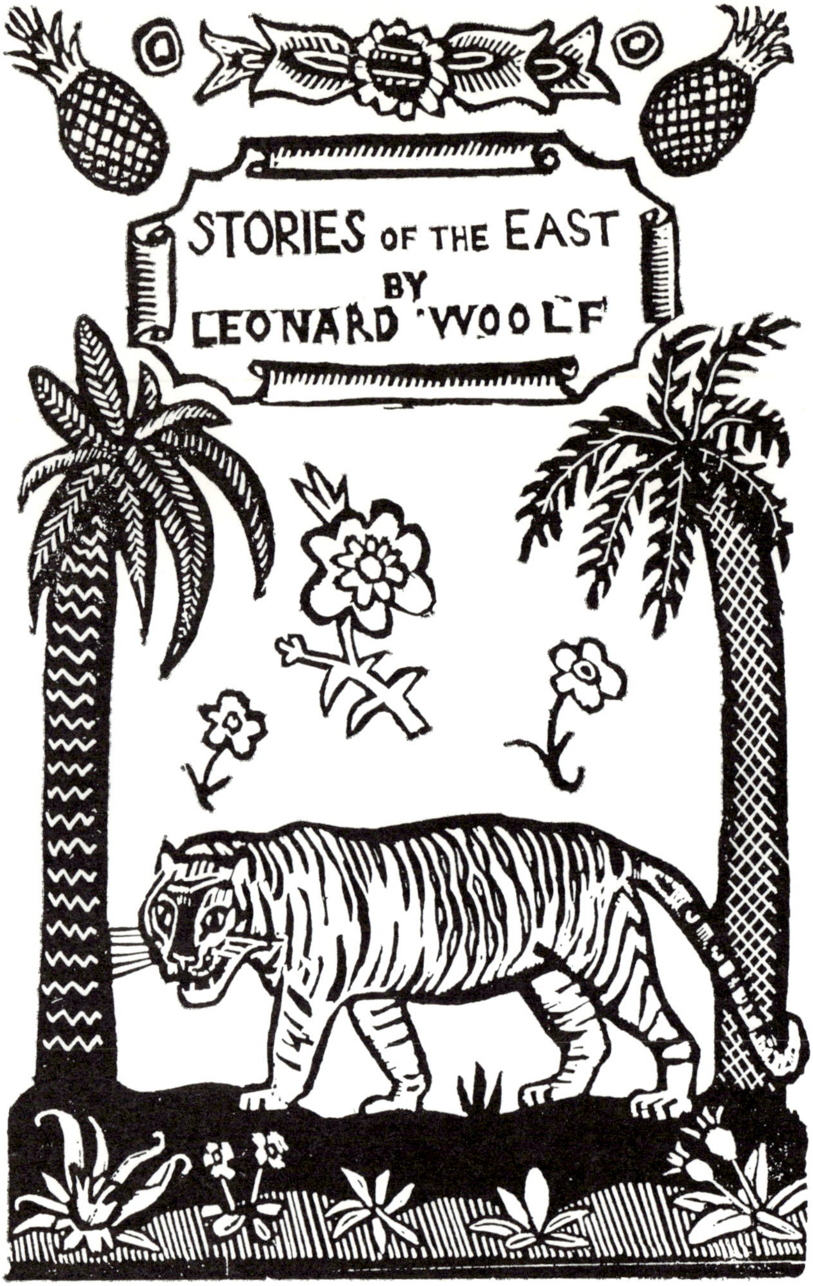

Carrington: woodcut title page for *Stories of the East*, Leonard Woolf, Hogarth Press, 1921. Printed from a line block.

Index

This is essentially a name and place index and is based on the text alone; references to picture titles and actual illustrations are not included.

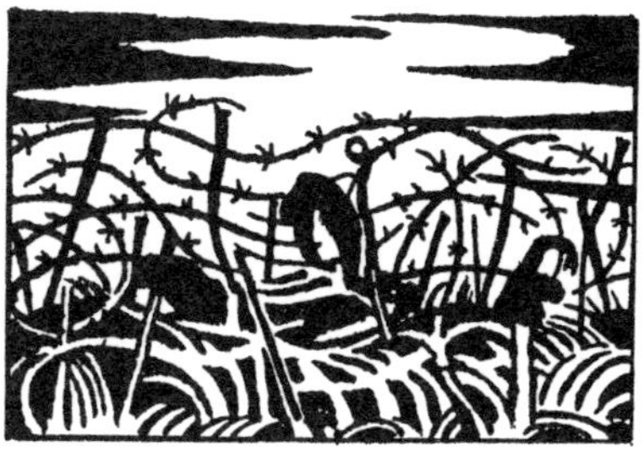

This was the first book to be printed at the Fleece Press's new workshop in Cawthorne, South Yorkshire, and is a marvellous story told so well.

There were 300 copies, all bound in quarter cloth and a Paul Nash pattern paper newly put together from one of the drawings he made for Images of War, *1919, another of which, a torn and abused landscape appears above. As Ronald Blythe says in his Introduction, the passion for landscape united these four friends.*

The first edition was set in Centaur, printed on Zerkall and bound in Otley by Smith Settle. Few books have been so satisfying to put together as this one, for both author and publisher.